THE HISTORY OF NATIONS

India

Jann Einfeld, *Book Editor*

Daniel Leone, *President*
Bonnie Szumski, *Publisher*
Scott Barbour, *Managing Editor*

GREENHAVEN
PRESS®

THOMSON
™
GALE

San Diego • Detroit • New York • San Francisco • Cleveland
New Haven, Conn. • Waterville, Maine • London • Munich

For more information, contact
Greenhaven Press
27500 Drake Rd.
Farmington Hills, MI 48331-3535
Or you can visit our Internet site at http://www.gale.com

Cover credit: © Victoria & Albert Museum, London/Art Resource, NY

LIBRARY OF CONGRESS CATALOGING-IN-PUBLICATION DATA

India / Jann Einfeld, book editor.
p. cm. — (History of nations)
Includes bibliographical references and index.
ISBN 0-7377-1599-5 (lib. : alk. paper) — ISBN 0-7377-1600-2 (pbk. : alk. paper)
1. India—History. I. Einfeld, Jann. II. History of nations (Greenhaven Press)
DS436 .I46 2003
954—dc21 2002034716

Printed in the United States of America

Contents

Chapter 2: British India

Chapter 4: Post-Independence India

Foreword

In 1841, the journalist Charles MacKay remarked, "In reading the history of nations, we find that, like individuals, they have their whims and peculiarities, their seasons of excitement and recklessness." At the time of MacKay's observation, many of the nations explored in the Greenhaven Press History of Nations series did not yet exist in their current form. Nonetheless, whether it is old or young, every nation is similar to an individual, with its own distinct characteristics and unique story.

The History of Nations series is dedicated to exploring these stories. Each anthology traces the development of one of the world's nations from its earliest days, when it was perhaps no more than a promise on a piece of paper or an idea in the mind of some revolutionary, through to its status in the world today. Topics discussed include the pivotal political events and power struggles that shaped the country as well as important social and cultural movements. Often, certain dramatic themes and events recur, such as the rise and fall of empires, the flowering and decay of cultures, or the heroism and treachery of leaders. As well, in the history of most countries war, oppression, revolution, and deep social change feature prominently. Nonetheless, the details of such events vary greatly, as does their impact on the nation concerned. For example, England's "Glorious Revolution" of 1688 was a peaceful transfer of power that set the stage for the emergence of democratic institutions in that nation. On the other hand, in China, the overthrow of dynastic rule in 1912 led to years of chaos, civil war, and the eventual emergence of a Communist regime that used violence as a tool to root out opposition and quell popular protest. Readers of the Greenhaven Press History of Nations series will learn about the common challenges nations face and the different paths they take in response to such crises. However a nation's story may have developed, the series strives to present a clear and unbiased view of the country at hand.

The structure of each volume in the series is designed to help students deepen their understanding of the events, movements, and persons that define nations. First, a thematic introduction provides critical background material and helps orient the reader. The chapters themselves are designed to provide an accessible and engaging approach to the study of the history of that nation involved and are arranged either thematically or chronologically, as appropriate. The selections include both primary documents, which convey something of the flavor of the time and place concerned, and secondary material, which includes the wisdom of hindsight and scholarship. Finally, each book closes with a detailed chronology, a comprehensive bibliography of suggestions for further research, and a thorough index.

The countries explored within the series are as old as China and as young as Canada, as distinct in character as Spain and India, as large as Russia, and as compact as Japan. Some are based on ethnic nationalism, the belief in an ethnic group as a distinct people sharing a common destiny, whereas others emphasize civic nationalism, in which what defines citizenship is not ethnicity but commitment to a shared constitution and its values. As human societies become increasingly globalized, knowledge of other nations and of the diversity of their cultures, characteristics, and histories becomes ever more important. This series responds to the challenge by furnishing students with a solid and engaging introduction to the history of the world's nations.

Introduction

"The whole history of India for thousands of years past shows her essential unity and the vitality and adaptability of her culture."[1]
—Jawaharlal Nehru, Indian prime minister, 1947–1964

India is the world's largest democracy, second most populous country, and third oldest civilization. It is the birthplace of the spiritual traditions of China and Japan, Tibet and Thailand, Burma and Sri Lanka. This sacred land of mystics, saints, and seers covers an area the size of Western Europe (excluding Russia), from the icy peaks of the Himalayas in the north to the lush, fertile central valleys known for their sweltering, humid heat. India's people are as diverse as its terrain. Over 1 billion inhabitants belong to several races and ethnic groups, seven prominent religions (Hinduism, Islam, Buddhism, Sikhism, Christianity, Jainism, and Zoroastrianism), and over three thousand castes. They speak roughly two thousand dialects of fourteen major languages, each with its own literary tradition.

Within this mosaic, there are many incongruities: Jeweled marble domes of the world's architectural wonders are perched amid squalid one-room shanties; elephants adorned with violet silk and gold brocade parade through streets lined with limbless beggars; and great and learned sages rub shoulders with illiterate peasants. In addition to this economic inequality, there are also apparent contradictions among Indians' beliefs and ideals. An ideology of nonviolent humanism sits alongside deep-seated discrimination; tolerance for all faiths coexists with violent communal clashes; social revolution is preached by autocrats; and Hindu fundamentalists pursue the material rewards of Western capitalism.

Yet beneath these contrasts lies a culture that has brought unity and continuity to the inhabitants of India for more than four thousand years. Historian Vincent Smith writes of "the underlying fundamental unity of India . . . which transcends the diversities of blood, color, language, dress, manners and sect."[2] India has one of the longest continuous cultural traditions in the world. It has endured many onslaughts by outside forces and shown a remarkable ability to absorb and synthesize external influences while still retaining its essential elements. This capacity to synthesize apparently conflicting ideas into a whole is based on a Hindu tradition that seeks to embrace contradiction, not for the sake of expedience but as a spiritual obligation. Historian A.L. Basham describes this distinctly Indian worldview:

> It is through [its] inclusive spirit that Hindu culture has always found it easy to incorporate new elements, and the process has not ceased. . . . It is a spirit of striving to assimilate apparently opposing elements. . . . [The] perennial vitality of Hinduism [is] largely due to the fact that it [succeeds] in assimilating local elements from all over the subcontinent, as it [assimilates] ideas and practices introduced by successive invaders. . . . Hinduism has shown all through its existence a remarkable assimilative character.[3]

Indus Civilization

This pattern of assimilation goes back to 2500 B.C. to a sophisticated civilization that thrived along the banks of the Indus River in what is now Pakistan. The unearthing of the ancient cities of Harappa and Mohenjo Daro by archaeologists in the 1920s revealed well-planned urban commercial centers with distinct socioreligious beliefs and patterns. This Indus civilization left a number of physical and spiritual legacies that support former Indian prime minister Jawaharlal Nehru's claim that Indian history is like "an ancient palimpsest [where] layer upon layer of thought . . . has been inscribed, [but] no succeeding layer has completely hidden or erased what had been previously written."[4]

The Indus culture made architectural and religious contributions that still shape modern-day India and Pakistan. An aerial view of contemporary houses in Pakistan reveals floor plans and building materials similar to those used in ancient days. Rectangular tanks, much like the great baths found in these ancient cities, are still found in Hindu temples, and Indus religious symbols, like the Buddhist pipal tree, have remained sacred to the present day. The discovery of seals and figurines among the Indus ruins revealed the common worship of animals, trees, a mother goddess, and an early prototype of Lord Shiva, one of the three main Hindu gods.

Cultural practices that trace their origins to these ancient times include the adorning of women in gold and silver jewelry, the use of *kajal* (eye makeup), the decimal system for weights, and the game of dice. Historian Stanley Wolpert says that the layout of the cities, with modest homes found clustered in some areas, suggests a class hierarchy, which may have been the early root of the more complex Indian caste system. According to Wolpert, "the more we study the . . . remains of these remarkable Indus sites, the more it appears that early Indic civilization contained many of the cells of the later Indian socioreligious organism."[5]

The Aryan Invasion and the Evolution of Hindu Thought

Beginning around 1500 B.C., waves of Aryan immigrants from Iran invaded northern India, encountering little resistance from the indigenous people of the Indus Valley. By this time, great Indus cities like Harappa and Mohenjo Daro had declined, mostly because of vast climatic changes that destroyed the agricultural base of their economies. Although the Indus civilization was past its heyday, it retained its distinct traditions, which blended with those of the Aryans to form the first Indian cultural synthesis.

Knowledge of the Aryan period of Indian history comes from the oral tradition of their priests, the Brahmans, who passed thousands of verses of Sanskrit poetry known as the Vedas (Books of Knowledge) down through the ages. From the Vedas, historians gleaned that the Aryans filtered through the Indus Valley and the Punjab from about 1500 to 1000 B.C. Their simple nomadic lifestyle evolved as they absorbed many of the customs, beliefs, and cultures of the more sophisticated people they conquered. Further religious texts—India's two great epics, the Mahabharata and Ramayana—provide more information about this period of the intermingling of cultures. As Wolpert explains, "the Aryan 'conquest' of North India was . . . a process of gradual institutional assimilation and sociocultural integration."[6]

In about 800 B.C., after more than seven centuries of Aryan and pre-Aryan intermingling, a later text, the Vedanta (or Upanishads), reflected the merging of the strongest attributes of the pre-Aryan and Aryan cultures and laid down the basic tenets of the emerging Hindu synthesis. Specific deities, central religious concepts, and caste social division were assimilated by the Vedic religion, then known as Brahmanism. Historian Ainslie T. Embree describes how the Aryans assimilated deities from the people they conquered:

> Often . . . gods that had originally no connection with [the major Hindu gods] Shiva or Vishnu were pictured [in religious texts] as their wives and children. Thus Ganesh, the elephant-headed god, had probably been an extremely ancient deity of some primitive non-Aryan tribe, but he was brought into the Shiva cult by making him the son of Shiva and his wife Parvati, who herself was a mother goddess imported from some ancient source.[7]

Many central concepts of Hinduism were adapted from the beliefs of the indigenous groups conquered by the Aryans. As Hinduism evolved in the Late Vedic period, the simple, polytheistic worship of nature gods gave way to a more sophisticated philosophy and religious doctrine based around a belief in reincarnation. Central Hindu concepts that date back to the Vedic period include the belief that all human beings have an immortal soul (*atma*) that passes through many lifetimes of suffering until it is liberated from the cycle of rebirth and reunited with the divine; that the moral quality of one's actions in this life determines the conditions of the next life (karma); and that good deeds are determined by the duties of one's social position (dharma).

The institution of caste also emerged from the synthesis of the Aryans and the peoples they conquered. India was subject to many invasions and evolved a complex racial mix of dark-skinned Dravidians, yellow-skinned Mongols, and lighter-skinned Aryans. Persians, Greeks, and Scythians who settled in the subcontinent added to the melting pot. Originally, caste was a functional division of society into four classes, or *varnas,* based on occupation: Brahmans were the learned priests; Kshatriyas, the warriors; Vaisyas, the merchants; and Sudras, the cultivators. The Untouchables, usually the darkest-skinned people, were outside the caste structure and subject to strict codes regarding physical contact and ceremonial purity. The Brahmans occupied a privileged position as intermediaries between the people and the many manifestations of God.

Buddhism and Jainism

In response to abuses of authority by the Brahmans in the sixth century B.C., two major outgrowths of the Hindu synthesis challenged key concepts of the evolving religion. Both Buddhism (founded by Kshatriya prince Siddhartha Gautama) and Jainism (founded by another Kshatriyan, Mahavira) rejected caste social division in favor of more egalitarian creeds. They initially claimed to be part of the Aryan Hindu tradition, offering new paths to the liberation of the soul from the cycle of rebirth. So, orthodox Brahmans did not grasp the challenge these breakaway sects would eventually pose to their social order. Yet while Buddhism and Jainism competed for the loyalty of the Indian people for the next several centuries, many of the tenets of both Jainism and Buddhism were eventually absorbed into mainstream Hinduism, further demonstrating the latter faith's capacity to absorb new ideas.

For example, *ahimsa,* the Jainist concept of nonviolence, made a lasting impression on Hindu thought. Based on the notion of the unity of all living things as manifestations of God, *ahimsa* encouraged Hindus to adopt vegetarianism and would play a central role in Mahatma Gandhi's philosophy during India's independence struggle of the twentieth century.

Buddhism's emphasis on understanding the true nature of the universe through meditation was also incorporated into Hinduism, and by the fifth century A.D., when Vishnu and Shiva became the major Hindu gods, "Lord Buddha" was drawn into the Hindu faith as an incarnation of Vishnu. Indian historian Ranbir Vohra says, "Because of this absorptive power of Hinduism, even well-defined heterodox sects, such as Buddhism and Jainism, got fitted into the Hindu order and their members came to form separate castes."[8]

Imperial Unification: The Flowering of Hindu Life and Culture

Hinduism further evolved during two great periods of imperial unification, with an interlude of significant religious inquiry and scholarship. The first unification came when Chandragupta Maurya (322–298 B.C.) unified the people of the Gangetic and Indus Valleys under his imperial administration. According to historian Percival Spear, the Mauryan dynasty was itself a synthesis, drawing on Persian influences that had been brought when Persian ruler Darius I conquered the Indus Valley and Western Punjab in 518 B.C. The idea of divine monarchy, solar cults, reverence for fire, and the Mauryan imperial organization all bear the Persian imprint.

While Chandragupta Maurya established a sophisticated administrative framework across India, it was Ashoka (ca. 272–232 B.C.), Chandragupta's grandson, who tried to forge a spiritual bond among his diverse subjects. Attracted to the nonviolent doctrine in Buddhism, Ashoka provided a Buddhist-centered ethical framework to morally uplift and unite his people. He preached nonviolence, religious tolerance, and right moral conduct on rock edicts placed throughout his empire. Wolpert observes that, under the emperor Ashoka, "India's diverse peoples and tribes . . . received their first infusions of what we would now call national ideology and culture."[9]

The five centuries between the first and second imperial unification of India were a time of great intellectual creativity. New forms of devotional religion emerged around the main Hindu gods, Vishnu and Shiva. The Ramayana and the Mahabharata were edited into their present-day form, and the Bhagavad Gita, the most influential text in the Hindu religion, was composed. The Bhagavad Gita first imparted the doctrine of inclusiveness and tolerance for all faiths, which is at the root of the Indian ability to embrace alternative viewpoints and pursue apparently conflicting courses with equanimity. As Vohra notes,

> What makes Hinduism the most tolerant of all religions is its syncretic nature and its acceptance of the fact that there are many paths that lead to God . . . and that God accepts all of them. [This was first stated] in the words of Lord Krishna (from the Bhagavad Gita) "And even those who worship other gods with a firm faith in doing so, involuntarily worship me, too."[10]

Further consolidation of Hinduism took place during the second great imperial unification of north India under the Guptas: Chandra Gupta I (A.D. 320–335), Samudra Gupta (335–376), and Chandra Gupta II (376–415). During this vibrant and creative period, Hinduism was honed and refined to its modern shape. The major contemporary deities, including the mother goddess, were adopted, and image worship became common practice as numerous temples were constructed throughout India to house the many gods and goddesses. Hindu cultural and intellectual life blossomed: Kalidasa, named the Shakespeare of India, wrote his greatest Sanskrit plays; brilliant Indian minds contributed to world knowledge in mathematics, astronomy, physiology, and medicine; and artists produced some of the finest religiously inspired paintings and sculptures of ancient India.

Muslim Invasion and the Hindu-Muslim Synthesis

The invasion of the Huns from central Asia at the close of the fifth century marked the decline of the Gupta Empire. It served as a prelude to two other invasions—first by Muslims in the eighth century, then by the British in the nineteenth century—that would dominate India for more than a thousand years.

Aggressive Islamic marauders first invaded the subcontinent in A.D. 711. The monotheistic and austere faith of the invaders clashed with the Hindu belief in many gods and reincarnation, as well as the music and revelry that surrounded Hindu religious life. The Islamic doctrine that all men are equal before God was also antithetical to Hindu caste divisions. "Not since the Aryan invasion had so powerful, persistent, unyielding a challenge been launched against Indic civilization and its basic beliefs and values,"[11] says Wolpert.

This challenge was mounted in earnest when the Mughal Empire was established in India in the sixteenth century. The Mughal period was marked by several outstanding emperors: Akbar (1556–1605), Jahangir (1605–1627), Shah Jahan (1628– 1658), and Aurangzeb (1658–1707). They created an imposing empire and each played a role in the synthesis of Muslim and Indian cultures. According to Wolpert, "Each [of the emperors] in his own way epitomizes some aspects of the complex syncretism within which they lived and over which they presided. The courts they maintained, the courtiers they chose, reflected a new syncretic patina of civilization that was a blend of Indian, Persian, and Central Asian manners and mores."[12]

In the sphere of religion, a number of new sects reflected syntheses of Hindu and Muslim beliefs. Sufism, which emerged in reaction to orthodox Islam (outside of India at first), cultivated a determination to know God through seclusion, meditation, and the study of metaphysics. Sufi ideas were attractive to Hindus, and the tombs of Sufi saints became places of worship for both communities. In the fifteenth century, Kabir (1440–1518) synthesized

Islam and Hinduism into one faith and inspired millions of Hindus and Muslims to pursue his religion, which emphasized the simple love of God. Another religious synthesis was developed by Nanak (1469–1539), a Hindu by birth who opposed the caste system and idol worship. His new religion of Sikhism aimed at a reconciliation between the faiths, emphasizing monotheism, derived from Islam, and karma and rebirth from the Hindu tradition.

The Hindu-Persian synthesis had a particular impact on high culture. Hindu society adopted certain Muslim fashions, such as seclusion of women and the wearing of Muslim dress. Urdu, a synthesis of Hindi, Persian, and Arabic, developed as a major literary language. In art, a blend of Perso-Islamic and Rajput-Hindu styles evolved, and in architecture the Arabic dome and arch merged with indigenous architecture to produce a hybrid style known as "Indo-Islamic."

The mingling of cultural practices went both ways. Muslim military penetration into India came in successive waves, which ensured that each invading group was influenced by local culture. Muslim soldiers married Hindu women who introduced Hindu practices into Muslim households. And while Hindus adopted Muslim dress, Muslims wore the Hindu turban. Even some caste conventions spread to the Muslim community. After many centuries of this close contact, the differences in the everyday lives of Hindus and Muslims were lessened. As Wolpert concludes, "Over time the process of cultural accommodation and synthesis—linguistic, artistic, genetic—rubbed off many sharp edges of doctrinal difference between Hindus and Muslims."[13]

There were, however, limits on the level of synthesis or fusion between the two fundamentally different religions and worldviews. Although the Mughal period witnessed a great deal of adaptation, Islam was not absorbed into mainstream Hinduism. As historian Percival Spear notes, "There was much give and take, but no fusion. . . . In daily life, there was much day-to-day tolerance and consideration, but behind it all was a permanent tension between the two ways of life. Indo-Persian culture spread a mantle of elegance over the whole of Indian aristocratic society, but Hinduism and Islam remained apart."[14]

Contemporary historians assert that tension between Hindus and Muslim rulers, court infighting, and overspending by the emperors were some of the factors leading to the slow decline of the Mughal Empire in the eighteenth century. The vacuum of authority was soon filled by enterprising European traders, heralding the second great alien intrusion into the subcontinent.

The Assault of the West

The European presence in India began in 1498, when Portuguese explorer Vasco da Gama was lured to India's western seaboard by spices, silk, and gold. The Portuguese traders who set up the first European trading post at Goa were soon followed by the Dutch, the French, and the English. After years of conflict among the European powers, British military supremacy in India was established with the victory of Robert Clive over local Bengal ruler Siraj U. Daula at the battle of Plassey in southern India in 1757. Clive's British East India Company expanded its authority throughout southern and western India, until the British dominion embraced

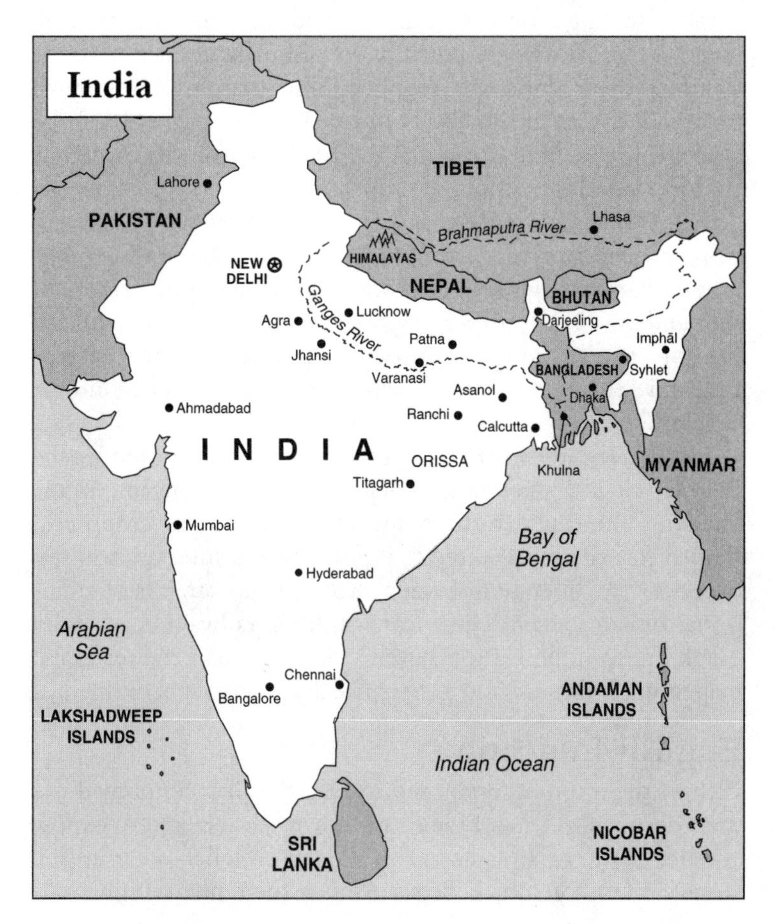

the whole subcontinent. The mighty British rule, or Raj, would dominate India for the better part of the next two centuries.

Although of far shorter duration than the Mughal period, the Raj was in many ways more intrusive in its character and more pervasive in its influence on the Indian subcontinent. Traditional Indian life was challenged on many levels by modernization, the industrial revolution, and the Western intellectual tradition. "Not only have political and economic structures of Indian society been far more profoundly modified by the Western impact than they were by the Islamic," notes Embree, "but the cultural and religious life of the people has been challenged by the pervasive forces of Western modernity."[15]

The century following Clive's victory witnessed a dramatic change in the relationship between Great Britain and India. Though trading officials continued to be concerned mostly with increasing profits, a new breed of Englishman, imbued with the teachings of utilitarian philosopher John Stuart Mill, was drawn to India's shores in the 1830s and 1840s. As early as 1813 the British Parliament declared that the British East India Company should amend the "moral condition" of its subjects. This encouraged British evangelists and social reformers, who wanted to help "civilize" and modernize India. The British reformers' attitude of patronizing superiority was best expressed by British author and poet Rudyard Kipling, who helped popularize the notion of "the white man's burden," a phrase that euphemized England's efforts to control its colonies' cultural and economic development.

Ultimately, however, many of the reforms imposed by the British helped India win its independence from England in the twentieth century. In the realm of economic development, British free traders asserted that government intervention was necessary to "liberate free trade" from the constraints of traditional Indian society. This meant building railways, roads, telegraph lines, and irrigation systems. Railways and the telegraph helped unify the vast and geographically diverse subcontinent.

English Education

Perhaps the most important reform that the British imposed was their decision to teach English in Indian schools, and to expose an elite group of Indians to the Western intellectual tradition taught in London's top colleges. Among the numerous linguistically diverse ethnic groups in India, English helped serve as a common language essential to the development of national unity.

When the British Parliament renewed the East India Company's charter in 1813, it also allocated a modest 10,000 pounds for Indian education. There had been debate in Britain over whether the funds should be spent promoting traditional literary languages (Sanskrit and Arabic) or English. British politician Thomas Babington Macaulay, in his famous "Minute on Education," asserted the superiority of the English language, literature, and race. He wrote that the British should create a local educated elite "Indian in blood and color, [but] English in taste, in opinions, in morals and in intellect,"[16] to act as an intermediary between the Raj and the people of India. "Macaulay envisaged a new type of conquest," says historian Michael Edwardes. "The invaders of India before the British had slowly been absorbed into the Indian scene, but Macaulay saw English education as the means of assimilating India into the English tradition."[17]

Macaulay's "Minute" proved persuasive. India's best and brightest scholars went abroad, and, steeped in the West's powerful intellectual tradition, they began to reassess their culture. This had profound implications for India's future. Historian Judith M. Brown explains:

> The new education . . . had ideological and political . . . repercussions which were of almost immeasurable consequence in the making of modern India. . . . It stimulated radical consideration of Hindu tradition and society . . . as western religious and secular values became available as a source of comparison. . . . The result was a commitment to social reform among a small group of educated Indians.[18]

English education and social reform raised important questions about Hindu traditions. Among Indians, there was a diverse range of responses to the British presence and their philosophies. Many Indians embraced Western ideas, and a relatively small proportion converted to Christianity. In contrast, by mid–nineteenth century, fears among some orthodox Hindus that the British wanted to make India a Christian nation led to fear, hostility, and in some cases violence.

The most common Indian reaction to the Western assault on

their traditions was more critical and selective. Indian reformers advocated adopting some features of Western society, especially those involving political and technological progress. The reevaluation of the Indian worldview in the light of Western rational doctrine provided a highly charged intellectual atmosphere. Percival Spear writes,

> Out of the mingling of these reactions came the intellectual ferment of the nineteenth and twentieth centuries. Perhaps nowhere else in the history of the world can one see a meeting of cultures and traditions comparable to that which took place in India, as western civilization, confident of its own greatness and proud of its achievements, met Hindu tradition. Although for a time uncertain and confused, Hinduism rallied to assert an equal pride and confidence in its greatness. . . . One of the most important features of the period was the reinterpretation that took place of the meaning of many of the values and ideals of [Hindu] tradition. . . . This task of reinterpretation was necessary for the renaissance of Hinduism to meet the conditions of the modern world.[19]

Hindu Renaissance

The father of Hindu Renaissance, Ram Mohan Roy (1772–1833), was the first and most influential Indian reformer of the nineteenth century. A Western-educated Bengali intellectual, Roy advocated going back to the first principles set out in the Vedas, while also incorporating worthy elements from the West. In 1828 he founded the Brahmo Samaj (the Divine Society), which subscribed to both Eastern and Western traditions and sought to reform Hindu practices such as suttee (the practice of widows throwing themselves on their husbands' funeral pyres), idolatry, and the extremes of the caste system.

Roy's ideas provided a principle that effectively linked the new Western ideas with Indian tradition. He took the Western concept of reason and demonstrated how this same principle was at the base of classical Vedic philosophy in the Upanishads. This had important consequences. Spear elaborates:

> Hinduism could [now] be justified . . . on the grounds that it provided a reasonable explanation of reality.

> Everything from the west could be considered in the same light. There could be assimilation and not merely borrowing at random. It was a case of one philosopher examining the system of another, not of a man adrift in a sea of new ideas clutching at the flotsam and jetsam of other worlds drifting by. Rammohan Roy's approach restored Indian intellectual and moral self respect and gave Indians a sense of choosing rather than receiving the gifts of a new world.[20]

Roy's outlook permeated the Indian middle-class response to the West throughout the nineteenth century. Indians supported the banning of infanticide and adopted English education and the Western professions of law and medicine. Roy undermined the notion of Brahman superiority and the caste system by accepting the dignity and equal value of all human beings. His belief in people's equality provided a basis within Hindu thought for democratic principles and pioneered the creative synthesis between Eastern and Western cultures, a process that continues in India today.

Muslim Response

The cultural synthesis advocated by Roy was not confined to the Hindu community. Political scientist Vera Micheles Dean notes that India's spirit of inclusiveness, though based on Hindu traditional thought, also infiltrated the Muslim population: "[The assimilation of conflicting views] . . . deeply rooted in Hindu religion and philosophy, [is not] prevalent solely among Hindus. It has also come to affect the thinking and attitudes of the Muslims who ruled India for three centuries, [and] have been . . . deeply imbued with the Hindu state of mind."[21]

Western-education Muslim leader Sayyid Ahmad Khan (1817–1898), like Roy, provided an ideological connection between Islam and the West by linking Western rationality to classical Islamic thought. Wolpert views Ahmad Khan as "the first human bridge between Islamic tradition and western thought."[22] Although Ahmad Khan's interpretation of the Koran (the Muslim holy book) was rejected by Muslim orthodoxy and in its specifics found little following, it had important symbolic appeal. "In detail the religious thought of Sayyid Ahmad Khan . . . had no general following; but its general affect was tremendous," writes

Muslim historian Aziz Ahmad. "He liberalized Indian Islam and made it susceptible to new ideas and new interpretations."[23]

The Rebellion of 1857 and the Indian Nationalist Movement

Both Muslim and Hindu religious reform movements were pushed into the background in the wake of the Indian Rebellion of 1857. In May of that year, a localized revolt by Hindu and Muslim sepoys (Indians employed as soldiers by Britain) over their unjust dismissal for refusing to violate dietary laws escalated into a widespread two-year war, with brutal retribution on both sides. British military superiority coupled with poor coordination on the part of the Indians settled the dispute in Britain's favor, but not without serious consequences.

The first consequence was Queen Victoria's 1858 proclamation making India a formal part of the British Empire, removing governing authority from the British East India Company and vesting it in the British Parliament. Another consequence of the rebellion was Britain's abandonment of its liberal agenda that promoted political, economic, and social change in India. The Raj now pursued a more conservative approach, while strengthening its military control.

The third and most important consequence of the rebellion was that it gave birth to India's nationalist movement. From India's viewpoint, the unsuccessful 1857 war proved the futility of violent revolt. Many of the brightest Indian minds, heirs to Macaulay's education policy, knew they must unite to press peacefully for political concessions from Britain. On December 28, 1885, seventy-three representatives, from every province of British India, met under the leadership of Calcutta barrister Womesh Bonnerjee for the first meeting of the Indian National Congress. At that meeting, Congress members declared that the Indian people "should have their proper and legitimate share [in the government]."[24]

While the Congress united Indian intellectuals from all over the subcontinent, it attracted strong personalities with different ideas concerning means and ends, particularly in regard to religious and social reform. Two approaches emerged, representing alternative ideologies that continue to shape modern Indian politics. As historian J.T.F. Jordens explains, "Nationalism developed two patterns, a religious one and a secular one, and each assigned a different place to social reform."[25]

The secular, Western-oriented approach of the nationalist movement was championed by Indians like Mahadev Ranade (1842–1901), an English-educated Brahman who was a high court judge in Bombay. Ranade and his disciple Gopal K. Gokhale (1866–1915) represented the moderate faction of Congress, who believed that Indians had to reform their society before they could govern it. Their views were an extension of Roy's work advocating the equal treatment of men and women of all castes and creeds or, in Gokhale's words, "assimilation of all that is best in the life and thought and character of the west."[26]

The second approach, adopted by the extremist faction of the Congress, was based on traditional Hindu rhetoric and was embodied in Poona Brahman B.G. Tilak. Tilak was appalled by the subservient attitude of the moderates. He instead called on the glories of the Hindu past to rouse popular support. Tilak quoted the Bhagavad Gita to justify acts of aggression and terrorism against the British and demanded immediate *swaraj* (home rule). Despite the extremists' use of traditional heroes and symbols, their methods also represented a synthesis between Eastern and Western ideas. As historian H.F. Owen writes,

> The very turning back to an idealized national cultural past for inspiration was in the mainstream of nineteenth century European romanticism and its offspring, nationalism. The Extremist nationalists used largely Western techniques—trying to mobilize the support of public opinion through newspapers and public meetings, employing passive resistance . . . and occasional terrorist tactics. . . . The whole notion that self-government is somehow the individual's and the nation's right has a . . . Western ring about it.[27]

Muslim reaction to the Indian nationalist movement was also divided, though this debate was about whether Muslims should join forces with the Hindu-dominated Congress or seek separate representation. Although some Muslims supported the cause of Indian unity and the Congress, a number of educated Muslims, including Sayyid Ahmad Khan, were concerned for the fate of their people if the British withdrew. "India is inhabited by different nationalities," said Ahmad Khan "and the experiment which the Indian National Congress wants to make [independence] is fraught with dangers and suffering for all the nationalities of India, especially the Muslims."[28] Ahmad Khan's Aligarh University, established as part of his Islamic reform program, became the intellectual base that sprouted the Muslim League, a political party formed in 1906 to represent the minority Muslim viewpoint. By the 1940s, the League was championing the cause of separatism and the demand for a separate Muslim state in Pakistan.

British Repression

The first three decades of the Indian National Congress were dominated by the debate between the moderates and extremists. During World War I, under Tilak's inspiration, agitational politics increased. Through his use of traditional symbols, Tilak began to deepen the base of support for the nationalist movement, building it from an elite-based party into one of mass appeal. As this nationalist movement gathered momentum, the British became more determined to suppress it.

The pinnacle of British repression came with the provocative Rowlatt Acts and the subsequent Amritsar Massacre of 1919. Alarmed by the activities of Hindu extremists, the British extended the suspension of civil liberties that had been in force during the war. Under the Rowlatt Acts, people were imprisoned without trial, and freedom of speech and of the press were denied. Indians protested these indignities. In the tense atmosphere created by these protests, British general R.E.H. Dyer ordered the murder and maiming of sixteen hundred people who were peacefully protesting the Rowlatt Acts. Dyer justified his actions, saying it was "the least amount of firing which would produce the necessary moral and widespread effect it was my duty to produce . . . throughout the Punjab."[29]

From then on, the nationalist movement took on a new character. Motilal Nehru, father of Jawaharlal Nehru, told the eight thousand delegates at the 1919 December meeting of Congress, "If our lives and honor are to remain at the mercy of an irresponsible executive and military, if the ordinary rights of human beings are denied to us, then all talk of reform is a mockery."[30] The era of cooperation with the British was over. The Western-educated and once-loyal British supporter Mohandas Karamchand Gandhi condemned the "Black Acts" and led a protest march calling on Indians to refuse to obey such "unjust subversive laws" and instead join a nationwide suspension of work for twenty-four hours in the first week of April 1919.

Mahatma Gandhi's Synthesis

This was the first of a number of Gandhi's satyagraha ("Hold fast to the truth") campaigns, based on *satya,* meaning truth, which came from the ancient Hindu Vedic literature, and *ahimsa,* or nonviolence, drawn from the Jain, Buddhist, and later Hindu traditions. From 1919 to 1947, Gandhi was the leading figure in the struggle for Indian independence. His revolutionary movement had two levels. On one level, Gandhi implored Indians to protest British rule through nonviolent noncooperation. In response, Indians resigned from government office and boycotted foreign goods. On a second level, Gandhi advocated civil disobedience, calling for noncompliance with or even the breaking of British laws that Indians felt were morally wrong (for example, they defied the government's monopoly on salt by making salt from seawater).

Gandhi urged his people to take a stance for independence and to submit to violence and punishment without responding in kind. His strategy created a moral force that at first baffled and finally defeated the British. Gandhi's methods also represented a unique and creative synthesis of different traditions. Much of his philosophy came from Hindu concepts like *apasya* (self-inflicted suffering) and the call for traditional *hartals* (closing of businesses in protest). Gandhi practiced *brahmacharya* (celibacy), which his countrymen believed invoked superphysical powers, and, drawing on ancient Hindu stories, he called for *Ram Raj* (the rule of the Hindu god-king Rama) to replace the British Raj. In this manner, Gandhi used Hindu scripture to inspire national unity in a revolutionary way.

Gandhi combined this creative interpretation of Hindu scriptures with political and philosophical ideas from the West. His civil disobedience and passive resistance programs were inspired by philosophers Henry David Thoreau and Leo Tolstoy, and his emphasis on love and self-effacing poverty was drawn in part from Christianity. Egalitarianism, embodied in his championing of the cause of the Untouchables, drew on Western doctrines of liberalism and humanism. In this fusion of ideas and beliefs, Gandhi developed a unique cultural synthesis. "He followed the long established Hindu pattern of syncretism," says Judith M.

Brown, "and 'imported' from the West the notions of the dignity of labor and equality of the sexes, without any sense that he was threatening the Hindu heritage, rather that he was enriching it."[31]

Mohammed Ali Jinnah and the Partition of India

While Gandhi's eclectic approach using Hindu symbols drew India's masses into the independence struggle, it unwittingly alienated the Muslim community. The actions of Hindu extremists, coupled with Congress leaders' neglect of Muslim concerns, led Western-educated lawyer Mohammed Ali Jinnah to take up the cause of independence for India's Muslims. Convinced that the British Raj would be replaced by a Hindu government, the once-staunch supporter of a united secular independent state of India became the champion of a separate Muslim nation based on the Islamic faith.

During the 1930s and '40s, Jinnah deepened the base of support for the Muslim League and united disparate Muslims from all over India. He also drew from a number of traditions in his bid to articulate a modern Muslim persona. Jinnah created a national culture based on Urdu as the language of Islamic nationalism and wore a national dress drawn from all parts of India—the *sherwani* (long black coat) and *karakulki* cap from north India, the *shalwar* (pajamas) from the Indus region, and the *kurta* (Muslim shirt) from Delhi. He also wore elegant English suits with the *karakulki* cap, suggesting his comfort with modern Western and Eastern traditions.

With his own particular blend of East and West, Jinnah created a contemporary Muslim identity and gave his people a vision for the future of a modern Muslim nation. In his Lahore Resolution to the Muslim League in 1940, Jinnah presented the two-nation theory that became the justification for the creation of Pakistan:

> The Hindus and Muslims belong to two different religious philosophies, social customs, literatures. . . . Their outlooks on life are different. . . . To yolk together two such nations under a single state, one as a numerical minority and the other as a majority, must lead to . . . final destruction of any fabric that may be so built up for the government of such a state. . . . The problem in

> India is not of an inter-communal character but manifestly of an international one.[32]

Jinnah's Lahore Resolution proved prescriptive. Despite efforts by Gandhi, Congress leaders, and the British to prevent the partition of the Indian subcontinent, negotiations between the two sides broke down. Under threat of civil war, the British hastily drew up boundaries in the final weeks before their departure. On August 14, 1947, the Muslim nation of Pakistan was created, and on August 15, India was freed from foreign domination for the first time in more than a thousand years.

Vision of a Republic

"Long years ago, we made a tryst with destiny," said Jawaharlal Nehru to the gathering of India's Constituent Assembly on the eve of independence, "and now the time comes when we shall redeem our pledge. . . . At the stroke of the midnight hour, when the world sleeps, India will wake to life and freedom."[33] The eloquent and visionary Nehru was prime minister of India from 1947 to 1964. His vision came to dominate the Indian landscape for the first forty-five years of freedom, first through his premiership and then through that of his daughter Indira Gandhi (not related to Mohandas Gandhi) and grandson Rajiv. Nehru advocated a strong secular democratic state to guide an economic and social revolution designed to put an end to poverty. He sought to bring India on a par with advanced industrial nations, while at the same time reforming society from within based on the rights of the individual.

Nehru's program embraced a number of contradictory impulses. India was to be a modern democracy with an independent judiciary, but a strong central authority would direct a centrally planned economic development program. Nehru envisioned a socialist pattern of society but one based on Gandhian principles. This drew heavily on India's cultural tradition of assimilating conflicting principles. Political scientist Francis Carnell writes that "Nehruism" was an example of "the Indian sponge trick" or "the belief, common to the ruling elite, in the infinitely absorptive capacity of Hinduism [where] what look like disharmonies, inconsistencies and contradictions to a Western eye can be made compatible with each other by an Indian. . . . They can exist side by side without giving rise to conflict or the urge for a strictly logical solution."[34]

The doctrine of synthesis that underlay Nehru's modernizing program was an operating principle in the drafting of India's constitution from December 1946 to December 1949. Indian leaders were able to resolve the dilemma posed by wanting India to be a republic but also wanting it to remain part of the British Commonwealth. (Other countries such as Ireland were not able to reconcile being a republic and part of a monarchy.) The doctrine of synthesis was also used to deal with seemingly irreconcilable demands for a strong central government and devolution of power to the local level. Indians applied both principles to different levels of government: The power of the provincial governments would be centralized at a national level, while decentralization of power would dominate politics below the provincial level.

The First Fifty Years of Freedom

Nehru's unorthodox approach met with mixed success. While strong democratic institutions were established, the dominance of the Congress Party (also known as the "Congress Raj") preempted the formation of a vibrant multiparty system. Congress monopolized the control and distribution of resources at the expense of popular participation; large industrial development projects failed to address chronic poverty; higher education expanded and improved at the expense of the basic literacy of the people; traditional caste divisions continued to operate in practice despite the growth of India's middle class; and reforms of the Hindu code permitting intercaste marriages and giving women rights to divorce and to inherit property incurred an orthodox backlash in practice. "In most areas we find an air of half-achievement, of a process stopping short,"[35] says Percival Spear.

Shortly after his death, Nehru's daughter Indira Gandhi was elected prime minister. During her term (1966–1984), she shook to the core the strong democratic structures and freedoms so prized by her father. In 1975, after the High Court of Allahabad found her guilty of using illegal campaign practices and ordered her to resign, Gandhi declared a state of emergency under which she had her political foes imprisoned and strictly censored the press. She also allowed her elder son, Sanjay Gandhi, to abuse his political powers. Indira Gandhi's authoritarian tactics, personal patronage, and sometimes questionable political dealings eroded both the unity and the popular support of the Congress Party.

Her younger son Rajiv, who succeeded his mother after her assassination in 1984, failed to restore the edifice created by his grandfather. Ranbir Vohra comments,

> Nehru's daughter and grandson, lacking his self-discipline and vision for India, turned democracy into a patrimonial system that personalized and corrupted power and impaired the proper functioning of the party, the cabinet, the Parliament, the judiciary, and the bureaucracy by diminishing their authority and political role. By [the 1990s], the Congress had lost all prestige and had become a moribund party.[36]

The Congress Party regained power from 1991 to 1996, however, under the premiership of P.V. Narasimha Rao. Rao embraced a new approach. After years of tight government controls, bureaucratic inefficiency, and disincentives to foreign investment, Rao abandoned Nehru's socialism for liberal capitalism. Rao's bold economic reforms had telling results: In the first three years, he reversed India's economic stagnation and recorded an annual growth rate of 7 percent. Yet despite success with the economy, Rao lost popularity amid accusations of corruption, and for failing to prevent the most serious Hindu-Muslim clashes since partition.

In May 1996, 330 million Indians voted for several thousand candidates competing for 545 seats in New Delhi's Lok Sabha (the lower house of Parliament). No single party, among more than three dozen contenders, won a majority. Instead, a multiparty coalition led by the Hindu fundamentalist Bharatiya Janata Party (BJP), under the leadership of Atul Behari Vajpayee, took office. BJP leaders forged their coalition around an emphasis on Hindu traditions. Vajpayee called freely on symbols of India's past to promote a unified modern nation (the BJP election logo—the lotus—was an ancient Hindu and Buddhist symbol, and its flag used saffron and green, the holy colors of Hinduism and Islam). Yet like Indian leaders before him, Vajpayee drew his own meanings from traditional concepts to fit the imperatives of his modern context. Contrary to its election manifesto, which preached *swadeshi* (the purchase of homemade goods only), the BJP continued with Rao's liberal capitalism. Vajpayee justified the actions, saying, "Swadeshi in today's context, is anything that [strengthens] India's economic base."[37]

The Road Ahead

The synthesis of seemingly irreconcilable ideologies continues to be a major thread woven through Indian political, social, and economic life. The assimilative character of Indian culture provides a formula for creative and experimental approaches to life in the twenty-first century. At the start of the new millennium, India's record in assimilating radical new ideas is impressive. In 1997, K.R. Narayanan, a dalit (Untouchable) by birth, was sworn in as India's president, a position occupied by both a Muslim and a Sikh since 1980, which is significant in a nation more than 80 percent Hindu. India's Supreme Court staunchly advocates civil rights and has not shied away from taking top government officials to task over corruption. In addition, the free press continues to provoke lively public debate, and democracy deepens as peasants and the lowest caste members gain a voice in government affairs.

With economic liberalization, India has taken a leading global role in information technology (Indians founded major firms like Sun Microsystems and Hotmail). The new middle class provides a huge market for the country's goods and services, which augurs well for continued economic growth. But on the other side of the coin, the gap between the haves and have-nots has never been more obvious. Indian unity is under duress from class conflict, erosion of power at the center, communal violence, regional demands for succession, and the disintegrating caste system, which, despite its inequality, has brought social stability to the subcontinent through the millennia. Strained relations with Pakistan (which have worsened since the mid-1990s because of both countries' testing of nuclear weapons) adds to the mix. Some critics have even claimed that India's problems have made the country ungovernable.

Others, like author V.S. Naipaul, believe that India is on the brink of the biggest transformation in its history. Freed from foreign domination, central government control, and rigid caste social divisions, optimists claim the nation is pulsating with vibrant new energy. "The idea of freedom has gone everywhere," writes Naipaul. "Independence was worked for ... by people at the top; the freedom it brought has worked its way down. People everywhere have ideas of who they are and what they owe themselves."[38] In the dawning of the new millennium, with India projected to be the most populous country on earth by 2050, the world looks on with wonder, awe, and apprehension.

Notes

1. Quoted in Granville Austin, *The Indian Constitution: Cornerstone of a Nation.* Oxford, England: Clarendon Press, 1966, p. 321.
2. Vincent Smith, *Oxford History of India.* Oxford, England: Oxford University Press, 1919, p. x.
3. A.L. Basham, *Aspects of Ancient Indian Culture.* New York: Asia Publishing House, 1966, pp. 35, 43.
4. Jawaharlal Nehru, "The Discovery of India: Part II, the Quest," in Thomas R. Metcalf, ed., *Modern India: An Interpretive Anthology.* London: Macmillan, 1971, p. 8.
5. Stanley Wolpert, *India.* Berkeley and Los Angeles: University of California Press, 1991, p. 26.
6. Stanley Wolpert, *A New History of India.* New York: Oxford University Press, 2000, p. 37.
7. Ainslie T. Embree, ed., *The Hindu Tradition: Readings in Oriental Thought.* New York: Vintage Books, 1972, p. 209.
8. Ranbir Vohra, *The Making of India: A Historical Survey.* New York: M.E. Sharpe, 1997, p. 31.
9. Wolpert, *A New History of India*, p. 35.
10. Vohra, *The Making of India*, p. 31.
11. Wolpert, *India,* p. 39.
12. Wolpert, *India,* p. 40.
13. Wolpert, *India,* p. 41.
14. Percival Spear, *India: A Modern History.* Ann Arbor: University of Michigan Press, 1972, p. 101.
15. Embree, *The Hindu Tradition,* p. 273.
16. Quoted in Michael Edwardes, *A History of India.* New York: Farrar, Strauss, and Cudahy, 1961, p. 264.
17. Edwardes, *A History of India,* p. 255.
18. Judith M. Brown, *The Origins of an Asian Democracy.* Delhi, India: Oxford University Press, 1985, p. 77.
19. Spear, *India,* pp. 266–67.
20. Spear, *India,* p. 296.
21. Vera Micheles Dean, *New Patterns of Democracy in India.* Cambridge, MA: Harvard University Press, 1959, p. 3.
22. Wolpert, *A New History of India,* p. 263.
23. Aziz Ahmad, "Islamic Reform Movements," in A.L. Basham, ed., *A Cultural History of India.* Oxford, England: Clarendon Press, 1975, p. 387.

24. Wolpert, *A New History of India,* pp. 258–89.
25. J.T.F. Jordens, "Hindu Religious and Social Reform in British India," in Basham, *A Cultural History of India,* p. 373.
26. Quoted in Basham, *A Cultural History of India,* p. 392.
27. H.F. Owen, "The Nationalist Movement," in Basham, *A Cultural History of India,* p. 393.
28. Quoted in Wolpert, *India,* p. 60.
29. Quoted in Wolpert, *A New History of India,* p. 299.
30. Quoted in Wolpert, *A New History of India,* p. 300.
31. Brown, *The Origins of an Asian Democracy,* p. 207.
32. Quoted in C.H. Philips, *The Evolution of India and Pakistan: Select Documents on Indian History.* London: Oxford University Press, 1962, pp. 353–54.
33. Jawaharlal Nehru, *Independence and After: A Collection of Speeches, 1946–49.* New York: John Day, 1950, p. 123.
34. Francis Carnell, "Political Ideas and Ideologies in South and South-East Asia," in Saul Rose, ed., *Politics in Southern Asia.* London: Macmillan, 1963, pp. 281–82.
35. Spear, *India,* p. 255.
36. Vohra, *The Making of India,* p. 227.
37. Quoted in Barbara D. and Thomas R. Metcalf, *A Concise History of India.* New York: Cambridge University Press, 2001, p. 289.
38. V.S. Naipaul, *India: A Million Mutinies Now.* New York: Viking Penguin, 1990, p. 518.

Chapter 1

Ancient and Medieval India

The Rise and Fall of Early Indus Civilization

By Hermann Kulke and Dietmar Rothermund

From the discovery in the 1920s by archeologists of the two great cities of Harappa and Mohenjo-Daro in northwestern India, historians know that early civilizations of the Indus Valley engaged in sophisticated city planning and international trade and held religious beliefs echoed in India today. In the following extract from A History of India, *historian Hermann Kulke points to more recent archeological findings of the 1950s and '60s that have thrown light on the reasons for the decline of Indus culture. Once thought to be an offshoot of Mesopotamian civilization, newer evidence suggests that the people of the Indus Valley had their roots in a much older, pre-Harappan civilization dating back to the sixth millennium* B.C. *The view that Indus civilization was destroyed by Aryan invaders has also been revised. Historians now believe vast climatic changes affected the economic viability of the great Indian cities of the period, many of which reverted to villages. Hermann Kulke specializes in ancient and medieval Indian history at the University of Kiel in Germany. Dietmar Rothermund is a professor of South Asian history at Heidelberg University in Germany.*

When the great cities of Harappa and Mohenjo-Daro were discovered in the 1920s the history of the Indian subcontinent attained a new dimension. The discoveries of these centres of the early Indus civilisation were certainly major achievements of archaelogy. Before these centres were known, the Indo-Aryans were regarded as the creators of the first early culture of the subcontinent. The Vedic Indo-Aryans had come down to the Indian plains in the second half of the second millennium BC. But the Indus civilisation proved to be much older, reaching back into the third and fourth mil-

Hermann Kulke and Dietmar Rothermund, *A History of India*. New York: Routledge, 1992.

lennia. After ancient Egypt and Mesopotamia, this Indus civilisation emerged as the third major civilisation of mankind.

Harappa and Mohenjo-Daro show a surprising similarity although they were separated by about 350 miles. In each city the archaeologists found an acropolis and a lower city, each fortified separately. The acropolis, situated to the west of each city and raised on an artificial mound made of bricks, contained large assembly halls and edifices which were obviously constructed for religious cults. In Mohenjo-Daro there was a 'Great Bath' (39 by 23 feet, with a depth of 8 feet) at the centre of the acropolis which may have been used for ritual purposes. This bath was connected to an elaborate water supply system and sewers. To the east of this bath there was a big building (about 230 by 78 feet) which is thought to have been a palace either of a king or of a high priest.

A special feature of each of these cities was a large granary. In Mohenjo-Daro it was situated in the acropolis; in Harappa it was immediately adjacent to it. The granary of Mohenjo-Daro, constructed next to the Great Bath, is still particularly impressive. Its foundation, running east to west, was 150 feet long and 75 feet wide. On this foundation were 27 compartments in three rows. The 15-foot walls of these are still extant. This granary was very well ventilated and could be filled from outside the acropolis. At Harappa there were some small houses, assumed to be those of workers or slaves, and a large open space between the acropolis and the granary.

The big lower cities were divided into rectangular areas. In Mohenjo-Daro there were nine such areas, each about 1200 by 800 feet. Broad main streets, about 30 feet wide separated these major parts of the city from each other. All the houses were connected directly to the excellent sewage system which ran through all the numerous small alleys. Many houses had a spacious interior courtyard and private wells. All houses were built with standardised bricks. The width of each brick was twice as much as its height and its length twice as large as its width.

But it was not only this excellent city planning which impressed the archaeologists, they also found some interesting sculptures and thousands of well-carved seals made of steatite. These seals show many figures and symbols of the religious life of the people of this early culture. There are tree gods among them and there is the famous so-called 'Proto-Shiva' who is seated in the typical pose of a meditating man. He has three heads, an erect phallus, and is surrounded by animals which were also worshipped by the Hindus of a later age. These seals also show evidence of a script which has not yet been deciphered.

Both cities shared a uniform system of weights and measures based on binary numbers and the decimal system. Articles made of copper and ornaments with precious stones show that there was a flourishing international trade. More evidence for this international trade was found when seals of the Indus culture were found in Mesopotamia and other seals which could be traced to Mesopotamia were discovered in the cities on the Indus.

Before indigenous sites of earlier stages of the Indus civilisation were found it was believed that Harappa and Mohenjo-Daro were merely outposts of the Mesopotamian civilisation, either constructed by migrants or at least designed according to their specifications.... In analogy to the Mesopotamian precedent, the Indus culture was thought to be based on a theocratic state whose twin capitals Harappa and Mohenjo-Daro obviously showed the traces of a highly centralised organisation. Scholars were also fairly sure of the reasons for the sudden decline of these cities since scattered skeletons which showed traces of violent death were found in the uppermost strata of Mohenjo-Daro. It appeared that men, women and children had been exterminated by conquerors in a 'last massacre'. The conquerors were assumed to be the Aryans who invaded India around the middle of the second millennium BC. Their warrior god, Indra, was, after all, praised as a breaker of forts in many Vedic hymns.

New Archaeological Discoveries

However, after the Second World War, intensive archaeological research in Afghanistan, Pakistan and India greatly enhanced our knowledge of the historical evolution and the spatial extension of the Indus civilisation. Earlier assessments of the rise and fall of this civilisation had to be revised. The new excavations showed that this civilisation, at its height early in the second millennium BC, had encompassed an area larger than Western Europe.

In the Indus valley, other important cities of this civilisation such as Kot Diji to the east of Mohenjo-Daro and Amri in the Dadu District on the lower Indus, were discovered in the years after 1958. In Kathiawar and on the coast of Gujarat similar centres were traced. Thus in 1954 Lothal was excavated south of

Ahmadabad. It is claimed that Lothal was a major port of this period. Another 100 miles further south Malwan was also identified in 1967 as a site of the Indus civilisation. It is located close to Surat and so far marks the southernmost extension of this culture. The spread of the Indus civilisation to the east was documented by the 1961 excavations at Kalibangan in Rajasthan about 200 miles west of Delhi. However, Alamgirpur, in Meerut District in the centre of the Ganga-Yamuna Doab, is considered to mark the farthest extension to the east of this culture. In the north, Rupar in the foothills of the Himalayas is the farthest outpost which is known. In the west, traces of this civilisation were found close to the border of present Iran at Sutkagen Dor. This was probably a trading centre on the route connecting the Indus valley with Mesopotamia. Afghanistan also has its share of Indus civilisation sites. This country was known for its lapis lazuli which was coveted everywhere even in those early times. At Mundigak near Kandahar a palace was excavated which has an impressive facade decorated with pillars. This site, probably one of the earliest settlements in the entire region, is thought to be an outpost of the Indus civilisation. Another one was found more recently further to the north at Shortugai on the Amu Darya.

This amazing extension of our knowledge about the spatial spread of the Indus civilisation was accompanied by an equally successful exploration of its history. Earlier strata of Mohenjo-Daro and Harappa as well as of Kalibangan, Amri and Kot Diji were excavated in a second round of archaeological research. In this way continuous sequence of strata, showing the gradual development to the high standard of the full-fledged Indus civilisation was established. These strata have been named Pre-Harappa, Early Harappa, Mature Harappa and Late Harappa. The most important result of this research is the clear proof of the long-term indigenous evolution of this civilisation which obviously began on the periphery of the Indus valley in the hills of eastern Baluchistan and then extended into the plains. There were certainly connections with Mesopotamia, but the earlier hypothesis that the Indus civilisation was merely an extension of Mesopotamian civilisation had to be rejected.

Stages of Harappan Culture

The early stages of the indigenous evolution of the Indus civilisation can be documented by an analysis of four sites which have been excavated in recent years: Mehrgarh, Amri, Kalibangan, Lothal. These four sites reflect the sequence of the four important phases in the proto-history of the northwestern region of the Indian subcontinent. The sequence begins with the transition of nomadic herdsmen to settled agriculturists in eastern Baluchistan, continues with the growth of large villages in the Indus valley and the rise of towns, leads to the emergence of the great cities and, finally, ends with their decline. The first stage is exemplified by Mehrgarh in Baluchistan, the second by Amri in the southern Indus valley and the third and fourth by Kalibangan in Rajasthan and by Lothal in Gujarat. . . .

The conclusions about the Indus civilisation and its great cities which can be derived from study of [these] four sites [are significant]. The new excavations at Mehrgarh show that in this area of Baluchistan there was a continuous cultural evolution from the sixth millennium BC throughout the subsequent four millennia. Earlier it was thought that this evolution started in Baluchistan only in the fourth millennium, but now we must conclude that the transition from nomadic life to settled agriculture occurred in Baluchistan simultaneously with the transition in Iran.

The excavations of Amri show that the decisive step towards the establishment of settlements in the Indus valley was made in the fourth millennium and that it was an extension of indigenous developments and not a mere transfer of a cultural pattern by migrants from Mesopotamia, Iran or Central Asia. The discovery of Neolithic settlements in Baluchistan has led to the conclusion that the Indus civilisation was the outcome of an indigenous evolution which started in the northwest of the Indian subcontinent. The many settlements of the fourth millennium which have been traced in recent years provide added evidence for this new hypothesis.

The rise of indigenous crafts obviously led to an increase in long-distance trade with Central and Western Asia but this trade did not have the unilateral effect of cultural borrowing as an earlier generation of scholars had thought—scholars who were naturally puzzled by the discovery of a mature civilisation which did not seem to have any local antecedents.

Whereas we do have a much clearer idea of the indigenous roots of the Indus civilisation by now, we still know very little about the rise of the specific Mature Harappa culture. The exact date of its rise is still a matter of debate. The dates 2600 to 2500 BC, suggested by those who first excavated the great cities, have not been revised so far, although recent research suggests that the most mature stage of this civilisation is probably limited to 2300 to 1800 BC. Where and how this stage was first attained still remains a puzzle. The archaeologists who initially excavated the two great cities were not very careful about establishing the stratigraphy of the various settlements. Moreover, Mohenjo-Daro, the most important site, is badly affected by groundwater which covers the earliest strata. The original foundations of Mohenjo-Daro are now approximately 24 feet below the groundwater level. The rising of the groundwater level was, presumably, one of the reasons for the decline of that city and it also makes it impossible to unravel the secrets of its birth. This is why it is necessary to excavate parallel strata in other sites of the Indus civilisation which are more accessible and whose age can be found out by means of radiocarbon dating.

Excavations of Amri and Kot Diji on the Lower Indus show that a new type of ceramics made its appearance there around 2600 BC—a type unknown in Harappa and Kalibangan at that time. This new type of ceramics and the culture connected with it must have arisen at Mohenjo-Daro. Changes in the pattern of settlement reaching from total extinction at Mehrgarh to a reduction at Amri and fortification and conflagration at Kot Diji were obviously due to this rise of Mohenjo-Daro. The Upper Indus region, Panjab and Rajasthan, with their later centres at Harappa and Kalibangan were not yet affected by this early development in the south. But they shared the cultural period referred to as Early Harappa.

First South Asian Empire

State formation in Mohenjo-Daro, Harappa and Kalibangan was probably not yet uniform at this stage, each centre serving as an independent capital of its particular region. But then from about 2200 BC onwards there is evidence for a striking uniformity of all these centres. This was probably achieved at the cost of war and conquest. The sudden extinction of Kalibangan around 2250 BC and its reconstruction in the uniform Harappan style about 50 to 100 years later seems to point to this conclusion. There was also a spurt of fortification at Harappa at that time where some city gates were completely closed with bricks. Kot Diji witnessed a second conflagration around 2100 BC from which it never recovered. But Lothal was built at about that time and several other settlements which have been found in recent years can also be traced to this phase of rapid expansion and uniform construction.

All this evidence seems to support the conclusion that this period witnessed the first emergence of a major empire in South Asia. Mohenjo-Daro was obviously the capital of that empire and Harappa and Kalibangan subsidiary centres. Such subsidiary centres may have enjoyed some regional autonomy; perhaps Mohenjo-Daro held sway over the whole empire only for a relatively short period. If this interpretation of the evidence is correct, state formation in the Indus valley proceeded along similar lines as that in the Ganges valley some 1,500 years later. In the Ganges valley, too, state formation in some nuclear areas preceded the establishment of a larger regional context until one of the centres emerged as the imperial capital. But all such questions about early state formation in the Indus valley cannot be finally settled until the script on the Indus seals is deciphered.

Climatic Changes Cause Decline

Recent research has not only shed more light on the antecedents of the Indus civilisation, it has also helped to explain the reasons for its sudden decline. All excavations support the conclusion that this decline occurred rather suddenly between 1800 and 1700 BC, but they do not support the theory of a violent end as no traces of 'last massacres' were found in any of the centres, apart from Mohenjo-Daro. Moreover, recent research has also exculpated the Vedic Aryans; they most probably arrived in the Indus valley almost half a millennium after its great cities had been extinguished. The excavations have revealed many striking symptoms of endogenous decay in those cities during the Late Harappa period. Some settlements seem to have been abandoned rather suddenly, e.g. kitchen utensils have been found scattered around fireplaces. Other places were resettled for a short period in a rather rudimentary fashion, before they were finally abandoned. The archaeologists call this the 'Squatters period' because there was no planning any longer, broken bricks were used for construction and no attention was paid to a proper sewage system. There are traces of this period at Kalibangan, Amri and Lothal. But there are no such traces in Mohenjo-Daro and Harappa, perhaps because their last inhabitants simply died out or were exterminated by marauders as in Mohenjo-Daro's 'last massacre'. But the decline of the big cities was obviously due not only to the raids of marauders, but also to other forces, against which man was helpless.

Research in different disciplines has led to the conclusion that the decline of the Indus civilisation was precipitated by a great change in environmental conditions which set in at the beginning of the second millennium BC. Geologists have pointed out tectonic changes which may have thrown up a kind of dam in the lower Indus valley, thus inundating a large part of the plains. This would explain the existence of thick layers of silt in the upper strata of Mohenjo-Daro which are now about 39 feet above the level of the river. Other scientists have suggested ecological reasons for the decline of the great civilisation: over-grazing, and deforestation caused by the operation of innumerable fireplaces and kilns for burning bricks. But the population in the Indus valley at that time was not large enough to have caused such severe damage. Even Mohenjo-Daro had, at the most, about 40,000 inhabitants in the period of its greatest extension.

Palaeobotanical research in Rajasthan has recently provided a new and amazing explanation of the decline of the Indus civilisation. According to these findings there was a slight increase of rainfall and vegetation in the Indus region in the sixth millennium, and during the third millennium there was a sudden and steep rise in rainfall which reached its peak around 2500 BC. But by the end of the third millennium this rainfall had receded as rapidly as it had increased, and by about 1800 to 1500 BC it had come down to a level well below that of 3000 BC. There was another slight increase of rainfall between 1500 and 1000 BC then it decreased once more. The period around 400 BC was probably one of the driest periods of all. Subsequently, rainfall became more abundant but never again reached the peak which it had attained around 2500 BC. The last 2,000 years up to the present have witnessed a pattern of rainfall and vegetation in South Asia which conforms to a mean value between the extremes of 2500 and 400 BC.

It is fascinating to see the course of history in the context of these findings. The rise and fall of the Indus civilisation could thus have been strongly influenced by changes in climate and even the immigration of the Aryans and their settlement in the northern Indus region could then be attributed to the renewed increase of rainfall and vegetation in the period after 1500 BC.

Similarly the decline of the fortunes of the Aryans in that region after 1000 BC and their movement eastwards into the Ganges valley could be explained by means of these climatological data. The *dry period* would have made the jungles of the Gangetic plains penetrable and when the climate improved again after 500 BC the migrants would have already established their footholds along the Ganges and have started cutting and burning the forest, thus reclaiming fertile lands for agriculture. The improvement of the climate would then have contributed to the second wave of urbanisation which started in South Asia at that time. But only more detailed palaeobotanical research can prove that these hypotheses derived from the findings in Rajasthan are applicable to other regions of South Asia as well.

Socioeconomic Factors

In addition to changes in climate and perhaps an inundation caused by a tectonic upheaval, there must have been also socioeconomic factors which contributed to the decline of the great civilisation. At their height around 2000 BC, the centres of this civilisation had become far removed from their agricultural roots and yet they were more dependent than ever on the land's produce. The traces of destruction at Kot Diji and the abandonment and reconstruction of Kalibangan show that in their prime the great cities were obviously able to hold sway over a vast hinterland. But a perennial control of trade routes and of the agricultural base would have required the maintenance of a large army and of a host of administrators. The excavations have shown no evidence for the existence of such armies. The agricultural surplus of the countryside was probably used for trade or for some kind of religious obligations. Thus, the cities depended on the wellbeing of their immediate hinterland, and their size was a direct correlate of the agricultural surplus available to them.

When the climate changed and agricultural production declined, the cities were probably in no position to appropriate surplus from farther afield. Under such conditions the people simply had to leave the city and this reduction of the population may have had an accelerating effect on the decline of the cities, the big cities being affected by it earlier and more severely than the smaller ones. Perhaps some inhabitants of the big cities in the Indus valley may have migrated to the new and smaller towns on the periphery, such as the towns of Gujarat. But with the decline of the centres the peripheral outposts also lost their importance and became dependent on their immediate hinterland only. In this way some of the smaller places like Amri and Lothal survived for a few generations in the Post-Harappa time when the big cities were already extinct. Finally these smaller places also lapsed back to the stage of simple villages as urban life had lost its sustenance. This was not a unique event in South Asian social and political development. History repeated itself when the flourishing cities of northern and central India, for instance, Kausambi, declined around 200 AD as long-distance trade, the most important factor in their rise, disappeared. It was only several centuries later that the medieval cities, capitals of kings or pilgrimage centres with great temples, signalled a new phase of urbanisation.

Hindu India Under the Aryans

BY MICHAEL EDWARDES

In the following extract from A History of India, *author Michael Edwardes explains that historical information on the Aryan invasion of northern India, which began in the second millennium* B.C., *is based on Hindu religious texts known as the Vedas. From the Vedas, historians have learned the Aryans were a primitive nomadic people who became more sophisticated as they absorbed Indus Valley culture. As they expanded their reach across the subcontinent, the Aryans instituted the idea of caste, or social stratification, based on the superiority of the fairer Aryan conquerors to the darker-skinned people of the Indus Valley. Some current religious practices and the worship of certain Hindu gods date back to the time of the Aryans.*

The Mahabharata and the Ramayana, also religious texts, give information on Indo-Aryan society in the post-Vedic stage. At that time, the early Aryan religion of Brahmanism began to lose its popular appeal, and Jainism and Buddhism arose in revolt against the abuse of power by Brahmin priests. Ultimately Brahmanism evolved into the more popular Hinduism.

The sole source of information on the Indo-Aryans (*arya*—meaning 'noble, well-born, free') is the Vedic hymns or *Vedas*, the oldest literary remains in the Indo-European language group. The word *Veda* means knowledge and to Hindus the *Vedas* are—as is the Bible to Christians and the Koran to Muslims—the primary source of religious belief. These hymns are invocations to various deities and were passed orally from generation to generation of *Rishis*, or 'seers'. There are three principal *Vedas*, the *Rig,* the *Sama*, and the *Yajura*. A fourth, the *Atharva-Veda,* is a compilation of magical spells. The *Sama-Veda* and the *Yajura-Veda* are mainly ceremonial recapitulations of the

Rig-Veda which consists of 1,028 hymns of varying ages, divided into ten books.

The original homeland of the Aryan peoples is not known for certain, but it is probable that they came from Iran to India and were to some extent the heirs of the civilization of Sumer. There is no characteristic Aryan 'culture' nor does it seem that they were a 'race' in any genetic sense, though they had sufficient group-identity to permit Darius I of Persia to have inscribed on his gravestone (486 B.C.) the claim that he was '*Parsa, Parsahya puthra, Arya, Arya cithra*'—'A Persian, son of a Persian, an Aryan of Aryan descent.'

The Aryans were pastoral tribesmen and warriors, tall and fair with straight noses. Their first move into India, about the beginning of the second millennium B.C., was as settlers, with their wives and children and their herds of animals. This peaceful immigration was followed by others which resulted in expansion, and conflict with the people living in fortified areas which now appear possibly to have been outposts of the Indus Valley civilization. These peoples were crushed and destroyed, probably because of that characteristic historical movement in which decadent high-level civilizations fall so easily to the vigour of the barbarians.

That the Aryans of the first invasion remained a nomadic people, an administration in the tent rather than the city, can be assumed from the Rig/Veda. [The high god of the Vedas, Indra, is known as the breaker of cities, but no mention is made of a builder or possessor of cities.] The Aryan people lived in camps. The peoples whom they conquered are described in the *Vedas* as short, black, and noseless, as *dasyu* or 'slaves', and the Vedic hymns constantly refer to wars against them. But later the Aryan conquerors intermarried with the female slaves they captured and, in time, produced a mixed race adopting many of the customs of their mothers.

A second invasion appears to have taken place not later than 1000 B.C., and the Aryans moved outwards from the Punjab towards the east. They had become much more sophisticated, inheriting, from the Indus civilization, the plough and the techniques of pottery, weaving, and carpentry.

The Aryans were continually fighting among themselves, and the Vedic hymns record great battles fought by infantry armed with bows and arrows, spears, swords, and battle-axes, and nobles dressed in armour, fighting from chariots—all to the sound of music and drums. It would seem from the *Rig-Veda* that many of the battles were fought for the control of water, an essential factor in nomadic agriculture. This continual inter-tribal strife and the pressures of the second invasion compelled the Aryans to move eastwards.

Social Organization

The *Rig-Veda* gives us a clear picture of the social life of these Indo-Aryans. The unit was the family, sharing its wealth and its responsibilities. The head was the father (*dama-pati*) whose control was absolute. At his death the property was divided. Women played an important role in society—the wife ruled the female members of the household and the slaves. There was no child marriage and polygamy seems to have been unknown. The wife's duties were to grind the corn, cook her husband's food and serve him, clean the pots and pans, and spread cow-dung on the floor. Above all, she was to provide him with a son. Later, when about eight years old, this son would be given the sacred cord of *manja* grass, tied over the left shoulder and under the right arm, while the priest whispered the Gayatri *mantra*.

> 'Let us meditate on the excellent glory of the Sun;
> the God may he enlighten our understanding.'

The village (*grama*) consisted of a group of families, with a headman and hereditary officers. Oxen were used for ploughing and drawing carts and a man's wealth was assessed by the number of his cows. Horses were kept for drawing chariots and dogs were used in hunting. They grew barley but not wheat or rice. Their diet generally consisted of parched barley, unleavened cakes, vegetables, clarified butter (*ghi*), and milk, but meat, including the flesh of the cow, was eaten at festivals and weddings. A sort of beer made from barley was drunk and, at religious ceremonies, an intoxicating drink made from the juice of a plant called *soma*. A whole book of Vedic hymns in praise of *soma*, which was supposed to confer immortality, survives.

Houses were made of wood with thatched roofs and mud walls. Clothing was usually of wool or skins, a skirt and a shawl for the shoulders. Hair was elaborately dressed and earrings and necklaces were worn.

The Indo-Aryans practised the arts, and that of the potter, the weaver, the jeweller, the carpenter, and the smith are mentioned. But though they used copper and gold, silver and iron were unknown. Their favourite amusements were chariot-racing, wrestling, dancing, and music. . . .

The tribe consisted of a number of families or clans living in villages. The head was the *Raja*, or 'king', usually hereditary but sometimes elected with the approval of the people. He was surrounded with a retinue of nobles who wore armour and fought from chariots with bow and arrow, sword, and spear. The king was no absolute ruler. His acts needed the sanction of a popular assembly (*sabha*) consisting of the males of fighting age. The king was the personification of justice. There was no capital punishment, a murderer having to pay a fine of a certain number of cows as compensation to the family of the victim. In administering law or tribal custom the king was advised by his *purohit*, or 'family priest'. Like the Brahmin of later times, the priest also composed hymns in his master's honour and invoked protection of the gods over his acts.

The Beginnings of Caste

The original idea of caste (a Portuguese word meaning purity of race) is that of colour (*varna*) and it emerged when the conquering Aryans absorbed the conquered population into a new system of society. The name given to these peoples by the invaders was *dasyu* (enemy) which later came to mean a slave. But the *dasyu* was not a piece of *private* property but of the Aryan tribe as a whole, very much in the same way as cattle. These *dasyu* were dark-skinned, the Aryans were white or at least lighter in colour.

The division into castes was a sort of occupational identification: the Brahmins were priests, the Kshatriyas, warriors, and the Vaisyas the commercial classes; the latter including cultivators, traders, goldsmiths, weavers, potters, and so on. Traces of such social divisions can be found amongst Iranians and in early Greece and Rome. To these, the Indo-Aryans added that of the Sudras or 'serfs'—the descendants of the *dasyus*. This functional structure was given divine origin in the *Rig-Veda* which describes how, when Purusha, the archetypal man, was sacrificed, the Brahmins rose from his head, the Kshatriyas from his arms, the Vaisyas from his thighs, and the Sudras from his feet.

In Vedic times, caste was not exclusive; a warrior could become a priest, and the king, though a warrior, had certain priestly

The Bhagavad Gita on Reincarnation

The Bhagavad Gita, the best known of all Hindu scriptures, contains the most profound teachings of the Hindu religion. The Gita is an allegorical poem that tells the story of a great warrior, Arjuna, who is filled with misgivings at the prospect of engaging in a war with his relatives. Krishna (who is the Lord acting as his charioteer) guides Arjuna through the war and explains to him the true nature of human existence. The following extract of Krishna's explanation is one of the most famous passages of the Gita, and refers to the Hindu belief in transmigration of souls and eternal life.

The Blessed Lord [Krishna] said:

You grieve for those who should not be mourned, and yet you speak words of wisdom! The learned do not grieve for the dead or for the living.

Never, indeed, was there a time when I was not, nor when you were not, nor these lords of men. Never, too, will there be a time, hereafter, when we shall not be.

As in this body, there are for the embodied one [i.e, the soul] childhood, youth, and old age, even so there is the taking on of another body. The wise sage is not perplexed thereby.

Contacts of the sense-organs, O son of Kuntī, give rise to cold and heat, and pleasure and pain. They come and go, and are not permanent. Bear with them, O Bhārata.

That man, whom these [sense-contacts] do not trouble, O chief of men, to whom pleasure and pain are alike, who is wise—he becomes eligible for immortality.

For the nonexistent there is no coming into existence; nor is there passing into nonexistence for the existent. The ultimate nature of these two is perceived by the seers of truth.

Know that to be indestructible by which all this is pervaded. Of this imperishable one, no one can bring about destruction.

These bodies of the eternal embodied one, who is indestructible and incomprehensible, are said to have an end. Therefore fight, O Bhārata.

He who regards him [i.e., the soul] as a slayer, and he who regards him as slain—both of them do not know the truth; for this one neither slays nor is slain.

He is not born, nor does he die at any time; nor, having once come to be will he again come not to be. He is unborn, eternal, permanent, and primeval; he is not slain when the body is slain.

Whoever knows him to be indestructible and eternal, unborn and immutable—how and whom can such a man, O son of Prithā, cause to be slain or slay?

Just as a man, having cast off old garments, puts on other, new ones, even so does the embodied one, having cast off old bodies, take on other, new ones.

Weapons do not cleave him, fire does not burn him; nor does water drench him, nor the wind dry him up.

He is uncleavable, he is unburnable, he is undrenchable, as also undryable. He is eternal, all-pervading, stable, immovable, existing from time immemorial.

He is said to be unmanifest, unthinkable, and unchangeable. Therefore, knowing him as such, you should not grieve [for him].

And even if you regard him as being perpetually born and as perpetually dying, even then, O long-armed one, you should not grieve for him.

For, to one who is born death is certain and certain is birth to one who has died. Therefore in connection with a thing that is inevitable you should not grieve. . . .

Unmanifest in their beginnings are beings, manifest in the middle stage, O Bhārata, and unmanifest, again, in their ends. For what then should there be any lamentation? . . .

The embodied one within the body of everyone, O Bhārata, is ever unslayable. Therefore, you should not grieve for any being.

Ainslie T. Embree, ed., *The Hindu Tradition: Readings in Oriental Thought.* New York: Vintage Books, 1972, pp. 120–22.

functions. Caste-rigidity was the result of the claim for a monopoly in religious rites by the Brahmins. Social imitation is a characteristic of an evolving society, and the lower orders formed similar special-interest groups based mainly on occupation. These groups ensured their continuance by a strict observance of the rule of marriage within the caste, i.e. men must marry women of their own caste and no other.

Later, religious sects such as the Jains, Sikhs, and Lingyats, while being antagonistic to caste, found themselves forced to assume caste status. In time, the four main castes divided into sub-castes, each exclusive and dedicated to a particular economic or religious function. In a detailed census of tribes and castes in 1901, 2,378 separate groups are listed, some with numbers running into millions, others with as few as a hundred members. The largest numbers were fourteen million Brahmins, and eleven million Chamars, who are dressers of hide and leather and the lowest caste of all.

Caste is the steel frame of Hindu society and an organization of almost incredible complexity, but the basis is the belief in the divine origin of the Conquerors and invaders, Buddhist, Muslim, and Christian, have been forced to accept its all-pervading strength.

The Religion of the Aryans

The Aryans worshipped the Devas or 'Shining Ones', who represented the powers of Nature. The most important of these gods was the sky father, Dyaus (*Zeús*, Jupiter), though he later gave way to Varuna, the lord of sky and sea. The Sun was worshipped in five forms, symbolizing various aspects of solar energy and effect. . . . Indra, god of the rains, was one of the foremost of Aryan gods. He was conceived as an ideal warrior, armed with a thunderbolt and riding in a chariot and bringing the boon of rain to the parched earth. These are only few of the Vedic pantheon. Rivers were worshipped for their life-bringing function.

Though the Vedic gods have human attributes—they eat milk, *ghi,* and flour-cakes, and drink *soma*—they were not clearly anthropomorphized. No temples and no images play a part in the Vedic religion. Ritual, however, was precise as this was the only way of approaching the gods. The middleman between the god and his suppliant was the Brahmin.

The Aryans cremated their dead and the ashes were scattered, as today, in a river. The wife was not burned with her husband but was called away from the pyre with the words: 'Rise up, O woman, into the world of the living.' Vedic ideas of the after-life were crude. They believed the soul departed to the 'fathers' where it was received by Yama, king of the dead. . . . The concept of rebirth had not yet appeared.

In later Vedic literature, particularly in the tenth *mandala* (section) of the *Rig-Veda,* we have the first expression of Indo-Aryan philosophical ideas. . . . Here the concept of the One, the ultimate behind the many manifestations, emerges. Also came the idea of *Rita,* the 'Moral Law' which is unchanging and unchangeable.

Indo-Aryans in the Post-Vedic Stage

As the social and economic order of the Indo-Aryans crystallized into a new society, the need for new pastures forced territorial expansion. At the time when the *Vedas* were composed, they had not moved farther east than present-day Ambala, but when more evidence appears in the form of the Epics, they have occupied the fertile country between the Jumna and the Ganges, known as the Madyadesa or 'Middle Land', and the Ganges replaces the Indus as the sacred river.

Our knowledge of this period of expansion is contained in two great works—the *Mahabharata*, 'the Great Epic of the War of the Descendants of Bharata', and the *Ramayana*, or 'Story of Rama'. The *Mahabharata* is the longest poem in the world consisting as it does of 100,000 *slokas* (verses). . . .

From the *Mahabharata* and the *Ramayana* emerge a view of Indo-Aryan society in its post-Vedic stage. The caste system has become rigid, though there are passages which declare that there is no distinction of caste. Descriptions are given of the qualities of the four main castes. The Brahmin, for example, is one who is never angry or infatuated, speaks the truth, pleases his elders, controls his senses, is virtuous, and devoted to study. . . .

In Epic times, the Aryans had produced a vast number of small kingdoms along the banks of the Jumma, the Ganges, and their tributaries. The Aryans seem to have spent much energy and time in battle and the forming of alliances for war. The king still led his army in battle. Towns were appearing and there are descriptions of well-watered and lighted streets, and fortifications to protect them. Copper and silver money is used for the payment of taxes as well as produce and cattle. The cow is now regarded as sacred, but meat other than beef is still eaten. Polygamy is practised. Chivalry abounded and, like the knights of mediaeval Europe, the Indo-Aryan prince is caught in a vast web of chivalric protocol.

The two great Epics, are, next to the *Vedas,* the most famous works of Sanskrit literature. The *Mahabharata* and the *Ramayana* are part of the popular life of the people, supplying ideal heroes and heroines. The stories have been used over and over again by dramatists, poets, and storytellers. The *Mahabharata* contains one of the most profound philosophical poems of all time when, before the battle, Krishna addresses Arjuna on the duty of a warrior. His words form the *Bhagavad Gita* or 'Song Celestial'.

A number of important changes in religion were taking place and the older Vedic gods became less prominent though mention is still made of Indra the warrior god, and Varuna. But the now familiar trinity, the Trimurti, of Brahma the Creator, Siva the Destroyer, and Vishnu the Preserver, becomes the object of worship. Ritualism becomes all-important. New divinities are introduced. The cosmos is conceived as a perpetual process of creation and destruction, filling eternity with an everlasting rhythm.

The world of the Epics is one in which human activity is shown to be inspired by ancient ideals. Great emphasis was placed upon morality. But it is also the period of the beginnings of sectarianism and religious petrification.

The Revolt Against Brahminism

By the sixth century B.C., the old religion of the *Vedas*, which was pragmatic and sacrificial, had lost its appeal with the masses. Yet the ideas of the *Upanishads*, a highly scholastic, metaphysical doctrine of the direct realization of God, could not in any way supply the spiritual needs of the people.

The period of the *Upanishads* (*c.* 800–600 B.C.) is significant for the growth of pessimism, and the main object of religion came to be the release from life—which was evil. . . .

Here too appears the concept of metempsychosis, the migration of the soul on death into another body until, after a series of wanderings, it finds release in returning to the World Soul. Conduct in a previous incarnation determines the position in the next—the good man returns as a Brahmin, Kshatriya, or Vaisya; the evil as a dog, a hog, or a Chandala (the offspring of a Brahmin woman and a Sudra, lowest of all in the social scale).

The consequences of action (*Karma*) could be overcome by penances from which probably resulted the practice of Yoga, later made into a discipline by Patanjali (*c.* 300 B.C.).

The Sankya school, founded by Kapila about the time of the *Upanishads*, was basically materialist. The concept of *Atma* [the 'World Soul'] was rejected, [and] rebirth was due to ignorance and could be avoided. Sankya ideas had profound influence both in India and elsewhere, for example on the later Gnostic schools in Greece.

Jainism and Buddhism

The two great reformers Vardhamana Mahavira and Gautama Buddha were born into a religious climate saturated with the Sankya system and this had considerable effect upon the doctrines they formulated.

Jainism and Buddhism have much in common. Both were revolts, not against Hinduism itself, but against the diverse polytheism and the arrogant claims of the Brahmins. *Karma* and rebirth are fundamental to both, each regarded existence as evil and offered a path to ultimate release. Mahavira and Gautama were both Kshatriyas and their systems were practical rather than philosophical. In the course of time, both religions have changed from the concepts of their founders, but in the beginning both attempted to reveal a pragmatic 'Way', attainable by all, without mediation by a priesthood which cherished the mysteries. Originally, the earlier records were composed not in classical Sanskrit but in the language of everyday speech, called Prakrit.

Vardhamana Mahavira, the man to whom Jainism owes its establishment as a faith, probably lived from 540 to 468 B.C. According to Jainist tradition, he was the last of twenty-four *Tirthankaras,* or 'prophets', and the sect seems to have existed for some time before the appearance of Mahavira—though there is little satisfactory evidence for this other than tradition. It seems probable, however, that the twenty-third *Tirthankara,* Parsva, *was* a historical personage. At the age of thirty, Mahavira became an ascetic and, after twelve years of wanderings, set out to teach the truth he had learned. Followers gathered around him and he was welcomed at the court of Magadha. His first adherents were found among the mercantile classes and the pattern today remains the same. There are now some one and a half million Jains, mainly in the Rajputana and Gujarat.

Siddhartha Gautama, or Sakyamuni, who was known after his Enlightenment as the Buddha, lived approximately between 560 and 480 B.C. The son of a Sakya chief of Kshatriya caste, who ruled in Kapilavastu on the Nepalese border—about one hundred miles north of Benares, in the foothills of the Himalayas—he was traditionally said to have been born in the Lumbini gardens, a belief which has now been reinforced by the discovery of an Asokan pillar erected in 250 B.C. and inscribed 'Here was born Buddha, Sakyamuni.' Overcome by the miseries and sorrows of everyday life, he tried many of the disciplines and doctrines current at the time, but finally received what he believed to be the truths of life and death.

The essence of the teaching of the Buddha was a call to take the Middle Way. This 'Way' was based on the recognition of the four truths: the Truth of Pain—birth, sickness, etc.; the Truth of the Origin of Pain—desire; the Truth of the End of Pain—by eliminating desire; and the Truth of the way to its elimination—the Noble Eightfold Path.

The appeal of the Buddha's message was immense, for it offered a new revelation, almost a classless religion—though strictly speaking Buddhism was not a new *religion* at all but the restatement of social truths in a new and dynamic form. It was also an *accessible* revelation couched in the common speech, undisguised by an elaborate ritual and a secret language. All castes and none were its converts.

The Buddha's message was simple, his teaching ethical and not metaphysical.

> 'Let a man overcome anger by love, let him overcome evil by good.
> Let him overcome the greedy by liberality, the liar by truth.'
> 'This is called progress in the discipline of the Blessed One, if one sees his sin in its sinfulness and refrains from it in the future.'. . .

Jainism and Buddhism represent similar ideas in extreme and moderate degrees. The Jains practised extensive penances and believed it meritorious to take one's own life. The Buddhists were more moderate. Both believed it a sin to kill but the Jains took extreme precautions to avoid even the death of an insect.

Both sects in their attitude to caste caused a social revolution but this was incidental to the teachings of the two Masters, for both claimed no break with Aryan tradition—only a new way to liberation. As a result, Brahmin opposition was slow to challenge, and by the time the social consequences of the Buddha and Mahavira were plain, powerful kings had already adopted the tenets of the reformers.

The Great Ancient Empires: The Mauryan Dynasty and the Glorious Gupta Age

By B.G. Gokhale

In the fourth century B.C., *Chandragupta, the founder of the Mauryan empire, unified the diverse territories and people of India for the first time within an imperial state. His grandson Ashoka, known for his great humanity and religious tolerance, built on this foundation to provide a spiritual unity to the many cultures and races of his people. After Ashoka's death, poor leadership and bureaucratic abuses led to the decline of the Mauryan empire. After several centuries of local revolutions, the Gupta Empire emerged as the next major empire heralding India's Golden Age where great art, literature, and the sciences flourished. Under the Guptas India was again unified, peaceful, and prosperous. Modern Hindu revivalists view these two ancient empires as symbols of the greatness that India, freed from foreign domination, might again recapture.*

B.G. Gokhale was the head of the history department at Siddarth College in Bombay, India, when he wrote The Making of the Indian Nation, *from which the following article is excerpted.*

With the year 326 B.C. India entered the age of historical certitude and imperial unity. The identification of the Sandracottus of the Greek annals with Chandragupta Maurya, the founder of the Maurya dynasty, led to the

B.G. Gokhale, *The Making of the Indian Nation*. New York: Asia Publishing House, 1960.

recognition of the first firm date in Indian history and this became the starting point of a system of historically valid chronology. . . . The decipherment of the Inscriptions of Chandragupta's grandson, Ashoka, have provided ample material for a somewhat detailed history of political and cultural events in India of the 4th and 3rd centuries B.C., a luxury comparatively unknown in earlier periods . . . and hence what the historian may present is no longer of the genre of conjecture and guesswork. It is also with this period that a history of India as a whole becomes possible for the Maurya empire covered almost the whole of India. . . .

India's First Emperor

Chandragupta Maurya has been rightly described as the first historical emperor of India. From his rich and populous capital he ruled over a vast empire which stretched from Kabul in the northwest to Mysore in the south and from Saurashtra in the west to Assam in the east. For the first time in the history of the country there was power, the strength of which could be felt all over the land and by which the multiplicity of kingdoms and principalities was transformed into the unity of an imperial state.

The administration of such a large empire raised intricate problems demanding the highest wisdom and tact. . . . Faced with the problem of maintaining a large empire based on primitive means of communications the Maurya empire became a finely wrought balance of power whereby a maximum centralization of authority was paralleled by a large measure of devolution of power in the provinces, districts and villages, the units of imperial administration. Over the provinces ruled the viceroys who were often princes of the imperial family. The smallest unit was the immemorial village with its own village government in the work of which the central authority participated through the headman who collected revenue and maintained law and order. To maintain close contacts with the officers on the one hand and the people on the other the Mauryas made an extensive use of reporters, agents and spies who kept the emperor constantly informed on all matters of importance to the state. . . .

The backbone of the empire was the large and efficient army maintained by the Mauryas. The standing army numbered 600,000 men who were paid regular salaries. Military administration was organized through six boards with five members on each board. These were the departments of the navy, infantry, cavalry, war-chariots, elephants and supply. Chandragupta, a warrior of no mean achievements himself, took great personal interest in the care and efficiency of the army and its strength was amply demonstrated to Seleucos when he invaded India. The Maurya state was highly bureaucratic and the hierarchy of officials working for it offers striking resemblance to governmental work in modern days. . . .

Chandragupta [ruled] for 24 eventful years, from 322 B.C. to 298 B.C.

Perhaps no other Indian ruler, with the exception of Akbar in the 16th century A.D., could claim such magnificent achievements as this founder of the Maurya dynasty. Raised as an orphan, he owed all his success to his own character and ability. . . . He was as great as an administrator as he was a mighty warrior. Under his vigorous rule, peace reigned throughout the empire and prosperity characterized the life of the people. . . . [He] created a mighty empire [and] tempered [justice] with sympathy. . . .

The Reign of Ashoka

The successor of Chandragupta was his son Bindusara whose long reign of 25 years was almost completely devoid of any spectacular or memorable events. . . .

Bindusara died in 273 B.C. leaving behind him the large empire which he had inherited from his illustrious father. The Buddhist chronicles would have us believe that there was a war of succession in which Ashoka killed all his brothers save one—and the number of brothers is stated to be 100—and waded through a sea of fraternal blood to the ancestral throne. This story is obviously inspired by a desire to present a sharp contrast in the character of Ashoka before and after his conversion to Buddhism. But there is some reason to suppose that there was an interval of four years between Ashoka's accession and coronation and these two events may be placed in 273 and 269 B.C. respectively.

Of Ashoka's early life we only know that he served as a viceroy in central India at Vidisha where he married a lady named Devi. Of this union were born Mahendra and Sanghamitra; the former became a Buddhist monk and the latter joined the order of nuns and both went to Ceylon as Buddhist missionaries. At least for the first eight years after his accession Ashoka did nothing unusual. He liked good food, often went hunting and took great interest in gardening and his horses. But in 261 B.C. the province of

Kalinga—modern Orissa—rose in revolt. This was promptly crushed and with great slaughter. But it had an extraordinary effect on the mind of Ashoka and it became a turning point in his life. The sight of the captives effectively quenched his aggressive ambitions, for the maimed ones his heart bled, and from the dead a new king was born. Never before in the history of humanity, nor ever afterwards, has a king publicly expressed genuine grief for a deed commonly regarded as the legitimate business of kings. The war of Kalinga was the first and the last war waged by Ashoka and the sword that he sheathed then was never unsheathed again. From that time on for Ashoka the drums sounded only to preach the truth. The promising warrior had been transformed into a practising evangelist.

At this point the thirty-odd inscriptions, graven on rocks and pillars, become documents of great human interest. Very probably the text of these inscriptions was prepared by the Emperor himself, and through their archaic words they certainly convey the impression of a personal confession of a great soul in anguish and in hope. They are located at all prominent points on the frontiers and central areas of the empire and were obviously meant to be read by the people. Through them the voice of Ashoka comes to us across the centuries, so ancient yet so familiar. With characteristic candour Ashoka tells us as much of his culinary preferences as of his ethical ideas. Soon after the Kalinga war Ashoka turned to Buddhism, though for some time he was not as enthusiastic in the practice of his faith as he should have been. But that phase soon ended and as the years matured into decades, his faith became firm and his enthusiasm for practising and preaching it unbounded. He undertook the customary pilgrimages to the holy places of Buddhism and interested himself in the affairs of the Buddhist order of monks and nuns. He is reputed to have built numerous stupas and the Buddhist tradition avers that the Third Great Synod was held in the 17th year of his reign.

Religious Tolerance and Morality

But Ashoka was no bigot for he never forgot that he was a king ruling over subjects who professed different faiths. In this he was truly catholic, for, with remarkable impartiality he distributed his patronage to Brahmins, Buddhists and Jains alike. Indeed, he sternly disapproved of the all-too-human weakness of extolling one's own faith and speaking disparagingly of the faith of others. He had little patience with meaningless ritual and regarded with abhorrence the practice of immolating animals as sacrificial victims. He banned the slaughter of many different kinds of animals and birds and disapproved of those public fairs at which there was much drinking and licentiousness. In his capacity as the temporal head of India he preached a simple creed of commonly accepted morals and endeavoured to bring humanity in the place of cruelty, ethical earnestness in the place of empty form. He commended good behaviour within the family and without and exhorted his subjects to act in such ways as to be ever mindful of the hereafter.

Of his positive undertakings the most prominent may be mentioned here. What Ashoka strove to establish was nothing less than the welfare state dedicated to righteousness. He had roads built and had shade-giving trees planted along them; he established rest-houses and set up hospitals for men and animals. In this he was far ahead of his times for the earliest hospital in Europe does not appear before the tenth century A.D. He had medicinal herbs planted and, in order to ensure that his policies were properly implemented, created a new cadre of officers called the "morality officers" whose tasks it was to carry out his beneficial policies and act in the best interests of the people. Ashoka strongly disapproved of sectarian rivalries and it was also the duty of these officers to see that all the sects lived in peace and amity with each other.

Having worked with zeal for the moral uplift of his own people Ashoka wanted his contemporary kings in foreign lands to know what he was doing. He sent envoys to the border peoples in India and also to the kings of the Middle Eastern and Hellenistic worlds. He mentions Antiochus II, Theos of Syria (261–246 B.C.), Ptolemy II, Philadelphos of Egypt, Antogonas Gonatas of Macedonia (278–239 B.C.), Magus of Cyraene (300–250 B.C.) and Alexander of Epirus (272–258 B.C.) as the kings to whom he sent his missions. At this time the Buddhist Order also sent its own missions to the Himalayan region, to western India and to the lands beyond the seas and thus the joint efforts of the Buddhist Order and Ashoka helped Buddhism develop from a small sect into a national and international religion claiming the allegiance of millions of people. His forefathers had built an empire that embraced the most diverse races and cultures in the country and Ashoka gave it the spiritual meaning that transcended the narrow limitations of caste and region, priesthood and ritual, in the hope that it would endure as the kingdom of righteousness so long as the sun and the moon shone on this earth of ours.

Ashoka's contribution to Indian history does not stop at religion and morals alone. In the field of art he is the originator of a great tradition in sculpture. His pillars are examples of the highest art of the stone-cutter and indeed, before his period, the history of Indian art is "philologically a blank page" and "archaeologically an empty show-case". A proper history of Indian art begins with Ashoka and with him it reveals a maturity of idealism and technical skill. Incidentally, his Sarnath capital is now used as the State seal of the Government of India and the Buddhist Wheel, popularised by this art, adorns the Indian national flag. . . .

Such was Ashoka, the greatest of kings. H.G. Wells has paid a well-deserved tribute to him in the following words: "Amidst the tens of thousands of names that crowd the columns of history, their Majesties and Graciousness and Serenities and Royal Highnesses and the like, the name of Ashoka shines, and shines almost alone as a star. From the Volga to Japan his name is still honoured. China, Tibet, and even India, though it has left his doctrine, preserve the tradition of his greatness. More living men cherish his memory today than have heard the names of Constantine or Charlemagne." Born a king Ashoka became an evangelist; where others were content to conquer and rule, Ashoka chose to conquer himself and build the Kingdom of the True, the Good and the Beautiful in the hearts of men.

The Decline of the Mauryan Empire

With the death of Ashoka began the collapse of the mighty Maurya empire. Of his four sons only one, Jaluka, ruled and that too in the territory covered by the present state of Kashmir. Kunala was blinded by his step-mother, Mahendra joined the Buddhist Order of monks and went to Ceylon as a missionary, and Tivara did the same. We know of his grandson, Dasharatha, from an inscription in the Barabar caves while Jain tradition speaks of a Samparati. It is almost futile to try and bring some order in the narrative after Ashoka's death. The last of the Mauryas was Brihadratha who was assassinated by his Brahmin general, Pushyamitra Shunga, later the founder of the Shunga dynasty, in 187 B.C.

What were the causes leading to the disintegration of the

Maurya empire? Some historians have blamed Ashoka for it, arguing that his "Buddhist" policy led to a Brahmanical counter-revolution. This contains some truth though it cannot be accepted as the whole explanation. It is possible that the Brahmanical priesthood saw deep affront in the "Buddhist" policies of Ashoka. . . . Brahmanism saw in Buddhism a system of thought and practice, which, if allowed to flourish, would cut the very ground from under the feet of the priests by insisting on the equality of all men. But the most probable reasons must be sought in the very constitution of the Maurya empire itself. Like all other empires of antiquity, the Maurya empire depended for its continued life on the personality of the ruler. The successors of Ashoka clearly did not display that combination of strength and tact so necessary for the continued existence of the empire. It is also possible to argue that the weakness of the successors of Ashoka was paralleled by a growth in the oppressive proclivities of the bureaucracy

Ashoka's Edicts

Ashoka's rock and pillar edicts are the major historical sources for his reign. Rock Edicts XII and II describe Ashoka's belief in religious tolerance and summarize his law of piety or right duty, which underscored all his moral teachings.

Minor Rock Edict II: Summary of the Law of Piety or Duty

Thus saith His Sacred Majesty:—

"Father and mother must be hearkened to; similarly, respect for living creatures must be firmly established; truth must be spoken.

"These are the virtues of the Law which must be practised. Similarly, the teacher must be reverenced by the pupil, and fitting courtesy must be shown to relations."

This is the ancient nature of things—this leads to length of days, and according to this men must act. . . .

Rock Edict XII: Toleration

"His Sacred and Gracious Majesty the King does reverence to men of all sects, whether ascetics or householders,

against which popular revolt was the only redress. . . . Ashoka in his inscriptions gives us an indication that he too was apprehensive of the abuse of power by his officials and to counteract this he instituted three- and five-yearly inspections. Finally, a weak central authority invariably encouraged revolts by provincial and regional chiefs to set themselves up as independent rulers. The process of disintegration was further speeded by a Greek invasion led by Demetrios. . . .

The Gupta Empires

In the north, after centuries of local revolutions involving the rise and fall of the Shungas, Kanvas, Kushanas, Shakas, Nagas and others, there arose a new empire. This was the empire of the Guptas (A.D. 319–550). The chief source of information about the Guptas is the corpus of inscriptions left by them and their coins which have been found all over northern, north-eastern and large

by gifts and various forms of reverence.

"His Sacred Majesty, however, cares not so much for gifts or external reverence as that there should be a growth of the essence of the matter in all sects. The growth of the essence of the matter assumes various forms, but the root of it is restraint of speech, to wit, a man must not do reverence to his own sect or disparage that of another without reason. Depreciation should be for specific reasons only, because the sects of other people all deserve reverence for one reason or another.

"By thus acting a man exalts his own sect, and at the same time does service to the sects of other people. By acting contrariwise a man hurts his own sect, and does disservice to the sects of other people. For he who does reverence to his own sect while disparaging the sects of others wholly from attachment to his own, with intent to enhance the splendour of his own sect, in reality by such conduct inflicts the severest injury on his own sect.

William H. McNeill and Jean W. Sedlar, eds., *Classical India.* London: Oxford University Press, 1969, pp. 104–106

parts of western India. Among these inscriptions the most interesting and valuable is the Allahabad Pillar inscription of Samudra Gupta which gives us a detailed life-history of the great king. Soon after his accession Samudra Gupta embarked on his career of conquest. He fought three great campaigns, two in the north and one in the south, and defeated as many as 24 kings. His wars led him on a march of over 3000 miles and in all this he was never defeated, a great feat of military valour and ability! His empire now became very extensive, comprising the whole of Bengal with the exception of the south-eastern parts and extended in the west to the Punjab and to the south to Jabalpur in the present Madhya Pradesh. His fame had spread all over the country and the kings of the south, the republican tribes, the Shaka and Kushana rulers and Nepal, all recognized his suzerainty. At this time king Meghavarna of Ceylon sent an embassy requesting permission from the Gupta emperor for building a monastery at Bodhgaya and it seems probable that the kings of the Indianized kingdoms of South-east Asia also maintained friendly relations with him.

The Golden Age

But Samudra Gupta was no mere warrior. His coins, issued in six different types, reflect his many-sided personality. He was well-versed in classical literature and was a patron of learning, if not a poet himself. He was fond of music and hunting and was a devout follower of Brahmanism. He performed a horse-sacrifice signifying a revival of the old Brahmanical faith at this time. In his personality he combined physical vigour with intellectual and artistic refinement and in this it was a fitting symbol of the Golden Age which his activities were helping to usher in. His long and distinguished reign ended around A.D. 380.

His successor was equally illustrious. Chandra Gupta II liquidated the power of the Shakas and the acquisition of the western areas meant for his empire a flourishing sea-borne trade with the Roman world. His campaign against the Shakas was carefully planned and he strengthened his position through a number of matrimonial alliances. He married a Naga princess. His daughter, Prabhavati Gupta, was married to Rudrasena II, the Vakataka king, and after her husband's death carried on the administration of the kingdom of the Vakatakas in the central areas of India with great efficiency. A daughter of Kakusthavarman, the

Kadamba ruler, was married to one of his sons and all these meant an extension of the Gupta influence in major parts of the country. He assumed the title of Vikramaditya (Sun of Valour) and many of his achievements recall to our minds the exploits of the legendary Vikramaditya who is presumed to have ruled in the first century B.C. from Ujjain. . . .

Chandra Gupta's glorious reign ended in A.D. 412–13. His successor was his son Kumara Gupta I (414–15 to 455–56) who is not known for any warlike activities. Towards the end of his reign, however, there was an invasion which was repulsed with great effort by the young prince Skanda Gupta who, in 456, became the Gupta emperor. He ruled until 468 and his greatest achievement was his successful fight against the Huns. Migrating from Central Asia the Huns descended on Europe and India in two groups. In A.D. 375 they ravaged Europe and shook the Roman empire to its very foundations. The India-bound group, called the White Huns, was beaten back by Skanda Gupta in 460–61 and this saved the country from suffering the kind of brutality Europe was subjected to. There was another Hun invasion of India in the opening years of the 6th century A.D. and inscriptions speak of two kings Toramana and Mihiragula, who appear to have been Huns. The Huns were finally defeated by a confederacy of northern Indian kings led by Narasimha Gupta Baladitya and supported by Yashodharman of Mandasore. Subsequently the Huns were assimilated into Indian society.

Skanda Gupta died in A.D. 468 and after him the Gupta empire began to disintegrate. Wars of succession, revolts by provincial rulers and assumption of sovereignty by the feudatory kings were some of the factors active in this process of disintegration. . . .

India's Classical Age

Thus ended the Gupta empire. But while it lived, it released great creative forces in the spheres of literature, science and the arts. The Guptas gave India, especially northern India, the much-needed sense of unity, security and peace. The Chinese pilgrim, Fa Hien, who came to India during the time of Chandra Gupta II, speaks in glowing terms of the happy life of the people. Though Buddhism still claimed numerous followers it was clearly on the decline. There was a great revival of Brahmanism and at this time arose the new popular Hinduism, that of the *Puranas,* the faith of millions of people even today. Vaishnavism and

Shaivism had won a national following and image worship and pilgrimages had become important parts of religious practice. The Gupta age, thus, was an age of peace and prosperity, urbanity and refinement, religious revival and intellectual achievement, classical literature and artistic eminence, and is aptly described as the Golden or Classical Age of ancient India. Possessed of self-confidence Indian culture freely and readily assimilated foreign influences; but while it borrowed it took care to see that the winds of all lands, as they blew around the house, did not sweep it off its feet. The essential "Indianness" of India was realized and enriched and given a lasting and classical expression in the sculpture, painting and architecture of the age.

Islamic Conquests and the Mughal Empire

By Stanley Wolpert

In the following extract from his book India, *eminent historian Stanley Wolpert underscores the enormity of the impact of Mughal invasion in India in* A.D. *711. Amidst the fierce military assaults by Muslim generals, there developed an antipathy between Hindus and Muslims which still exists in many areas. For many years Muslims were acculturated into Hindu society, adopting some of its features, such as caste social divisions. This tendency was encouraged under the Mughal emperor Akbar, whose policy of religious tolerance included placing Hindus in positions of authority. Wolpert maintains that the Mughal empire's decline was heralded by the resurgence of Islamic orthodoxy, divisive infighting at the center, and the growing autonomy of provincial authorities.*

Adherents to the militant brotherhood of *Islam* ("Submission" to the will of Allah) slashed their sharp scimitars through the body politic of South Asia, starting in Sind in A.D. 711. The faith founded by Prophet Muhammad in the sands of Arabia a century earlier thus reached India's shore the same year as it did the Iberian Peninsula, borne with zealous fervor by its galloping legions of true believers in God Almighty and His awesome Last Judgment. Muslim armies were to continue their assault on Indian soil for the next thousand years, during the last 500 of which Muslim monarchs would rule most of India. Not since the Aryan invasions had so powerful, persistent, unyielding a challenge been launched against Indic Civilization and its basic beliefs and values. In many ways, the Islamic impact was more divisive, its legacy more deeply threatening to Indian Civi-

Stanley Wolpert, *India*. Los Angeles: University of California Press, 1991.

lization, than Aryan rule ever was, for the Aryan–pre-Aryan synthesis gave birth to Hinduism. The only major offspring of Hinduism and Islam has been the Sikh community, which may prove almost as disruptive a challenge to Indian unity as Islam has been.

The Arab conquest of Sind came by sea. The desert sands of that lower Indus province of modern Pakistan proved no springboard, however, for conquering the rest of the subcontinent. Sind remained an isolated Muslim outpost in South Asia for almost three centuries before emerging as a portent of India's "Muslim era." The true dawn of that era came when Mahmud of Ghazni, "Sword of Islam," led his first band of Afghan raiders down the Khyber Pass in A.D. 997 on what would for the next quarter century be an annual hunt. Mahmud's game were Hindus and their temples, whose icons offended his sensibilities as much as their gold and jewels roused his greed. The rapacious Ghaznavid raids were followed by those of their successors to Afghan power, Ghors, whose bloody "holy wars" (*jihads*) against Hindu India left an equally bitter legacy of communal hatred in the hearts and minds of India's populace. Those early centuries of fierce Muslim assaults upon "infidel" Indians confirmed Hindus in their views of Muslim "foreigners" as polluting "Untouchables," although far more predatory. The gulf of mistrust, fear, and hatred that was soon to divide India's population from its martial Muslim rulers subsequently served to undermine all attempts to reunify the subcontinent, whose political fragmentation since 1947 reflects in part the historic incompatibility of those early centuries of Muslim-Hindu intercourse. . . .

Cultural Accommodation and Synthesis

After 1206, Muslim Sultans of Perso-Afghan-Turkish descent made the rust-colored plains of Delhi their home for three and a quarter centuries. No fewer than thirty-five Muslim Sultans sat on thrones of five successive dynasties at Delhi, ruling over a kingdom aptly called "despotism tempered by assassination." Once Muslim rulers settled permanently on Indian soil, however, they encouraged doctrinal accommodation toward Hindu subjects, no longer given just the extreme options of Islam or "death." Like Christians and Jews, Hindus were permitted to retain their own faith at the price of paying a special head tax for "Peoples of the Book," those whose partially revealed Scripture raised them above "infidel" status. Not that Brahmans enjoyed paying for the privilege of remaining second-class subjects in their own land! Still, it was better than forced conversion or death.

Over time the process of cultural accommodation and synthesis, linguistic, artistic, genetic, rubbed off many sharp edges of doctrinal difference between Hindus and Muslims. Most of the Muslims, who represented close to one-fourth the total population of India by the late nineteenth century, were descendants of converts or Hindu mothers. After centuries of residence in India, the "Brotherhood" of Islamic faithful acquired some of the features of Hinduism's "caste" system, particularly with regard to marriage, Sheikhs and Sayyids, Afghans and Muslims, of Persian or Turkish ancestry preferring mates from within their "own" communities. In some circles Muslim eating habits became more restrictive. No "strangers" have ever remained totally aloof from the impact of India. Islamic iconoclastic fervor was also tempered by time and the impossibility of destroying every statue on every Hindu temple in the land. Muslims were soon sated by gestures of symbolic destruction of gods and goddesses, most of whose images, if they date from pre-Muslim times, have a broken nose, arm, or other fractured feature, hacked from their stone body by some angry Muslim sword.

Islam's final wave came out of Central Asia, led by a direct descendant of Ghengiz Khan and Tamerlane named Babur, "the Tiger," founder of the great Mughal Empire. From 1526 to 1530 Babur defeated every Sultanate and Hindu Rajput army that took the field to challenge his relentless march. Born to fight and rule, Babur turned Delhi and Agra into twin capitals of the Empire he bequeathed to his heirs, Great Mughals who ruled India for more than two centuries. The Mughal Empire was the strongest dynasty in all of Indian History, nominally retaining the throne of Delhi until 1858, although for most of its last century the Mughals ruled as puppets of British, Maratha, or Afghan power.

Akbar's Achievements

As had been true of the Mauryan and Guptan dynasties, the third Mughal Emperor proved to be the greatest monarch of his line. Akbar, "the Great," reigned almost half a century (1556–1605), the high point of Mughal "national," enlightened rule, although not of territorial sovereignty. Akbar was the first Muslim monarch to initiate a general policy of religious toleration toward Hindus, wooing the Rajputs through marriages that forged potent "national" alliances, seated on his throne of inlaid marble as quasi-divine monarch of *all* Indians. Some orthodox Mullahs considered Akbar a traitor to Islam, raising battle cries of "Jihad" against him. The Emperor's elephant corps stamped out such rebellions with ease. Several of Akbar's leading advisers were Hindus, the head of his imperial revenue department had been born a Brahman, his military commander, a Rajput prince. Akbar chose his leading lieutenants personally, rewarding them lavishly with lands, whose revenues, generally about one-third of all crops, sufficed to support from 500 to 50,000 cavalry troops and their horses, always ready to gallop at the emperor's call. The system proved effective in securing the borders, expanding them over the Hindu Kush to incorporate most of what is now Afghanistan within the Delhi-Agra-Fatehpur Sikri imperium. Fatehpur was Akbar's own new capital, created to celebrate the birth of his son and heir, although an inadequate water supply

Destruction of Hindu Temples

During the reign of the Mughal emperors, Muslim historians were engaged to record the daily events of the period. The following extract from one such historian's account describes Emperor Shah-Jahan's (1628–1658) order to destroy Hindu temples.

It had been brought to the notice of His Majesty that during the late reign many idol temples had been begun, but remained unfinished, at Benares, the great stronghold of infidelity. The infidels were now desirous of completing them. His Majesty, the defender of the faith, gave orders that at Benares, and throughout all his dominions in every place, all temples that had been begun should be cast down. It was now reported from the province of Allahabad that seventy-six temples had been destroyed in the district of Benares.

John Dowson, ed., *The History of India as Told by Its Own Historians.* Calcutta: Susil Gupta (India) Private Ltd., 1963, pp. 37–38.

forced its abandonment after little more than a decade. Its haunting sandstone shell survives on the Jaipur road west of Agra, a tribute to Akbar's eclectic ingenuity, its ghostly ruins all that remain of his dream of uniting Hindus and Muslims within a single polity.

Persian poetry and arts added sophistication and colorful beauty to the Mughal court and its urbane culture during the effulgence of its seventeenth-century golden age. Persian became the official language of the Mughal Empire, rather than Babur's cruder native Barlas Turkish tongue, and was to remain so until English deposed it in 1835. Like their Persian neighbors, Indian monarchs have generally loved beauty, luxury, sensuality, pageantry, and the trappings of power. The Great Mughals pandered to such indigenous tastes, importing the best Persian artists and craftsmen to their sumptuous palaces, adding pearl mosques and peacock thrones encrusted with jewels to marble, fountained halls, engraved with Persian poetry, such as "If there be Paradise on earth, it is here, it is here, it is here!" Shah Jahan ("Emperor of the World") was the most extravagant of Mughal spenders. His profound remorse, or guilty conscience, following the death of his beloved wife, Mumtaz, resulted in the construction of the Taj Mahal, which provides breathtaking proof of the magnificence of Mughal art at its apogee. Little wonder that centuries later, a different sort of extravagant empire would dub its early filmmakers "moguls."

Return to Islam

The fatal weakness of later Mughal monarchs was not their spendthrift waste, however, but their return to narrow-minded Islamic orthodoxy. India's starving millions could at least derive vicarious pleasure from viewing the Red Fort at Agra or the Taj Mahal, but what joy or satisfaction could Hindu masses feel from Emperor Aurangzeb's (r. 1658–1707) reimposition of the hated head tax on non-Muslims? Or what pleasure could they take from his ban on alcoholic beverages? Or on repairs to Hindu temples? The "prayer-monger" *Padishah* ("Emperor") conquered more real estate than any of his ancestors, yet Aurangzeb did so only after wading to his throne through the blood of his brothers, and stirring up a storm of Hindu hatred throughout the Deccan, Rajasthan, and the Dravidian South. He also unified the Sikhs of the Punjab as no Mughal before or after him did, by torturing and beheading the ninth Guru, for refusing to convert to Islam. The first Guru, Nanak (1469–1538), had founded the Sikh faith, a peaceful blend of his own inherited Hinduism and Islam, which he learned from his dear Muslim friend. Following Aurangzeb's harsh persecution, however, Sikhs fused themselves into an "Army of the Pure" (*Khalsa*), changing their names from passive "Disciples" (*Sikhs*) to martial "Lions" (*Singhs*). Militant Sikhism was thus forged in the furnace of Mughal antipathy, the swords of that mightiest of Punjabi warrior communities initially sharpened against Muslims. After mid-1984, however, when Mrs. Gandhi ordered the Indian Army to "liberate" Amritsar's Golden Temple, Hindu-Sikh antipathy became modern India's most volatile internal problem.

Maratha opposition to Mughal rule was led by Shivaji (1627–1680), father of the Maratha confederacy, and spread from its Poona (Pune) base within half a century of his death to the environs of Delhi, Calcutta, and Madras. As the founder of Indian guerrilla warfare, Shivaji was reviled by Mughal generals as a "mountain rat," but his shrewd tenacity in battle was matched only by his Hindu faith in his motherland. Shivaji made *Sva-raj* ("Self-rule" or "Freedom") his mantra, launching the first major Hindu revolt against Muslim monarchs and their armies. His successors were so inspired by his fierce "national religious" passion that Pune would remain one of the key cradles of Indian Nationalism in the late nineteenth century. Brahman *Peshwas* ("Prime Ministers") of Pune administered the Maratha confederacy under nominal control of Shivaji's heirs. The singularly astute Peshwas remained a unique secular and religious dynasty ruling the Deccan for almost a century, until the British defeated their last incumbent in battle in 1818.

Decline of the Mughal Empire

After Aurangzeb's death in 1707, Mughal power started its slow decline. Court feuds and factional in-fighting at the center coincided with growing provincial autonomy and the emergence of several regional limbs more robust than the Delhi-Agra head. The Nizam was the first powerful minister to abandon Delhi and carve out his own southern kingdom in Hyderabad early in the eighteenth century. Nawabs of Oudh and Bengal, formerly mere deputies of the Great Mughal, became virtual kings in their own wealthy Gangetic domains by midcentury. Simultaneously, Afghanistan became a powerful threat from the west, under its own Amirs, who embarked on a series of bloody plundering raids into the Indus Valley, wresting the Punjab as well as the North-West Frontier from Delhi together with the peacock throne.

As the Great Mughal thus diminished in status, potent new forces appeared along India's coast, trading quietly, inconspicuously, at first. They came by sea from the West, and for most of the early eighteenth century were so busy fighting one another that they seemed uninterested in or incapable of challenging any Indian rulers, local or regional, not to speak of the awesome might of that empire, whose twin capitals were remote from the tiny British and French "factory" towns that dotted the Southern peninsular trunk of the slumbering elephant that was India.

Mughal Impact on India

BY PERCIVAL SPEAR

Mughal emperors ruled India from 1526 to 1761. In the following extract from A Cultural History of India, *British historian Percival Spear analyzes the impact of Mughal imperial rule. According to Spear, the cultivation of the idea during Akbar's reign that the emperor was divinely ordained has inspired devotion to Indian rulers ever since the Mughal period. The Mughals also implemented an effective administrative, bureaucratic, and revenue collection system. In art, architecture, and literature, the spread of Persian ideas, tastes, and language created a new Indo-Persian elite culture, the remnants of which are evident in India today.*

When Bābur [the first of the great Mughal emperors] descended into northern India he found a country still recovering from Tīmūr's[1] invasion of 1398 and the collapse of the Tughluq Dynasty of the Delhi sultanate which followed it. For two centuries a series of able Turkish soldiers had ruled with such ability that they had been able both to hold the formidable Mongols at bay and to extend their rule to south India. They had devised an effective administrative machine and made Delhi one of the great cities and cultural centres of Asia. In the next 120 years this ordered imperialism vanished. Hindūstān [as India was called] was ruled by Afghan chiefs whose kingdoms were tumultuous confederacies of nobles rather than well-organized states. Prosperity had departed to Bengal and the Deccan [central India] and the sultans of Delhi could barely hold their own against the *rājās* [Indian princes] of Rājasthān, whom once they had harried. The Mughals had thus very largely a free

1. Timur the lame, who became known as Tamburlaine throughout the West, led Mongol troops deep into the heart of India, leaving devastation in his wake.

hand in reorganizing the north, and the result of this work was largely handed on to the Deccan during the seventeenth and the south in the early eighteenth centuries.

The Mughals in general were a secular-minded race. In the late [Muslim historian] Sardār Panikkar's happy phrase they were 'kings by profession', more interested in ruling than in propagating religion. Bābur set greater store on Samarqand [a political and commercial center] than on Mecca, on musk melons and drinking parties than on strict religious observance. His descendants in general followed him. It is this aspect of their rule with which we are concerned.

Emperor Worship

The first contribution of their rule may be described as the imperial idea. There had of course been previous empires in India, and Hindus retained the idea of an overlord emperor or *chakravartin rājā*. But actual examples of such empires, like the [Hindu] Mauryan and the Gupta, lay so far in the past that they had ceased to exercise any practical influence. The ideal of unity lived on, but its actuality had ceased to be a memory. In their extension of empire from north to south India, an extension which, it is often forgotten, was still continuing while their power was collapsing in the north, the Mughals were only reviving or putting into practice a very ancient tradition. But their treatment of the idea of imperial authority was original and lasting. Briefly they removed the person and office of the emperor from the religious to the secular plane and at the same time surrounded it with a halo of mystical and religious sanctity.

The first step was the use of Persian titles and ceremonies which in themselves were neither Hindu nor Muslim. The *naurūz* ceremony, for example, was simply the Persian rite marking the solar new year in the spring. Persian also was the ceremony of weighing the emperor on his birthday against sundry grains and precious metals. These things were in themselves mere foreign importations: it was Akbar [emperor 1556 to 1605] who added the element of divinity that doth hedge a king. His new or Divine Faith is usually thought of as the eccentricity of genius or a dismal political failure. In fact, while we may grant the element of whim or eccentricity, the whole episode was a calculated political risk which in the long run became a brilliant success. Akbar never dreamt of producing a new religion in whose favour both Hindu and Muslim would abandon their own tenaciously held traditions. What he wanted was to find a way of canalizing the immense reservoir of Indian devotion towards an object distinct from the traditions of both communities. His method, which seemed fantastic both at the time and later, was to create a religious cult centred round the emperor. With his death the cult disappeared, but reverence for the imperial office remained. It secured, unlike the case of the previous Muslim dynasties, the succession and recognition of Mughal emperors when they had lost all imperial power. It was a potent factor, overlooked by the British, in rallying anti-British sentiment before and during the revolt of 1857.[2] One of the symptoms was the use of the halo for the imperial head by Mughal painters, which even the orthodox Aurangzeb [emperor 1658 to 1707] allowed; another the worship or veneration of the imperial person in the style of the Hindu *darshan* [holy men]; another the taking of disciples or *murīds* by the last emperors. The essence of the idea was that the emperor ruled, not only by divine permission, but with divine approval. He therefore had assumed a semi-sacred character and required not only obedience, but veneration as well.

Administration and Revenue Collection

A second Mughal gift to India was in the realm of administration. The Mughals as a race were not markedly original, but they had been 'charmed' by the Persian culture with which they had come into contact and of which they had proved apt pupils. They imported much of the Persian administrative apparatus into India and above all the idea of ordered bureaucratic authority. If it could hardly be called the rule of law it was certainly the rule of rule. There were regulations (as the *Ā'īn* testifies[3]) for everything, whether for the emblems of royalty and court ceremonial, the assessment and collection of revenue, the payment of troops, or the branding of horses for the imperial cavalry. Much Persian terminology is in use today. Setting aside details, we may note some major contributions to India in this sphere. It is true that Sher Shāh the Afghan (emperor 1540–5) made a significant start in this direction, upon whose foundations Akbar later built. But

2. In the Indian Mutiny of 1857, Muslim soldiers banded together against the British and harked back to the "days of glory" under the Mughal emperors. 3. The *Ā'īn i-Akbarī*, which laid down all the regulations for Muslim rule, was written when Akbar was emperor (1556–1605).

as he only reigned for five years, most of which were spent campaigning, his measures as recorded by the chroniclers must be regarded as a blueprint for the future rather than as an actual achievement. Outstanding in this department were the revenue arrangements, which are associated with the name of Akbar's revenue minister, Rājā Todar Mal. Their essence was an assessment of the revenue according to the extent of cultivation, the nature of the soil, and the quality of the crops. There was laborious measurement, analysis of possibilities, and calculation of prospects. The actual demand was adjusted to meet seasonal, price, and cultivated area variations. The system was administered whole or partially, well or ill, at different times and places. At times it broke down altogether. But it was never altogether abandoned or forgotten and it has never been superseded by something quite novel. It is the underlying basis of the revenue system today.

An Imperial Bureaucracy

In the political sphere the Mughals contributed the *mansabdār* system. This was a graded set of imperial officials who together formed an imperial military-cum-civil service. The higher grades were the 'omrah' described by European travellers like Bernier. They owed the appointment to the emperor and were paid, at first in cash and then by means of assignments on the revenue or *jāgīrs.* These grants had no resemblance to feudal tenures, for they were revocable at the imperial will and in any case lapsed at death. The *mansabdārī* service was not hereditary and in fact lacked a pension or its equivalent, since the *mansabdār*'s property was impounded at his death to offset cash advances made by the treasury during his life. This procedure amounted to a death duty of nearly 100 per cent. From this service were appointed governors of provinces (*sūbahs*), the high officers of state from the *wāzīr* downwards, administrators of districts, commanders of armies, cities, and forts. They were in fact the arteries of the Mughal system, the pulsating blood from the Mughal heart at court. They were the effective agents of the Mughal will. The titles and grades survived as aristocratic distinctions, like European titles of nobility, in the Nizām's [ruler of Hyderbad in the North] dominions until they were absorbed by India in 1948, but the system collapsed with the empire itself in the eighteenth century. Nevertheless the system as a whole permanently influenced the Indian consciousness. During the two centuries of its effective existence it accustomed nearly the whole country to the idea of an imperial bureaucracy representing and enforcing the central government's will. It replaced in the Indian mind as the symbol of government the feudal and clan relationships of the Rājputs [Hindu soldiers] and the loose tribal links of the Afghans. Though the extent of government may seem slight in modern terms, there was in fact during this period and thanks to this system more regular administration than most of India had known for a thousand years. In this respect the system provided a foundation upon which the British could build far more easily than would otherwise have been the case, because India had been conditioned already to a form of bureaucracy.

Rule by Foreigners

The *mansabdārī* system had another characteristic which was important for the future. Its personnel was mainly foreign. An analysis of the lists given in the *Ā'īn i-Akbarī* shows that approximately 70 per cent of the officers had come to India from the northwest within fifty years; the remaining 30 per cent were Indian, roughly half of these being Muslim and half Hindu. The service continued to be heavily recruited from abroad through the seventeenth century. India thus became used, not only to a regular administration, but also to a foreign one. Previous governments in north India had either been irregular or not foreign. This trait also was of value to their British successors. Indians were accustomed to rule by foreigners; the change for them was from one kind of foreigner to a stranger one.

A further feature of Mughal rule in general, remarked on by most non-governmental sources and particularly by European travellers, merchants, and ambassadors, was the arrogance and cupidity of the average official. The latter quality, as recorded by Sir Thomas Roe [British envoy] during his embassy to Jahāngīr, went right up to the heir-apparent himself. It was perhaps to be accounted for by the sense of insecurity of the nobles, liable, as they were, to be superseded or dismissed at any moment without a chance of appeal, and knowing that their property would be confiscated at death. They not only took presents, held up goods to ransom and so on, but also engaged largely in trade. Here again was a feature which smoothed the transition to the early British merchant official. What was strange in the British operations to the Indian observer was not their indulgence in commerce but the extent and method of their activities. The arrogance of the Mughal *nawāb* [governor] was proverbial, so that no surprise was caused by comparable conduct on the part of their British successors. But the Mughals treated each other in the same way as they treated the Hindus. What eventually caused complaint against the British was the discovery that they had one code of behaviour amongst themselves and another for their relations with Indians.

Religious Tolerance

Another characteristic of Mughal rule was tolerance. Toleration was not absolute, and was subject to considerable variations. There were times, notably in the reign of Aurangzeb, when the ruler aspired to be the head of an Islamic state rather than the Muslim head of an Indian state. But even so, though some discrimination was practised such as the imposition of the *jizya* [levies] on non-believers and the occasional demolition of temples, toleration was the general rule. Temples received grants as well as mosques, and were rarely demolished without a political motive. The emperor intermarried with Rājput families and Hindu customs were countenanced at court. It may be said that such regimes had existed before during the Islamic period, and that in any case religious toleration was an Indian tradition. But the duration and extent of the Mughal Empire, in contrast to the varying policies and briefer periods of other dynasties, served to stamp the policy afresh on the Indian mind as part of the accepted order of things.

Elaborate Art and Architecture

But perhaps the most striking of the Mughal legacies were the artistic and the cultural. Both of these began with Persian importations, which were exotics to the Mughals themselves who came from Central Asia. It was as if the Scots, having adopted the French language and culture, had conquered England and then introduced French as the language of government and society, covering the country with French-style chateaux and churches. Bābur brought with him a taste for all things Persian and the Persian invasion went on through several generations of talented and artistic rulers. But it encountered the current Indian forms and its genius was to form harmonious and original combinations with them. In the field of architecture the Mughals met the existing Indo-Muslim 'Pathān' style in north India, itself an earlier synthesis of Indo-Muslim forms, as well as the surviving Hindu style. Bābur began the artistic invasion by laying out Persian gardens wherever he went. Humāyūn [his successor] continued with his palace fortress in Delhi, the Purānā Qilā'. But it was Akbar who was the real parent of the Indo-Persian or Mughal school of architecture. In his palaces and mosques in Āgrā and Fatehpur-Sīkrī he employed Hindu masons under Mughal direction so extensively and skilfully as to produce a harmonious whole, neither Persian nor Hindu, but properly Indian in character. The proportion of Hindu elements was reduced without being eliminated by his successors, to produce a completer synthesis. His grandson Shāh Jahān was the director as well as the patron of Mughal building and it was in his time that the style attained its zenith with the Tāj Mahal, the palaces in Delhi and Āgrā, the Pearl Mosque of Āgrā, and the Jāmi' Masjid of Delhi. From Delhi and Āgrā the style spread to the far south. It became the norm of all domestic and official buildings in the north and even many small temples included the Mughal arch pattern. The style as a living tradition must now be pronounced moribund. But it is significant that when Western architects wished to draw on Indian tradition it was to this style that they primarily turned. The Mughals set the pattern for gardens, palaces, mosques, and houses.

The same Persian invasion occurred with painting. Bābur brought Persian miniature painters with him and Humāyūn encouraged them. Akbar, by employing Hindu artists steeped in their own tradition along with Muslims, created the Mughal School of painting. [Emperor] Jahāngīr, who was the artistic director of the school as his son was of architecture, expanded the range with his passion for nature and love of animals. With [Emperor] Shāh Jahān came the Mughal School of portraiture. Like architecture, Mughal painting lingered on in many branches long after the fall of the empire. But unlike the architectural heritage, it can still be said to be a living influence on modern Indian painting.

Literature and Etiquette

The third form of Persian influence was that of literature and manners. The Mughals did not, of course, introduce the Persian language and literature into India. This had been done by the Delhi sultans, so that under the Tughluqs Delhi was a leading Persian cultural centre; the traveller Ibn Battūta, who visited the city in the time of Muhammad Tughluq, considered it one of the principal cities in Asia. But the Persian spell was broken by Tīmūr, and not restored by the Afghans who ruled north India after him. The Mughals may be said to have re-established Persian influence, not so much by bringing in something which was not there before, as by the enthusiasm with which they propagated all things Persian. Though Turkish-speakers, they were Persian-lovers, and the love remained when their descendants became Persian-speakers. They spread the use of Persian from the court and diplomacy to the whole range of administration. Their conquests extended their administration to the south of India and with it a widespread and pervading Persian influence. Indo-Persian poets and historians there had been before, though none surpassed Faizī and Abu'l Fazl of Akbar's day. What was new was the spread not only of the Persian language, but of Persian ideas, tastes, and terminology to a wide Hindu class as well as the Muslim ruling class. The Hindu managerial and secretarial classes cultivated Persian and produced a school of poets which has persisted to this day. Along with literature went Persian manners and customs. Persian modes of address, dress, etiquette, and tastes (such as the love of formal gardens) spread with the new regime all over the country. Their traces were to be found in Rājput and Marāthā courts [in the northern and south-central parts of India], whatever their political or religious feelings towards the Mughals at any given time. They became the norm of social judgement and social deportment.

Indo-Persian Elite Culture

In fact the Mughals went a long way towards grafting upon Indian society a new aristocratic Indo-Persian culture. Under their aegis Persian and local influences combined to produce new forms of art and literature, new canons of behaviour, and a new type of speech. Mughal architecture and painting, though compounded of Persian and Hindu elements, were fused into something distinct from either. The same was true of language. Urdū was born under the sultanate, but it was the Mughals under whom it developed as a literary language in its own right and Muhammad Shāh Rangīla who admitted it to Court. In manners the Delhi Court became the Versailles of India. Akbar's religion, followed by the exaltation of the person of the emperor, provided an emotional centre for aristocratic loyalty, and the imperial services with their large employment of Hindus outside the *mansabdār* ranks, an administrative cement. The effort to create a new culture proved 'abortive' in the Toynbeian sense [referring to historian Arnold Toynbee's theories on the rise and fall of civilizations], perhaps because it was too confined to the aristocracy or perhaps because the middle class, which should have mediated it to the masses, was too small. But it left indelible marks on India in the developed Urdū language, in the arts of architecture and painting, and in manners and tastes.

THE HISTORY OF NATIONS

Chapter 2

British India

Origins of an Empire: The British East India Company

BY P.J. MARSHALL

The British presence in India dates back to trading contacts with western ports in the early seventeenth century. By the middle of the eighteenth century, limited commercial contact of the British East India Company blossomed into a substantial political role. Quite suddenly India was subsumed within the vast and growing British Empire. According to historian P.J. Marshall, in the following extract from The Raj: India and the British 1600–1947, *edited by C.A. Bayly, explanations for the transformation of British interests have focused on global theories—notably anarchy and economic deterioration in the wake of a declining Mughal empire, and the deliberate policy of imperialist aggression on the part of the British government. Marshall dismisses these theories and says a more accurate explanation can be gleaned from an analysis of local politics. In particular the rivalry and alliances formed between regional states and British settlements provided the context for the famous events that brought the British Empire into being.*

Direct contact between Britain and India dates back to the beginning of the seventeenth century. English merchants went to India, as they went to other parts of the world, to obtain exotic and expensive commodities for which there was an increasing demand throughout western Europe. In 1600 Elizabeth I granted a charter to a group which became 'The Governor and Company of Merchants of London Trading into the East Indies', known throughout its long history as the

P.J. Marshall, "The Seventeenth and Eighteenth Centuries," *The Raj: India and the British 1600–1947*, edited by C.A. Bayly. London: National Portrait Gallery Publications, 1990.

East India Company. In its early years the primary concern of the Company was to ensure that English merchants had a direct role in the supply of Asian spices and pepper to Europe, especially in the face of formidable Dutch competition. Indonesia was the major source of spice and pepper exports, and therefore the Archipelago rather than India was at first the main focus for the Company's operations. It was, however, attracted to Indian ports by the huge quantities of textiles—silk and cotton goods—that were sold there. These textiles were needed to barter for Indonesian spices and pepper, but some of them could be sold in Europe. To obtain Indian goods the Company sent ships on its third voyage in 1608 to the great port of Surat on the western coast of India. Surat became the site of the first English 'factory' or permanent trading post in India. . . .

By the early eighteenth century the commercial success of the English in India was impressive. The East India Company shipped more Indian goods to Europe than did any of its rivals, while the English communities in the ports of Bombay, Madras and Calcutta had won a considerable stake for themselves in India's seaborne trade with other parts of Asia. The strong position which the Portuguese had built up in Indian trade in the sixteenth century had been undermined in the seventeenth, when their lead passed to the Dutch. By 1740, if not earlier, the Dutch were being eclipsed by the British. . . .

Britain's undoubted success in India by the middle of the eighteenth century needs to be kept in perspective. From the British point of view Indian trade was still a small proportion of overseas trade as a whole. In terms of the whole of India, overseas trade was of limited significance and the British involvement in it was of no great consequence. On the other hand, from the perspective of coastal regions such as Bengal, where exports by sea were an important element in the economy, the growth in the British presence had serious implications. Nevertheless, even on a regional scale, by the middle of the eighteenth century the British had played virtually no political role outside their enclaves. The use of force had rarely been attempted, beyond some early seventeenth-century naval scuffles with the Portuguese and a disastrously unsuccessful attempt to coerce the Mughal empire in the 1680s.

Changes were to come thick and fast from the middle of the eighteenth century. The British quickly developed a spectacular political role. Their troops were to fight wars in southern India, in Bengal and even in the heartlands of the old Mughal empire. Out of war was to come a British empire. In 1765 the East India Company were awarded the *diwani* of Bengal by the Mughal emperor. This meant that they were recognised as the effective rulers of a province that probably contained something like 20 million inhabitants. By 1765 the British were also dominant along the Coromandel coast. The major Indian power on the coast ruled as their puppet, subject to their control. Through a garrison of their troops, the Company were also able to assert a decisive influence over the great north Indian state of Awadh.

Events in this great transformation such as the siege of Arcot or the battle of Plassey, or such personalities as Clive, Dupleix and Warren Hastings have, over the years, attracted a vast body of writing. Explaining why the transformation came about, however, now seems to be a complex and intractable business. Earlier generations were less troubled. If their sympathies lay with the empire that had emerged out of these events in the nineteenth century and which remained essentially intact until 1947, they tended to argue that a peaceful trading company had been compelled to take up arms because of the breakdown of ordered conditions and a slide to anarchy over much of India following the collapse of the Mughal empire. To make matters worse, the French had tried to exploit the Mughal failure by attacking the British first. Albeit reluctantly, the British found that they had no alternative but to resort to arms to protect their trade, chastise their enemies and eventually to restore India to what was usually taken as a much higher state of order than any that had existed under the Mughals. Those who were less well disposed towards the British Raj tended to argue that India in the mid-eighteenth century had been the first victim in a wave of systematic imperial aggression which Europe, and Britain in particular, was to unleash on the world in the nineteenth century.

Refuting Global Theories

These old certainties now seem flawed to most present-day historians. While there can be no denying that the Mughal empire had disintegrated, the eighteenth century is no longer seen as a period of disorder and anarchy affecting most of the subcontinent. In some cases Mughal rule was broken by persistent rebellion, as in the Punjab, but more commonly it withered away with relatively little disruption. It was succeeded by the regimes of great noblemen who had ruled provinces as governors in the name of the empire, as was the case in Bengal, Awadh or the Deccan; or by the rebels of the past who had reached accommodations with the empire, such as the Marathas. These regimes exercised authority over populations often comparable to those of an eighteenth-century European state. Within their domains some of the new rulers of the eighteenth century showed a capacity to develop new techniques of administration in order to enhance the revenue of their states and to maintain effective armed forces. If their courts lacked some of the splendour of those of the seventeenth-century Mughals, cities such as Hyderabad, Murshidabad and Lucknow became major centres of learning and artistic patronage, often reflecting the cultural traditions of the regions of which they were becoming the capitals. Some degree of economic growth, especially in the first half of the eighteenth century, seems to have underpinned this process of regional devolution. Cities like Delhi declined disastrously and some trade routes were disrupted by war, but other regions flourished and new commercial centres emerged. In short, it now seems difficult to portray eighteenth-century India in general as a land plagued by disorders so serious that they brought about a marked deterioration in economic conditions and thus compelled Europeans to intervene in order to maintain their trade.

On the other hand, it seems equally difficult to sustain an argument that India was the victim of calculated British aggression. Events were to show that, although there was as yet little qualitative difference between European and Indian military technology in the age of the cannon and the musket, armies of European soldiers and sepoys trained and organized by Europeans could be devastatingly effective in the eighteenth century. There is, however, very little evidence that would suggest that the British were aware in advance of their potential military advantages or that the Company, let alone the British Government, planned to exploit them. Both were very conscious indeed of the cost of war and of the absence of any obvious commercial benefits to be derived from it. Official policy was nearly always to avoid war and to concentrate on peaceful trade. Nevertheless, to deduce from this that the British were simply the victims of other people's bellicosity and only retaliated in self-defence would be a serious oversimplification. At a sailing distance of six months,

A Source of Immense Wealth to the Kingdom

Robert Clive was keen to enlarge British possessions in India after his military triumphs during the Battle of Plassey in 1757 in Bengal. The following extract is from Clive's 1759 letter to the British minister William Pitt. It is the first known document suggesting that the British East India Company's influence in Bengal could be extended to direct British rule in India.

Sir . . . The great revolution that has been effected here by the success of the English arms, and the vast advantages gained to the Company by a treaty concluded in consequence thereof, have, I observe, in some measure, engaged the public attention: but much more may yet in time be done, if the Company will exert themselves in the manner the importance of their present possessions and future prospects deserves. I have represented to them in the strongest terms the expediency of sending out and keeping up constantly such a force as will enable them to embrace the first opportunity of further aggrandising themselves; and I dare pronounce, from a thorough knowledge of this country government, and of the genius of the people, acquired by two years' application and experience, that such an opportunity will soon offer. The reigning Subah, whom the victory at Plassey invested with the sovereignty of these provinces, still, it is true, retains his attachment to us, and probably, while he has no other support, will continue to do so; but Musselmans [Muslims] are so little influenced by gratitude, that should he ever think it in his interest to break with us, the obligations he owes us would prove no restraint: and this is very evident from his having lately removed his Prime Minister, and cut off two or three principal officers, all attached to our interest, and who had a share in his elevation. Moreover, he is advanced in years; and his son is so cruel, worthless a young fellow, and so apparently an enemy to the English, that it will be almost unsafe trusting him with the succession. So small a body as two thousand Europeans will secure us against any apprehensions from either the one or the other; and, in case of their daring to be troublesome, enable the Company to take the sovereignty upon themselves. . . .

But so large a sovereignty may possibly be an object too extensive for a mercantile Company; and it is to be feared they are not of themselves able, without the nation's assistance, to maintain so wide a dominion. I have therefore presumed, Sir, to represent this matter to you, and submit it to your consideration, whether the execution of a design, that may hereafter be still carried to greater lengths, be worthy of the Government's taking it into hand. I flatter myself I have made it pretty clear to you, that there will be little or no difficulty in obtaining the absolute possession of these rich kingdoms; and that with the Moghul's own consent, on condition of paying him less than a fifth of the revenues thereof. Now I leave you to judge, whether an income yearly of upwards of two millions sterling, with the possession of three provinces abounding in the most valuable productions of nature and of art, be an object deserving the public attention; and whether it be worth the nation's while to take the proper measures to secure such an acquisition,—an acquisition which, under the management of so able and disinterested a minister, would prove a source of immense wealth to the kingdom. . . .

May the zeal and the vigorous measures projected for the service of the nation, which have so eminently distinguished your ministry, be crowned with all the success they deserve, is the most fervent wish of him who is, with the greatest respect,—Sir, Your most devoted and humble servant, Robt. Clive.

Adrian Sever, ed., *Documents and Speeches on the Indian Princely States*, Vol. I, letter from Robert Clive to William Pitt. Delhi: B. R. Publishing Corporation, 1985, pp. 72–74.

official policy from home could be defied with relative ease by men in India who, by the middle of the eighteenth century, had developed reasons of their own for resorting to force.

Focus on Local Politics

In seeking to explain why a British empire came so suddenly into being in the middle of the eighteenth century, historians are now inclined to look less for global explanations, such as the collapse of the Islamic empires or the unleashing of a new industrial imperialism from Europe, and more at local situations and the interaction between new regional states and such burgeoning colonial enclaves as Madras or Calcutta. The courts of seventeenth-century Mughal emperors and the factories of the East India Company had lived in entirely separate worlds which never met. The port cities of the mid-eighteenth century and the capitals of coastal regional states were part of the same world.

For Indian states a European settlement offered a mixture of advantages and threats, but it could hardly be ignored. As European trade grew it became an important element in the revenue of coastal states. The Europeans and their Indian partners took an ever larger proportion of the produce of artisans and peasant cultivators on which the state's taxation depended. The eighteenth-century Indian states, like contemporary states in Europe, required rich merchants to advance them money. The prosperity of such merchants was often based on their dealings with the Europeans. At the European ports Indian rulers could obtain arms for their new armies and could even hire the Company's troops. On the other hand, huge accumulations of wealth in towns like Madras or Calcutta, which were outside the jurisdiction of the local ruler, could not but cause resentment and apprehension. As European trade spread inland, immunities and privileges were claimed for it. Put crudely, eighteenth-century Indian rulers were facing a dilemma that was to become familiar to future generations in what has come to be called 'the Third World': how to balance the potential generation of new wealth through a foreign presence in their territories with the loss of autonomy which that foreign presence undoubtedly entailed.

Even though the English might resolve to live in a self-contained manner within their settlements, by the mid-eighteenth century they could no longer do so. With the increase of their trade, both corporate and private, they felt it necessary not only to protect the immunities of the settlements, but also to claim privileged access to markets and sources of commodities far inland. The ruler's needs could be their opportunities: they too could advance money to Indian rulers. The ultimate temptation was to intervene in the politics of the state to extract concessions or to support one faction against another in return for favours.

A world of new states and growing settlements, in which Europeans and Indians could be both partners and rivals, now seems to be the context in which to place the famous events that brought empire to the British in the eighteenth century. The first portents of what was to happen appeared on the Coromandel coast in the years after 1744. Here the English and French settlements of Madras and Pondicherry were locked in rivalry, which spread to draw in Indians on both sides. The French under the enterprising Dupleix may have been the first to see the possibility of winning greatly enlarged concessions from supporting Indian claimants to power, but the English were quick to match them by adopting the cause of other claimants. Along the Coromandel coast small armies of English and French regular and Company soldiers, regiments of sepoys and the forces of their Indian allies fought one another for strategic points, like the great fort at Trichinopoly. After many fluctuations of fortune, in 1761 the English under Sir Eyre Coote won a decisive victory at Wandiwash and besieged and captured Pondicherry. The outcome was that the British claimant to control of the Carnatic state on the Coromandel coast was confirmed in power. This was Muhammed Ali Walajah, the famous 'Nabob of Arcot'. For many years he maintained a nominally independent court which became a magnet for British clients. . . . The reality behind his independence was that the territory of the Carnatic was protected by British troops and that the Company claimed the right to seize and make use of his resources whenever emergencies arose.

Robert Clive and the Battle of Plassey

The French played a much less conspicuous role in the events that brought the British to power in Bengal. From early in the eighteenth century the British involvement in Bengal's trade had become very large indeed and the potential for conflict with the ruler, the Nawab, was accordingly very high. Tension had built up under the powerful Nawab Alivardi Khan, who reigned from 1740 to 1756. It boiled over under his successor, the young Siraj-ud-Daulah. The new Nawab seems to have been determined to curb Calcutta's autonomy and to extract what he regarded as proper financial contributions from the British. When the Company's servants refused to negotiate seriously with him, he attacked Calcutta in 1756 and took it with surprising ease. The death of part of the garrison in the Black Hole, an episode around which much later emotion was to be generated, was an unintended consequence of the Nawab's victory. Calcutta was, however, quickly recovered by an expedition of troops from the southern battle front on the Coromandel coast, dispatched from Madras under one of the officers who had most distinguished himself against the French, Colonel Robert Clive. Within a few months Clive became aware that his army could be used to support a conspiracy against Siraj-ud-Daulah, which promised to yield major gains for the Company and huge rewards for the individuals concerned. Clive came to terms with the conspirators, who ensured that the main part of Siraj-ud-Daulah's army would desert him. This they duly did at the battle of Plassey in 1757, leaving the British victorious. Siraj-ud-Daulah was deposed and killed and his successor, Mir Jafar conferred the promised benefits on the Company and its servants.

Clive's intention when he intervened in Bengal's politics was probably limited to obtaining a new Indian regime that would in future be a pliant ally of the Company. Within a very few years, however, the Company had destroyed even the semblance of an independent regime and had itself become the ruler of Bengal. Between 1757 and 1765 nothing could be done to protect a succession of Nawabs from ruthless demands for concessions, both public and private. The Company insisted on receiving ever larger allocations of taxation to pay for its troops, while individuals levied 'presents' for themselves and claimed the right to trade on their own terms in any commodity in any part of Bengal. Mir Kasim, one of the Company's appointed Nawabs, resisted these demands to the point of a new war in 1763. The war took the Company's troops out of Bengal and involved them in a fresh round of fighting with the Wazir of Awadh, who had joined in a coalition against the British. In 1764 the Company's army won the battle of Buxar in northern India. This left them in a position to dictate terms not only for the future of Bengal but for the territories adjoining it. The settlement was made in the following year by Clive on his return to India. At the Treaty of Allahabad of 1765 Clive accepted the *diwani* of Bengal, a recognition that the Company had made it impossible for any Nawab to retain even nominal authority. He also established a British diplomatic and military presence for the Company at Lucknow. . . .

British Rule of Bengal and Beyond

The 1765 settlement was to last in essentials until late in the eighteenth century. Clive's successors had, however, to work out the practical implications of what would be involved in British rule of Bengal. Clive's original intention had probably been to leave all the layers of Indian authority intact. In the event, British Company servants were placed in some of the senior positions of what was still essentially an Indian state apparatus. Calcutta, the residence of Warren Hastings, the first Governor-General, and of his Council, became the seat of government for the whole province. In what came to be known as 'districts' junior Company servants began to concern themselves with levying taxation, the central preoccupation of the new regime as of the old, and even with supervising the administration of justice.

On these foundations a bureaucratic colonial administration was eventually to be established, but for most of the eighteenth century it would be more realistic to describe what the Company was doing in Bengal as the management of the state apparatus that had emerged under the Nawabs through Indian intermediaries and collaborators such as Warren Hastings's famous *banian* (steward and business manager) Cantu Babu under the somewhat remote supervision of the East India Company's servants. Some of these men, like Hastings himself, were assiduous administrators and developed an interest in the country they governed that added greatly to Western knowledge of it. Most, not surprisingly, also showed a keen concern for the personal advantages that the conquest of Bengal offered them. With what they acquired some of them were able to live in considerable style in Calcutta or other centres of British power. . . .

By the end of the eighteenth century the British began to strike out of the bridgeheads which they had consolidated in Bengal and at Madras. Expansion from Madras brought the Company into bitterly contested wars with the powerful regional state of Mysore under the rule of Haidar Ali and his son Tipu Sultan. Until the Company could organize massive forces, they were by no means certain of victory over Mysore. In 1792 Tipu was worsted, and in 1799 his capital was taken and he was killed. By then he had acquired the reputation of being the Indian Hannibal, the dauntless enemy of the new Rome. . . . From Bengal the British tightened their grip on Awadh and in the first decade of the nineteenth century, under the direction of the Marquess Wellesley, their armies extended British rule beyond Delhi and imposed British hegemony over the Marathas. Their power over the subcontinent was now unassailable.

British Cultural Imperialism

By Thomas Macaulay

While members of the British East India Company focused on matters of trade and profit, by the early nineteenth century British social reformers were intent on "civilizing" the Indian people. British politician Thomas Macaulay saw English education as the means to assimilate India into the English tradition. His famous "Minute on Education," excerpted here, expresses the zeal of British reformers of the period. Ignorant of the breadth and depth of Indian culture and imbued with an unshakable belief in the superiority of the British race, Macaulay argues adamantly for English as the medium of instruction in India. On March 7, 1835, English became the official language of British India. Ironically, Macaulay's victory in providing geographically and culturally diverse Indians with a common language was a major factor in accelerating the end of British rule by arming India's elite with the words in which to demand their freedom.

We have a fund to be employed as government shall direct for the intellectual improvement of the people of this country. The simple question is, what is the most useful way of employing it?

All parties seem to be agreed on one point, that the dialects commonly spoken among the natives of this part of India contain neither literary or scientific information, and are, moreover so poor and rude that, until they are enriched from some other quarter, it will not be easy to translate any valuable work into them. It seems to be admitted on all sides that the intellectual improvement of those classes of the people who have the means of pursuing higher studies can at present be effected only by means of some language not vernacular amongst them.

What, then, shall that language be? One half of the Commit-

Thomas Macaulay, "Extract from Macaulay's Minute on Education 1835," *A History of India*, by Michael Edwardes. London: Thames and Hudson, 1961.

tee maintain that it should be the English. The other half strongly recommend the Arabic and Sanskrit. The whole question seems to me to be, which language is the best worth knowing?

I have no knowledge of either Sanskrit or Arabic.—But I have done what I could to form a correct estimate of their value. I have read translations of the most celebrated Arabic and Sanskrit works. I have conversed both here and at home with men distinguished by their proficiency in the Eastern tongues. I am quite ready to take the Oriental learning at the valuation of the Orientalists themselves. I have never found one among them who could deny that a single shelf of a good European library was worth the whole native literature of India and Arabia. The intrinsic superiority of the Western literature is, indeed, fully admitted by those members of the Committee who support the Oriental plan of education.

It will hardly be disputed, I suppose, that the department of literature in which the Eastern writers stand highest is poetry. And I certainly never met with any Orientalist who ventured to maintain that the Arabic and Sanskrit poetry could be compared to that of the great European nations. But, when we pass from works of imagination to works in which facts are recorded and general principles investigated, the superiority of the Europeans becomes absolutely immeasurable. It is, I believe, no exaggeration to say, that all the historical information which has been collected from all the books written in the Sanskrit language is less valuable than what may be found in the most paltry abridgments used at preparatory schools in England. In every branch of physical or moral philosophy the relative position of the two nations is nearly the same.

The Case for the English Language

How, then, stands the case? We have to educate a people who cannot at present be educated by means of their mother-tongue. We must teach them some foreign language. The claims of our own language it is hardly necessary to recapitulate. It stands pre-eminent even among the languages of the West. It abounds with works of imagination not inferior to the noblest which Greece has bequeathed to us; with models of every species of eloquence; with historical compositions, which, considered merely as narratives, have seldom been surpassed, and which, considered as vehicles of ethical and political instruction, have never been equalled; with just and lively representations of human life and human nature; with the most profound speculations on metaphysics, morals, government, jurisprudence, and trade; with full and correct information respecting every experimental science which tends to preserve the health, to increase the comfort, or to expand the intellect of man. Whoever knows that language, has ready access to all the vast intellectual wealth, which all the wisest nations of the earth have created and hoarded in the course of ninety generations. It may safely be said that the literature now extant in that language is of far greater value than all the literature which three hundred years ago was extant in all the languages of the world together. Nor is this all. In India, English is the language spoken by the ruling class. It is spoken by the higher class of natives at the seats of government. It is likely to become the language of commerce throughout the seas of the East. It is the language of two great European communities which are rising, the one in the south of Africa, the other in Australasia; communities which are every year becoming more important, and more closely connected with our Indian Empire. Whether we look at the intrinsic value of our literature, or at the particular situation of this country, we shall see the strongest reason to think that, of all foreign tongues, the English tongue is that which would be the most useful to our native subjects.

The question now before us is simply whether, when it is in our power to teach this language, we shall teach languages in which, by universal confession, there are no books on any subject which deserve to be compared to our own; whether, when we can teach European science, we shall teach systems which, by universal confession, whenever they differ from those of Europe, differ for the worse; and whether, when we can patronize sound Philosophy and true History, we shall countenance, at the public expense, medical doctrines which would disgrace an English farrier—Astronomy, which would move laughter in girls at an English boarding-school—History, abounding with kings thirty feet high, and reigns thirty thousand years long—and Geography, made up of seas of treacle and seas of butter.

Refuting the Arguments Against English

It is said that we ought to secure the co-operation of the native public, and that we can do this only by teaching Sanskrit and Arabic.

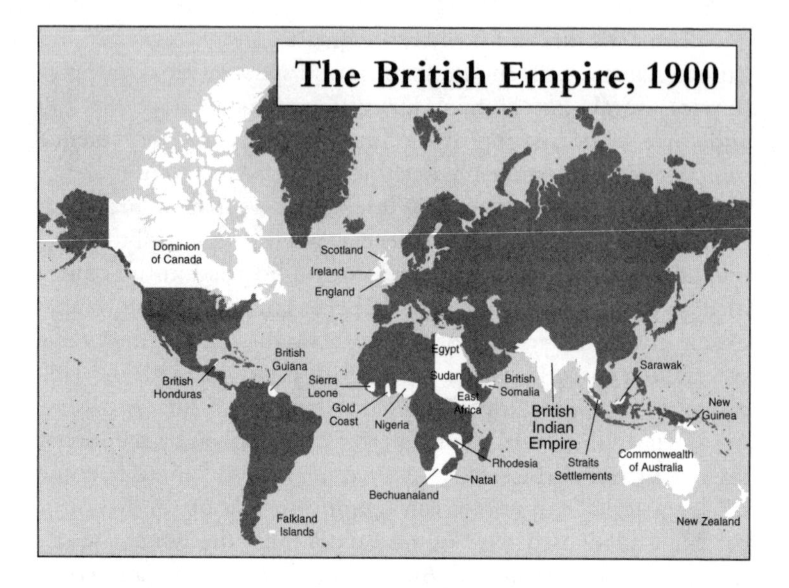

I can by no means admit that, when a nation of high intellectual attainments undertakes to superintend the education of a nation comparatively ignorant, the learners are absolutely to prescribe the course which is taken by the teachers. It is not necessary, however, to say anything on this subject. For it is proved by unanswerable evidence that we are not at present securing the co-operation of the natives. It would be bad enough to consult their intellectual taste at the expense of their intellectual health. But we are consulting neither—we are withholding from them the learning for which they are craving; we are forcing on them the mock-learning which they nauseate.

This is proved by the fact that we are forced to pay our Arabic and Sanskrit students, while those who learn English are willing to pay us. All the declamation in the world about the love and reverence of the natives for their sacred dialects will never, in the mind of any impartial person, outweigh the undisputed fact, that we cannot find, in all our vast Empire, a single student who will let us teach him those dialects unless we will pay him.

It is said that the Sanskrit and Arabic are the languages in which the sacred books of a hundred millions of people are written, and that they are, on that account, entitled to peculiar encouragement. Assuredly it is the duty of the British government in India to be not only tolerant, but neutral on all religious questions. But to encourage the study of a literature admitted to be of small intrinsic value only because that literature inculcates the most serious errors on the most important subjects, is a course hardly reconcilable with reason, with morality, or even with that very neutrality which ought, as we all agree, to be sacredly preserved. It is confessed that a language is barren of useful knowledge. We are told to teach it because it is fruitful of monstrous superstitions. We are to teach false history, false astronomy, false medicine, because we find them in company with a false religion. We abstain, and I trust shall always abstain, from giving any public encouragement to those who are engaged in the work of converting natives to Christianity. And, while we act thus, can we reasonably and decently bribe men out of the revenues of the State to waste their youth in learning how they are to purify themselves after touching an ass, or what text of the Vedas they are to repeat to expiate the crime of killing a goat?

It is taken for granted by the advocates of Oriental learning that no native of this country can possibly attain more than a mere smattering of English. They do not attempt to prove this; but they perpetually insinuate it. They designate the education which their opponents recommend as a mere spelling-book education. They assume it as undeniable, that the question is between a profound knowledge of Hindoo and Arabian literature and science on the one side, and a superficial knowledge of the rudiments of English on the other. This is not merely an assumption, but an assumption contrary to all reason and experience. We know that foreigners of all nations do learn our language sufficiently to have access to all the most abstruse knowledge which it contains, sufficiently to relish even the more delicate graces of our most idiomatic writers. There are in this very town natives who are quite competent to discuss political or scientific questions with fluency and precision in the English language. I have heard the very question on which I am now writing discussed by native gentlemen with a liberality and an intelligence which would do credit to any member of the Committee of Public Instruction. Indeed, it is unusual to find, even in the literary circles of the Continent, any foreigner who can express himself in English with so much facility and correctness as we find in many Hindoos. Nobody, I suppose, will contend that English is so difficult to a Hindoo as Greek to an Englishman. Yet an intelligent English youth, in a much smaller number of years than our unfortunate pupils pass at the Sanskrit college, becomes able to read, to enjoy, and even to imitate, not unhappily, the composition of the best Greek authors. Less than half the time which enables an English youth to read Herodotus and Sophocles ought to enable a Hindoo to read Hume and Milton.

Restating the Case

To sum up what I have said: I think it clear that we are free to employ our funds as we choose; that we ought to employ them in teaching what is best worth knowing; that English is better worth knowing than Sanskrit or Arabic; that the natives are desirous to be taught English, and are not desirous to be taught Sanskrit or Arabic; that neither as the languages of law, nor as the languages of religion, have the Sanskrit and Arabic any peculiar claim to our encouragement; that it is possible to make natives of this country thoroughly good English scholars, and that to this end our efforts ought to be directed.

In one point I fully agree with the gentlemen to whose general views I am opposed. I feel, with them, that it is impossible for us, with our limited means, to attempt to educate the body of the people. We must at present do our best to form a class who may be interpreters between us and the millions whom we govern; a class of persons, Indian in blood and colour, but English in taste, in opinions, in morals, and in intellect. To that class we may leave it to refine the vernacular dialects of the country, to enrich those dialects with terms of science borrowed from the Western nomenclature, and to render them by degrees fit vehicles for conveying knowledge to the great mass of the population.

I would strictly respect all existing interests. I would deal even generously with all individuals who have had fair reason to expect a pecuniary provision. But I would strike at the root of the bad system which has hitherto been fostered by us. I would at once stop the printing of Arabic and Sanskrit books; I would abolish the Madrassa and the Sanskrit college at Calcutta. Benares is the great seat of Brahmanical learning; Delhi, of Arabic learning. If we retain the Sanskrit college at Benares and the Mahomedan college at Delhi, we do enough, and much more than enough in my opinion, for the Eastern languages. If the Benares and Delhi colleges should be retained, I would at least recommend that no stipend shall be given to any students who may hereafter repair thither, but that the people shall be left to make their own choice between the rival systems of education without being bribed by us to learn what they have no desire to know. The funds which would thus be placed at our disposal would enable us to give larger encouragement to the Hindoo college at Calcutta, and to establish in the principal cities throughout the Presidencies of Fort William and Agra schools in which the English language might be well and thoroughly taught.

I believe that the present system tends, not to accelerate the progress of truth, but to delay the natural death of expiring errors. I conceive that we have at present no right to the respectable name of a Board of Public Instruction. We are a Board for wasting public money, for printing books which are less value than the paper on which they are printed was while it was blank; for giving artificial encouragement to absurd history, absurd metaphysics, absurd physics, absurd theology; for raising up a breed of scholars who find their scholarship an encumbrance and a blemish, who live on the public while they are receiving their education, and whose education is so utterly useless to them that, when they have received it, they must either starve or live on the public all the rest of their lives. Entertaining these opinions, I am naturally desirous to decline all share in the responsibility of a body which, unless it alters its whole mode of proceeding, I must consider not merely as useless, but as positively noxious.

The Indian Rebellion of 1857

By R.C. Majumdar and P.N. Chopra

Historians hold conflicting views on the significance of the Indian Rebellion of 1857. In the following extract, Indian historian R.C. Majumdar argues against the interpretation given by Indian nationalists, who assert that the outbreak of 1857 was India's first national war of independence. He says the rebellion was neither preplanned nor unified, nor was it an expression of nationalist sentiment. Majumdar says that Indians as a group did not yearn for independence in the mid-nineteenth century, for the people at that time had no conception of an Indian nation. Rather than a demand for progress or reform, concludes Majumdar, the uprising was a reactionary response aimed at the restoration of Mughal dynastic rule.

R.C. Majumdar is one of India's most eminent historians and a persistent critic of what he regards as attempts by Indian historians to falsify history to serve nationalist ends. P.N. Chopra is the author and editor of several authoritative works on Indian history, society, and culture.

The great outbreak of 1857 is one of those episodes of Indian history in the modern age which no educated Indian has ever regarded without interest, and a few without prejudice. While some regard it as the mutiny of the sepoys, as the popular name Sepoy Mutiny indicates, others describe it as the first national war of independence in India. The main facts or incidents are, however, fairly well-known and may be briefly stated as follows.

The Indian soldiers, generally known as sepoys (*sipahi*), always outnumbered British soldiers. It was mainly with the help of the sepoys that the British conquered India and maintained order and discipline over their vast dominions. The sepoys certainly welcomed their recruitment in the Indian army and preferred it to enrolment in the army of the India Princely States.

But gradually widespread discontent grew against British rule and vague apprehensions prevailed among all classes of people, both civil and military, that the British government intended to convert them wholesale to Christianity. The sepoys had additional grievances in respect of their pay and promotion, and there were mutinies of sepoys on a small scale on several occasions, prior to 1857. At last the introduction at the Enfield rifle served as the immediate cause of the Revolt. The Sepoys had to bite off the end of the cartridge which they believed were greased with the fat of cows and pigs, in order to pollute both the Hindus and the Muhammadans, and to convert them to Christianity. Subsequent inquiry showed that these apprehensions were not altogether unfounded and that the fat of cows and pigs had really been used in making these cartridges.

The rebellious spirit was evident at Barrackpur on 29 March 1857, when a sepoy struck a blow at his officer. It soon spread to Meerut and Lucknow. The sepoys at Meerut rose in a body, murdered the Europeans, burnt their houses, and then marched to Delhi. These rebels were soon joined by others at Delhi. There they murdered many Europeans, proclaimed Bahadur Shah, the last of the Mughals, as the rightful emperor of India. The rebellion soon spread to other parts of the United Provinces (U.P.) as well as to Central India, including Bundelkhand. The chief strongholds of the rebels were Delhi, Lucknow, Kanpur, Bareilly and Jhansi.

In these and other places the successful rebellion of the sepoys was followed by popular outbreaks and plunders. The British were taken by surprise and in most places the sepoys had no difficulty in driving away the officers and their families and becoming masters of the localities. But in some places like Kanpur and Lucknow where the British took shelter in forts, improvised entrenchments or some pucca [permanent] buildings, they defended themselves against the sepoys who far outnumbered them.

No Action Plan

The rebellions were merely sporadic outbursts in various isolated towns. Neither the mutinous sepoys nor the local people who revolted or rather took advantage of the absence of authorities to loot and fight among themselves—had any common plan of action. The people at large and most of the landlords, except the ryots and the taluqdars of Avadh, who took this opportunity to resume the lands of which they had been deprived did not make common cause against the British. The rulers of many of the Indian States also held aloof. The Sikh soldiers helped the British against the sepoys, who had defeated them only a few years ago and were the chief instruments of the ruin of their region. The Gurkha king of Nepal also helped the British. So the British were able to suppress the Revolt, which came to an end in 1858.

The Rani of Jhansi, the most distinguished leader in the Revolt, at first denounced the rebel sepoys, but when she found that the British suspected her of complicity in it and wanted to try her, she joined the sepoys and proved to be the ablest rebel leader against the British. She died fighting bravely, while two other leaders, Nana Sahib and the Begum of Oudh, fled to Nepal. Tantia Tope, the general of Nana, also fought bravely but was captured and hanged. Bahadur Shah was exiled to Rangoon.

The Revolt was marked by terrible cruelties and atrocities on both sides. Reference may be made to the grim tragedy at Kanpur.

At Kanpur the rebels were headed by Nana Sahib, the adopted son of Baji Rao. The English soldiers and residents, nearly a thousand in number, shut themselves up behind a feeble rampart. Nana promised to convey them safely to Allahabad, but as soon as they reached the river-side, the rebels opened fire, and massacred nearly all of them. Nana also murdered nearly two hundred women and children who were kept as prisoners (15th July), and threw their bodies into a neighbouring well.

But while suppressing the Revolt, some of the English officials were equally guilty of barbarities of the worst type.

Lord Canning showed wonderful tact and patience in handling a very dangerous situation. When the Rebellion was over, he did not wreak an ignoble vengeance on the deluded people, but showed mercy and moderation.

Direct Rule by the British Crown

One of the most important changes brought about by the Great Revolt was the final abolition of the authority of the East India Company. The shocking news of the revolts and massacres brought home to the people in England the incongruity of the administration of a great empire by a mercantile company. An Act for the "Better Government of India" was finally passed on 2 August 1858, and the responsibility for the Government of India was directly assumed by the Crown. A Secretary of State for

India took the place of the President of the Board of Control, and the Council of India, that of the Court of Directors. The Governor-General was henceforth styled as the Viceroy, or representative, of the Crown in India.

This momentous change was announced to the people and princes of India on November 1, 1858, by a solemn proclamation of Her Majesty Queen Victoria. It was translated into the vernacular, and read out in various parts of the country. As the first formal declaration of Indian policy by the Crown, its importance cannot be over-estimated. The more important portions of the document may be summarised as follows:

Viscount Canning was appointed the first Viceroy and Governor-General, and all the officers of the Company were confirmed in their posts. The existing treaty obligations were accepted, and any desire for further conquests was expressly repudiated.

Nature of the Outbreak

Divergent views have been expressed both by contemporary and later writers about the nature of the outbreak of 1857–58. These may be broadly divided into two classes. According to some, the outbreak was really a rebellion of the people against British rule and not merely a mutiny of soldiers. According to others it was primarily and essentially a mutiny of sepoys though in certain areas the civil population took advantage of it to break out into open defiance of authorities. Only a very few might have had any political motive, but not necessarily the achievement of freedom from the British yoke.

We find supporters of both these views among contemporary Englishmen. Eminent Indians, throughout the latter half of the 19th century almost regarded the outbreak as purely a mutiny of soldiers. Thus Kishorichand Mitra, an eminent Bengali wrote in 1858: "It is essentially a military insurrection. It is the revolt of a lac of sepoys. It has nothing of the popular element in it." The same view was expressed by other eminent Bengali leaders like Sambu Chandra Mukhopadhyaya, Harish Chandra Mukherji, Raj Narain Bose, and Syed Ahmad and three other Bengalis and one Maratha, Godse Bhatji, who were eye-witnesses of the events in different localities.

It was not till the beginning of the present [twentieth] century, when a genuine revolutionary movement of the people began, that the Sepoy outbreak of 1857 began to be looked upon not only as a great revolt of the people but also claimed to be the first Indian War of Independence, and this has now got wide currency. This view, first made popular by the publication, in 1909, of "The Indian War of Independence—1857" by the great patriot Vinayak Damodar Savarkar has now obtained great currency among Indians, but historically it is difficult to accept this view.

In the first place, the actual revolt, both of the sepoys and of the civil population, was confined to the U.P. and a fringe of territory just outside its boundary. There is hardly any justification, therefore, to characterise the movement as Indian or National.

India in the sense of a political or national unit had no meaning or existence in the conception of our ancestors in 1857. They talked of the Sikhs, Rajputs, Marathas, Hindusthanis, Bengalis, Oriyas, Tamils, etc., but had no clear conception of an Indian. We learn from Bishop Heber, who travelled widely over North India in 1824, that the people in U.P. regarded the Bengali as much a foreigner as the English. In spite of the slogan of Hindu Pad Padshahi, the Marathas had ravaged without compunction the territories of the Sikhs and Rajputs on the west, the Bengalis in the east, the Tamils and Kannadas in the south, and the Hindusthanis in the north. The conception of India, as a whole, was to be found only in the literary works of a past age, and still survived in theory, but it had no application to actual politics till the sixties or seventies of the 19th century.

So long as there was no conception of India, there could not have been any idea of freedom of India, far less any struggle for attaining it. But, in reality, the case was perhaps worse. For even among the smaller political units into which India was divided, there was not the same urge for freedom from British yoke. In Bengal, as mentioned above, British rule was regarded by the Hindus as only a change of masters, and for the better.

Nowhere in India did the conception of a national State supersede that of the dynastic State. The allegiance of the people, if any, was due to the ruler and his dynasty, but not to any regional State. There were attempts in 1857 to restore the Mughal dynasty in Delhi, the Peshwa's supremacy in Central Provinces and, the rule of the Nawab family of Oudh. But there was no question of establishing a national State in any of these regions. As such there could be no national war of independence before the Indians were conscious of forming a nation and imbued with a sense of patriotism or yearning for independence.

A Shift in British Imperialist Ideology

By David Washbrook

For much of the nineteenth century, the British pursued a liberal agenda, promising India moral and material progress, Western education, the beginnings of political representation, and equal rights to Indians as citizens of the British crown. The rebellion of 1857, however, shocked the British to the core. They abandoned this liberal approach and decided to leave traditional Indian society intact and untouched. No longer looking to promote modernity and change, Queen Victoria legitimized her authority by harking back to India's imperial past and proclaiming herself "queen-empress." From then on, the British pursued regressive measures designed to maintain their authority and keep a tight rein on the local situation. Under conservative administrators like Lord Lytton, this shift came to dominate the character of British imperialism until the end of World War I. According to David Washbrook, a professor of South Asian history at Oxford University, this emphasis on the past inadvertently provoked the Indian nationalist movement.

The [Indian] Mutiny [of 1857], which had seen the British lose control of much of the central Ganges valley, gave the imperial system a profound shock. Although its eighteenth-century antecedents had lain in Indian forms of government and its initial policies had stressed continuity with India's own traditions, the state presided over by East India Company in the nineteenth century had progressively come to see its purposes in a more radical light. The pre-Mutiny generation of British administrators had few doubts about the superiority of their own civilisation and many had committed themselves to transforming Indian society on its model.

But the Mutiny provoked a serious re-evaluation of Britain's 'mission' in the subcontinent. One theory of revolt, popular in certain quarters, was that it reflected a reaction against precipitate interference in indigenous traditions. Hindu and, more particularly, Islamic religious leaders had been driven into rebellion by the threat posed to their values by Christianity and Rationalism.

A second and related theory saw the problem more in economic and institutional terms. The encouragement given by the Company to the development of a competitive market economy had both undermined traditional 'aristocracies' and placed substantial sections of the peasantry under threat from merchants and money-lenders. Such theories moved the post-Mutiny Raj towards a more conservative agenda. Law courts and legislatures were called upon to foreswear interference in Indian custom and religion and to shoulder the burden of protecting tenants and landlords alike from the social consequences of economic failure. Indian society was now to be distanced from the modern world and preserved in its traditional and hierarchical forms.

Pressures for Modernization

Yet other analyses of the Mutiny promoted other policy inclinations and modernity was not easily denied access to the plains of Hindustan. The revolt, most obviously, had first arisen in the Company's army where a thin cadre of British officers had sought to discipline a mass of Indian troops. To prevent a recurrence, British line regiments were brought to serve in India on a much more regular basis and the 'white' segment of the army was substantially increased. But this substantially increased, too, the European population in India, which was further promoted by improved means of transport and communications. Could indigenous society be preserved in all its 'traditionality' while becoming, simultaneously, host to an ever expanding European presence?

The same dilemma affected many other areas of the state. In a variety of ways, the Mutiny introduced the principle of 'representative' government into India. Another theory of revolt attributed it to lack of consultation between British and Indian authorities and gave rise in 1861 to the creation of a Viceregal Council which included Indian members. At a more local level, the costs of suppressing the Mutiny had burdened the government with heavy debts and necessitated a devolution of power.

To raise more taxes, municipalities were authorised to associate 'respectable' Indians with their administrations, eventually by means of election. Although these beginnings were very limited in scope, they set a crucial precedent. But how far was a 'traditional' society compatible with principles of competitive political representation?

Elsewhere, too, the novel pressures of the Victorian Age bore in on India. Railway-building, which had begun just before the Mutiny, proceeded at a much greater pace thereafter, transforming commercial and demographic possibilities. Industry arrived in the 1860s, converting Calcutta and Bombay by 1901 into the second and third largest cities in the entire British Empire, overshadowed only by London. Western education also began to find a deeper response. The Indian Universities Act, passed in the same year as the Mutiny, established new institutions at Calcutta, Bombay and Madras, which attracted an ever larger flow of Indian talent and introduced it to both the mysteries and the powers of Western knowledge. By the end of the nineteenth century, Lord Macaulay's dream of a nation of 'brown Englishmen' was ceasing to be a mere fantasy. But would 'brown Englishmen', travelling the railways to offices and business premises in the major megalopolises of imperial wealth and power, be content with the rights and privileges merely of 'traditional' subjects?

British rule in the years after the Mutiny faced many divergent pressures. How far should it go in accommodating India to the new forces—economic, technological, cultural and social—then re-constituting the modern world? Might it not be more prudent to preserve a 'traditional' India which, whatever the price of its stagnation, would more easily accept an inferior colonial status and continuing British domination? These questions became the more urgent as the nineteenth century wore on and British world economic and political power were challenged by a reviving France and Russia and a new Germany and United States. British answers were often contradictory, but they rarely failed to appeal to the 'mystique' attached to Queen Victoria's Crown.

The Promise of Progress

The initial effects of Victoria's assumption of the throne of India were very much to emphasise the modern side of the colonial paradox. In responding to the 'grievances' against British rule expressed during the Mutiny, the new regime offered Indians glimpses of a future of unlimited moral and material progress, which became theirs by right as full 'subjects' of the Queen's Empire. On November 1st, 1858, a Royal Proclamation was issued to 'the Princes and Peoples of India', whose words were later to come back and haunt British colonial governors. While generally re-affirming all existing rights and privileges, the proclamation also announced that: 'We hold ourselves bound to the natives of our Indian territories by the same obligations of duty which bind us to all our other subjects' and that 'it is our further will that . . . our subjects of whatever race or creed, be freely and impartially admitted to offices in our services, the duties of which they may be qualified, by their education, ability and integrity, duly to discharge'.

This vision of equal rights for Indians with British 'subjects' under the Crown proved a powerful magnet in attracting Indian opinion in the new 'colony', especially the opinion of the Western-educated most qualified to benefit. This was not least because the social reality of India contrasted so starkly with the proclamation's aspirations. Since the turn of the nineteenth century, the Company's government had, as much by institutional practice as by any formal declaration, made itself progressively more 'British' and come to enforce a de facto race hierarchy in many areas. The Queen's sentiments appeared to challenge this and to construct a multi-racial imperial identity giving all her subjects equal access to the privileges accruing to members of the most powerful empire that the world had ever seen.

In another way, too, direct rule by the Crown opened possibilities for Indian advancement. It brought 'Indian affairs' much more centrally into British politics and emphasised metropolitan responsibilities for conditions in far-distant Eastern colonies. Previously, the anomalous status of the Company's India had been convenient in guaranteeing that large parts of its government could take place behind closed doors and that moral culpabilities could be deferred onto other authorities. Parliamentary debates on India had been confined to occasional scandals and to the renewal of the Company's charter, which took place only every twenty years. Now, however, a regular forum for more continuous dialogue was created and the ability of Indian administrators to conceal their deficiencies was reduced. By the 1870s, this was to have some important consequences.

In 1876, a serious famine had broken out in southern and

western India, killing several million people. Official propaganda on the progress brought by British rule stood contradicted by the visible evidence of mass starvation. Pressure exercised by the British Parliament called the Indian administration to account and played a role in constructing a more adequate famine code to deal with similar eventualities in the future. Equally, in 1878 the then-Viceroy, Lord Lytton, had launched a gratuitous, expensive and ultimately disastrous war in Afghanistan. Public reaction against this debacle was to prove so strong that it led to the defeat of Disraeli's government at the General Election of 1880.

Taking advantage of the new conduits created after 1858, Indians themselves also began to make their presence felt in the imperial metropolis. After the 1860s, when competitive examinations were established for entry to the Indian Civil Service, a steady stream began to see higher education at Oxford, Cambridge and London. When the India National Congress was formed in 1885, it established a permanent standing committee in London to pursue a programme aimed at opening up the services to the competition of the talents, reforming judicial administration and increasing Indian representative rights. In the 1890s, an Indian businessman resident in Britain, Dadhabai Naoroji, stood at the polls and was elected as a Liberal member of the 'imperial' Parliament itself.

England's Liberal Agenda in India

These activities brought some rewards. The viceroyalty of Lord Ripon (1880–85) was particularly distinguished for its responsiveness to Indian opinion. Ripon extended the powers of local self-government and introduced electoral procedures into them, and, through the notorious Ilbert Bill, even sought to remove racial privileges from the practices of the law courts. Ripon's government represented something of a honeymoon period in the early formation of 'modern' Indian politics, helping to imbue them with a strong sense of loyalty to the Empire and the Queen. Those politics pursued far more a liberal than a nationalist agenda and sought the increasing integration of Indians into the British Empire. They betrayed few thoughts of separation or 'independence': annual sessions of the Indian National Congress were opened and closed to the strains of 'God Save the Queen'. The Crown here was seen to symbolise a future of multi-racial amity and joint Indo-British cooperation.

The Pageantry Surrounding the Queen-Empress

In January 1877, Queen Victoria was pronounced queen-empress of India at a spectacular ceremony in Delhi reminiscent of those of the great Mughal emperors. The following extract from Britain's Viceroy Lord Lytton's letter to the queen gives a sense of the pomp and splendor of the occasion, which represented a departure from Britain's progressive agenda for India and a return to the glory of India's past.

The day before yesterday (December 23), I arrived, with Lady Lytton and all my staff, at Delhi, and received at the station by all the native chiefs and princes. I immediately mounted my elephant, accompanied by Lady Lytton, our two little girls following us on another elephant. The procession through Delhi to the camp, which we only reached towards sunset, lasted upwards of three hours. It was a magnificent and most successful pageant. The Viceroy and staff were followed by the chief functionaries, civil and military, of your Majesty's Indian Government, mounted on elephants spendidly caparisoned. The streets were lined for many miles by the troops; those of the native princes being brigaded with those of your Majesty. The crowd along the whole way, behind the troops, was dense, and apparently enthusiastic; the windows, walls, and housetops being thronged with natives, who salaamed, and Europeans, who cheered as we passed along. . . The infinite variety of the non-British native troops presented a most striking and peculiar appearance. Those who saw it will probably never again behold in one spot so vivid and various a display of strange arms, strange uniforms, and strange figures. . . .

My reception by the native princes at the station was most cordial. The Maharaja of Jeypore informed Sir John Strachey that India had never seen such a gathering as this, in which not only all the great native princes (many of whom have never met before), but also chiefs and envoys from Khelat, Burmah, Siam, and the remotest parts of the East, are assembled to do homage to your Majesty. He himself, he said, could hardly realise the difficulties which had been overcome, or the success which had been achieved, by this assemblage. . . .

Sir Dinkur Rao (Sindiah's great Minister) said to one of my colleagues: "If any man would understand why it is that the English are, and must necessarily remain, the masters of India, he need only go up to the Flagstaff Tower, and look down upon this marvellous camp. Let him notice the method, the order, the cleanliness, the discipline, the perfection of its whole organisation, and he will recognise in it at once the epitome of every title to command and govern which one race can possess over others." . . .

Two Burmese noblemen, from the remotest part of Burmah, said to me: "The King of Burmah fancies he is the greatest prince upon earth. When we go back, we shall tell all his people that he is nobody. Never since the world began has there been in it such a power as we have witnessed here." . . .

Monday was the day of the assemblage, which I cannot attempt to describe to your Majesty. The weather was fortunately most fine. Everyone who witnessed it is unanimous in the opinion that it was the grandest spectacle and the most impressive they had ever seen. . . . At a State banquet during the evening it was my privilage to propose the health of your majesty as Empress of India. . . .

With heartfelt prayers for all that can prolong and increase the happiness of your Majesty's life and the glory and prosperity of your great reign,

I have the honour to be, Madam, your Majesty's devoted and faithful humble servant.

(Signed) LYTTON

Adrian Sever, ed., *Documents and Speeches on the Indian Princely States*. Delhi: B.R. Publishing Corporation, 1985, pp. 280–85.

Yet this was a future which by no means all among the British welcomed. The warnings issued after the Mutiny about the dangers of interfering with Indian 'tradition' remained on the table—and tradition could hardly be interfered with more thoroughly than by a process converting India into a replica of Liberal Britain. Moreover, among British elites the values of liberalism and progress themselves were starting to face rejection. The onset of 'mass' society brought signs of a deepening cultural pessimism and a turning back to pre-industrial traditions to suggest alternative possibilities for the future.

The Mutiny had also sharpened racial tensions between Britons and Indians, which now found new forms of justification in the 'scientific' theories becoming fashionable in post-Darwinian Europe. If the supremacy of the white races was a fact of nature, what point was served by setting multi-racialism as a goal for the British Empire? Further, as the British economy came under increasing international competition and as British world power was threatened from new quarters, ought not the Empire to be seen, first and foremost, as a means of securing the wealth and prestige of Britons themselves—if necessary at the expense of their 'colonial' subjects?

Regressive Measures

Even by the 1870s, these questions—which betokened a hardening British 'nationalism'—were beginning to affect metropolitan politics, giving rise to a new kind of conservation which, in turn, preached a New Imperialism. Under Disraeli's government (1874–80), this New Imperialism reached out to Queen Victoria's India. In January 1877, she was proclaimed 'Queen-Empress' amidst extraordinary scenes of display. At an imperial durbah (public ceremony) held in the old Mughal capital of Delhi, she was represented as the direct heir of the Mughal dynasty in whose name her Viceroy proceeded to receive the ritual fealty of India's remaining princes and maharajas. Her erstwhile symbolic role, as India's link to a modern future, was abruptly terminated. Now she stood for, and took her legitimacy from, the Indian past: a past captured in a pseudo-historical pageant, at times bordering on pantomime kitsch, wherein she became the Great Mughal and committed herself to sustaining, changeless and unchangeable, the hierarchical order of a traditional Indian society.

The pantomime was presided over by Lord Lytton, a minor

Romantic poet whom Disraeli had plucked from an undistinguished diplomatic career to be Viceroy of India and co-architect there of his New Imperialism. Although Lytton's talent for the picturesque may temporarily have dazzled India's eyes, and his emphasis on the 'glories' of the Mughal past have flattered its sense of history, the real meaning of the change in imperial style was not long in becoming apparent. If Indian society was to be 'returned' to its historic traditions, it could have no claims on a modern future where British interests must predominate.

Elsewhere, Lytton launched an attack on Indian claims to racial equality and participation in the imperial state. In 1878, he passed a Vernacular Press Act which clamped down on the free expression of political opinion. In 1879, within months of the ending of the Great Famine, he pushed measures through his Executive Council, against the concerted opposition of most of its members, removing India's residual forms of tariff protection and opening its economy to unrestrained exploitation by British business. In the same year, he also began to campaign against Indian entry to the Indian Civil Service. Most famously, he fomented a war with Afghanistan, which served British strategic interests against Russia far more than it contributed anything to India's own security but cost the Indian tax-payer 4 million [pounds sterling].

Lytton's viceroyalty, with its centrepiece of the imperial durbah, signalled a conservative counter-offensive against the nostrums of liberal imperialism, which was to last through the rest of Victoria's reign and up to the First World War. Although it never succeeded in forcing an entire abandonment of the liberal agenda, it exercised a dominant influence over British imperial ideology. In 1883, Ilbert's Bill to bring racial equality to the judicial system provoked a 'White Mutiny' among European residents in India and had to be modified almost out of existence. In 1886, measures were introduced to restrict Indian entry and to preserve the 'British' character of the Indian Civil Service. By 1913, a Government of India would even pass legislation designed explicitly to protect 'the mystique of the white race'.

This deepening racism had its counterpart in an intellectual veneration of Indian tradition, typified in Kipling's classic writings, as the true repositary of Indian culture and identity. But, given also Kipling's stridently critical view of 'the Babu'—the Western-educated Indian—there was little doubting the political implications of such nostalgia. While the Queen-Empress invoked her Mughal heritage, Indians could not expect to gain any more rights under their British conqueror than they had possessed under her Central Asian predecessor.

The Indian Nationalist Movement

Yet the shift in royal symbolism was to be bought at a heavy price. By changing the focus of the monarchy's appeal, from the future to the past, Lytton also set another train of history in motion. Invited to seek the roots of their identity in their own traditions, Indian intellectuals soon began to doubt both that the Mughal heritage was truly theirs and that their past contained any reasons to accept British supremacy. Parallel to the imperial 'invention of tradition', a romantic voyage of Indian self-rediscovery began to get under way. Conducted preponderantly by the high-caste Hindus, who had first been drawn to Western education, it produced visions of an Indian civilisation based on Hinduism, which was inimical alike to the rule of Muslim Mughals and Christian British.

For some years, the romantic reconstruction of Hindu India remained a literary phenomenon with few immediate political implications. But, following the viceroyalty of that paragon of the New Imperialism, Lord Curzon (1898–1905), it exploded into action and revealed its full political meaning. If India's identity lay in its own past and if that past pre-dated both Mughal and Briton, then an authentic Indian 'nation' must be independent of both as well. The political movement which arose in reaction to Curzon's partition of Bengal made a definitive break with the imperial ideal in its several senses. Indian nationalists now looked to the ancient Hindu world for their inspiration, even introducing as the Indian National Congress' anthem a hymn which invoked the 'glories' of Bengali Hindu resistance to the Mughals. And they redefined their future political trajectory to insist on the severance of ties with Britain. The Swadeshi campaign of 1905–08 called for a boycott of British goods, the independent development of the Indian economy and a new programme of 'national' education and cultural regeneration.

The invocation of Indian tradition, undertaken by Lord Lytton, produced consequences unforeseen at the time but perhaps obvious in retrospect. It provoked the emergence of an Indian national identity which rejected incorporation with and subordination to the British Crown. The passage from 'Queen' to 'Queen-Empress' set the British monarchy in India on a path which by 1947 would see the King-Emperor George VI, albeit under rather different circumstances, passing into history alongside Bahadur Shah.

The British Impact in India: A British Viewpoint

By the Marquess of Zetland

In response to mounting criticism of British policies in India in the late 1920s, the Marquess of Zetland, a well-known British journalist on Indian affairs, wrote the following piece in The Times *lauding British achievements. The marquess maintains that British rule brought law, order, and effective administrative and education systems to India. Construction of the railway and communications networks linking all parts of the country accompanied the growth of large-scale industry. The marquess concludes that these developments served to forge a national identity, the crowning achievement of the British in a land traditionally divided along religious, ethnic, and linguistic lines.*

For 150 years and more Great Britain and India have been travelling a common road. On the horizon stands the goal, at first scarcely imagined, but now clearly outlined, towards which their onward march is carrying them. To that goal and to the remaining stages on the road that leads to it public attention will shortly be directed by the Report of the Statutory Commission,[1] and since with the attainment of the goal the crowning act of British statesmanship in the romantic drama of British Indian history will be consummated, we may profitably employ the brief interval that still remains to us before we are called upon to embark upon a fresh advance in taking stock of all that has emerged from the long and intimate contact between these two

1. In the late 1920s the Statutory Commission on India, comprised of British and Indian delegates, made recommendations to the British government re: granting independent status to India.

The Marquess of Zetland, "The British Achievement," *India: A Reprint of the Special India Number of the Times*. Great Britain: The Times Publishing Company Limited, 1930.

strangely dissimilar nations. That the relationship between Great Britain and India is unparalleled in history is undeniable. How, then, did it arise? Not, certainly, as the result of any premeditated plan—though a tendency has been observable in the controversies of recent times to attribute our presence there to-day to the prosecution of a policy of deliberate exploitation and aggrandizement. Such ideas are born out of the heat of controversy, and have little basis in fact.

History of British Involvement

[American poet and essayist Ralph Waldo] Emerson, viewing the achievements of the British in India with the detachment of an onlooker, arrived at a conclusion the historical accuracy of which is beyond challenge when he declared that the English did not calculate the conquest of India; and it is flattering to our national vanity to suppose that he spoke with equal insight and sincerity when he added that India fell to our character. That the bands of merchant adventurers who sailed round the Cape with charters granted by Queen Elizabeth in 1600, and by William III. in 1698, were inspired by the hope of material gain there is no need to deny. But if commerce had remained the sole motive of the British in India the history of British India would never have been written, for there would have been no British India about which to write it.

It was when the activities of the traders were diverted into other channels that they became the unconscious instruments of a new and wholly unforeseen destiny. They fought—and conquered—only because in no other way could they suppress the disorders which militated against the successful prosecution of their trade. Neither were these disorders due wholly, nor even mainly, to the rivalry of other competing European Powers. They were the inevitable outcome of the decline and fall of the Moghul Empire. Ballads still sung by village bards in the eastern districts of Bengal give a vivid picture of the insecurity of life and property on the confines of the Moghul Empire, even during the halcyon days when Moghul power was at its height; and by the close of the seventeenth century it was already clear that Moghul rule had reached and passed its zenith. The breadth of vision and tolerance of Akbar [Mughal emperor 1556–1605] had given place to the religious bigotry of Aurangzeb [emperor 1658–1707]; and if, after the latter's death, in 1707, Moghul Sovereigns continued to succeed one another upon a nominally Moghul throne, they passed fitfully across the scene like the figures of a shadow-show, outlined uncertainly against a background of ever-increasing anarchy and confusion. Throughout the eighteenth century India was a prey to all those tyrannies and disorders which have been the invariable experience of Eastern peoples when thrones have wilted and tottered to the dust.

Such, then, were the provocations which led to the imposition of the authority of the East India Company over the Peninsula. Here and there, as the tide of conquest flowed onwards over the land, it left behind it a number of islands, some large, some small, pieces of territory over which the Company did not establish its own direct authority, but which it left to the rule of Native Chiefs, with whom it contracted treaties. In this way there came into existence the Native States, which to-day cover nearly two-fifths of the total area of India and embrace not far short of one-quarter of its population. That the onward march of the Company's victorious troops was often welcomed with greater enthusiasm by the people who submitted to it than by the authorities at Whitehall [British politicians] is not the least striking feature of the gradual consolidation of British rule. It was at the request of a people groaning under tyrannous misrule that [British general Robert] Clive fought and won the battle of Plassey, which in its turn led to the assignment of the revenues of Bengal, Bihar and Orissa to the East India Company, which thus acquired for Great Britain, in 1765, the virtual sovereignty of these countries. And the distaste with which the Directors of the Company in London viewed the extension of their territorial responsibilities which was still in progress three-quarters of a century later is well illustrated by the witty paragraph in *Punch* [a popular cartoon] in 1844, wherein [British general] Sir Charles Napier was depicted conveying the news of his conquest of Sind to his superiors by means of a single word, "Peccavi" [Latin for "I have sinned"]. Viewing these crowded events in the truer perspective which is possible to-day, we can perceive that it was out of them that emerged that reign of peace and order which was the first great gift conferred upon the Indian people by Great Britain. And if she had done no more than this her achievement would have been no mean one.

But if the skill of her military commanders and the courage and perseverance of her troops, both British and Indian, have played their part in laying the foundations of a new and happier India, and have since secured to her peace within her borders and immunity from invasion from without, it is the success of her administrators, both military and civil, in bringing so vast a territory, inhabited by so many and such diverse races, under a just and orderly administration that history will regard as the outstanding achievement of her work in Asia. For it is by the labours of her administrators, her Judges, her educationists, her sanitarians, and her engineers that the contrast between the India of to-day and the India of two centuries ago has been effected. And how remarkable that contrast is! It is scarcely too much to say that to-day there is not an acre of British India—a territory more than a dozen times as large as the United Kingdom—over which the finespun web of the Administration has not been cast. From the point of view of the teeming masses of the Indian peasantry that alone is a matter of capital importance; for what does it mean? It means that there is not a field, however small, belonging to the humblest villager, which is not recorded in an official document, and for the possession of which he has not, therefore, that legal security which was so conspicuous for its absence from the picture of the India of two centuries ago. Statistics make heavy reading, but they have their uses, and incidentally they bear witness to the extent of what has been accomplished in evolving order out of chaos, for they are the offspring of orderliness and successful administration.

For anyone who cares to satisfy himself as to the thoroughness of British administration in India there is the Report on the most recent Census, that of 1921—a volume of 300 pages packed with statistical information of every kind. A few figures from a single table at the beginning of the volume will suffice as an example. From this small introductory table the curious may learn that the area of British India—that is to say, that part of the continent which is administered directly by Great Britain as distinct from the Native States—is 1,094,300 square miles; that it has a population of 247,003,293, composed of 126,872,116 males and 120,131,177 females; that the urban portion of the population lives in 1,561 towns and the rural portion in 498,527 villages; and, finally, that the number of occupied houses in the towns is 5,046,820 and in the villages 45,394,816. These figures bear striking testimony to the work, among others, of the Survey and Settlement Officers, that is to say, those who are responsible for the topographical survey of the country and those whose duty it is to make and maintain a record of all existing rights and responsibilities in land.

Transportation, Communications, and Industry

But great as the task of these painstaking officials has been, it represents only one aspect of the work of organization for which the British have been responsible. The land has been covered with a network of railways, steadily increasing, and already over 40,000 miles in extent, over which no fewer than 623,000,000 passengers have been carried in the course of a single year. Posts and telegraphs have been set up by whose agency letters are carried expeditiously, and at the cost of a penny only, from one end of this huge area to the other. Immense tracts of desert land have been made fertile by means of some of the greatest irrigation works in the world; and the yield of crops has been enormously increased as the result of scientific agricultural research. Great industries, which have added to the resources of the peasantry, have been built up by British enterprise and with the aid of British capital. The tea industry is a case in point. Nearly 750,000 acres are now under cultivation, producing annually not far short of 400,000,000lb. of leaf. The value of tea exported amounts to approximately £25,000,000 a year. Even more remarkable are the statistics of the jute industry. While in this case the fibre is cultivated by the peasantry, its manufacture for commercial use is almost entirely in British hands. There are in Calcutta and its neighborhood 90 mills with over 1,000,000 spindle and 50,000 looms having an authorized capital of £16,000,000, and employing 330,000 hands. Their output in 1927–28 amounted to 463,000,000 gunny [jute] bags and 1,552,000,000 yards of gunny cloth valued at £40,000,000. Some idea of what the creation of this industry has meant to the villagers of Bengal and Assam may be gained by a glance at the extent and value of the crop, which in 1926 amounted to more than 12,000,000 bales, worth in English money over £100,000,000.

Law, Education, Health, and Politics

Other services which have been rendered to the country include the establishment of Courts of Law, from village Benches up to the High Courts of Judicature of Calcutta and other provincial capitals, while law itself, both civil and criminal, has been codified and accorded the place of honour which it occupies in all modern civilized States. Schools and universities have been established. Plague, famine, and pestilence have been, and are being, fought. In the field of malarial research the name of Sir Ronald Ross at once occurs to one, while in the School of Tropical Medicine in Calcutta is to be seen a monument to another of India's benefactors in this domain—namely, Sir Leonard Rogers, whose work has been of special value in the treatment of cholera, leprosy, and kala-azar. In the political sphere a system of local self-government both in town and country has been established; and, finally, long strides have already been taken towards the institution of Parliamentary government on a federal basis.

So much, in brief, for British achievement in India. Not the least remarkable feature of the whole vast system of administration is the extent to which it has been manned by an Indian *personnel.* At no time has the British controlling agency—civilians, Judges, engineers, doctors, educationists, police officers, forest officers, agricultural and other experts—exceeded 5,000 men. It has in recent years been appreciably less, and is still in process of diminution. A detailed examination of the various activities for which these men have been responsible would prove both interesting and instructive; but space permits of a closer scrutiny of only a few of them; more particularly as something must be said of the peculiar conditions under which they have been undertaken, if a true view of Great Britain's achievement is to be obtained.

A Vast Region

If India had been a small, compact, homogeneous country such as Great Britain herself, or any one of the countries that go to make up the continent of Europe, her achievement would still have been great, though it would have been less remarkable than is actually the case. But in all these respects she is the very antithesis of the British Isles. Where Great Britain is small, India is vast; where Great Britain is compact, India is loosely knit; where Great Britain is homogeneous, India is polygenous and bewilderingly polyglot. From all directions contrasts, contradictions, and diversities stare one in the face. The contrasts in her physical characteristics alone provide intricate problems for solution. The soaking humidity of the south and east, and the awful aridity of the north-west; Cherrapungi [in southern India], with its annual rainfall of 450 inches, and Jhatput [in northern India], where rain may be looked for on six days only in a normal year, and where an annual fall of three inches is all that can be counted on, may be taken as examples. The one provides a problem of overwhelming magnitude for the custodian of the public health; the other for the irrigation engineer. For where water is excessive the problem for solution is its rigorous control, since stagnant pools left on the land with the seasonal recession of the waters provide deadly breeding ground for the malaria-bearing mosquito and other hos-

British Rule: An Indian Viewpoint

Indian historian Ranbir Vohra, whose grandfather was an Indian nationalist jailed by the British in the nineteenth century, refutes the British assertion that their rule unified the Indian subcontinent in the following extract from The Making of India, *published in 1997.*

"Unity" under the British not only allowed for hundreds of autonomous princely states but culminated in the partitioning of the country. The legal system was not uniform because it avoided interfering with personal law. The Indian Civil Service (ICS) was manned by arrogant bureaucrats who looked upon themselves as the rulers, not the servants, of the people. The introduction of English as the official language and the medium for higher instruction produced an Anglicized Indian elite who tended to acquire many of the negative attributes of the British ruling class. The electoral process, when inaugurated, was undemocratic because it was based on communal representation. And the British hardly made a dent in the poverty and illiteracy from which the country suffered. . . .

[Furthermore, contemporary India bears a heavy legacy of communal conflict which traces its roots to the British Raj.]. . . . Partition did not end the story of India's communal troubles. The heightening of religious hostility and the

tile forms of insect life. This is one of the outstanding problems of Bengal. On the other hand, great skill and vast expenditure are required to bring water to the desiccated highlands of the Deccan [in central India] and the thirsty reaches of the north-west.

Humanitarian Impulse

Much had already been done by the close of the nineteenth century; but great impetus was given to these as to all other measures designed to improve the lot of the teeming masses of the Indian peasantry by the lofty ambitions and the devouring energy of

trauma resulting from the bloodshed still casts a heavy shadow over the subcontinent. First, the formation of Pakistan did not solve the Muslim issue. The number of Muslims that migrated from India to Pakistan was a fraction of the Muslim population that remained behind. Today, the 100 million plus Muslim citizens of India—practically equal to the entire population of Pakistan—constitute nearly 12 percent of India's population. Since most of these Muslims had voted for the Muslim League, they were naturally looked upon with suspicion by the Hindus. Acceptance of these Muslims as citizens of a secular republic has been a long time coming.

Second, the introduction of a secular constitution in India has yet to completely destroy the notion, confirmed by the formation of Pakistan, that a religious-ethnic community can struggle for and gain a separate homeland. As a result, to name just a few of such conflicts, post-1947 India has witnessed the violent struggle for an independent Khalistan by the Sikhs, an independent Nagaland by the Naga tribes, and an independent Kashmir by the Kashmiri Muslims. The post-partition history of India begs the question: Has the dialectics of communalism [planted during the British period], got so strongly rooted in India's political system that it has come to undermine, if not to replace, the notions of secularism and democracy by consensus?

Ranbir Vohra, *The Making of India*. New York: M.E. Sharpe, 1997.

Lord Curzon [viceroy of India 1899–1905]. The story of what has been accomplished reads like a romance; and Lord Curzon himself declared that he had found the Report of the Commission on irrigation which he had set up "infinitely more interesting than a novel." The expectations which he based on its recommendations were high, but not unduly so. They were about to embark upon their programme, he told the public in 1905, with the consciousness that they were not merely converting the gifts of Providence to the service of man, but that they were labouring to reduce human suffering and, in times of calamity, to rescue and sustain millions of human lives. As a result huge tracts of sterile land have been converted into granaries. Twenty-eight million acres in British India alone are irrigated by works constructed by the State. Water pours down 67,000 miles of Government canals to raise crops whose estimated value is £105,000,000 a year. And immense projects are still in process of construction. The Sukkur barrage [a barrier dividing hostile Hindus and Muslims in modern-day Pakistan], stretching for a distance of 1,575 yards between the faces of the regulators on either side, will be the greatest work of its kind in the world; the Sutlej Valley project [in northwestern India], at a capital cost of approximately £18,000,000, will bring 3,750,000 acres of waste land under cultivation; in the Deccan the Bhandardara dam, 270ft. in height, recently completed, has been instrumental in converting great tracts of desert into prosperous gardens of sugar-cane, while in the same neighbourhood the Lloyd dam—the largest mass of masonry in the world—will hold up a perennial supply of water which will feed a total cultivable area of 675,000 acres. In short, a total area of 40,000,000 acres irrigated by all these great State systems may confidently be said to be in sight.

Diversity of People

These few facts give some indication of the problems provided by the abrupt contrasts in the physical features of the land; it remains to point out that these in their turn have been simple in comparison with those which have arisen out of the diversities of her many-visaged, many-hued, and many-tongued peoples. Within the confines of the continent are to be found representatives of every epoch in human history, from the Stone Age to the twentieth century; and legislation and administration have had to be devised to meet the needs of all of these. And to cultural differences have been added the schisms of religion. If in Europe differences between adherents of a single faith have often baffled statesmanship, it should be easy to imagine the task of an alien ruler confronted with peoples professing the creeds of the innumerable sects of no fewer than nine distinct religions. Religious sanction has sometimes been claimed for customs of immemorial antiquity but of barbarous cruelty. Against such antisocial practices, intimately affecting the religious and social life of the people, the ruler of an alien race and creed has necessarily had to proceed with caution. And if such delicate questions as that of child marriage have not yet reached a permanent solution, much has, nevertheless, been done. The inhuman custom of suttee [burning of widows] and the equally heinous practice of infanticide have disappeared, while throughout the public services bribery and corruption are giving way before the higher standards of morality inculcated over a long term of years by precept and by the example of the British *personnel.*

Educational Achievements

It is often claimed by the detractors of British rule in India that the fact that 229,000,000 of the 248,000,000 inhabitants of British India remain illiterate is a damning proof of failure. Such statistics are misleading, and it would be easy to quote figures on the other side which, taken by themselves, would convey an equally false impression of what has actually been done. The fact could be emphasized, for example, that India possesses 16 modern universities, and that in one of them—the Calcutta University—she can claim the largest university in the world. It is not too much to say, indeed, that Sir Michael Sadler and his colleagues on the Commission of 1917 were staggered by the magnitude of the institution, with its 58 affiliated colleges dotted over vast geographical areas and its 27,000 students. But the achievements of the British in this direction can only be properly assessed by those acquainted with the conditions under which the system of education has had to be set up. Religious and social custom has stood in the way of the provision of an adequate supply of women teachers, recognized as the essential instrument of elementary education in all Western lands. And side by side with this formidable disability has stood another arising from yet one more of the baffling diversities of the Indian peoples—that of language. For if in India the medley of creeds is great, the confusion of tongues is greater still. In the little province of Assam [in northeastern India] nearly one-half of the people speak Bengali, one-fifth Assamese, while the remaining two-fifths among them speak no fewer than 98 different tongues. In the Census Reports for India as a whole more than 200 dialects, belonging to six distinct families of speech, are officially recognized. The effect of this state of affairs upon the educational system has necessarily been profound, for it has led to the employment of a foreign language—English—as the medium of instruction in all but the more elementary stages of the curriculum, a handicap upon the pupil which it is impossible to ignore.

That the spread of education should in such circumstances have been slow is, perhaps, less surprising than that the system should have produced so versatile, so cultured, and, comparatively speaking, so large a minority—according to the Census of 1921, 2,500,000 passed the test of literacy in English—imbued with the culture of the Western world. For in the ranks of this minority are to be found great lawyers and eminent Judges, fine scholars and brilliant scientists, capable administrators, talented writers, engineers, doctors, artists, architects, and captains of modern industry. The deficiencies of the system may be readily admitted; but Indians themselves should be cautious in their denunciation of it, for it is an outstanding feature in a number of factors which have gone to make the appointment of the Statutory Commission possible.

National Unity

Without the unifying influence of British administration—a dynamic force of extraordinary power in view of the many and startling diversities of the Indian continent—no political Constitution, such as that which is now in sight, would have been conceivable. And, with all its drawbacks from an educational point of view, the imposition and wide diffusion of the English tongue has had a unifying influence of remarkable effect. No more striking proof of its value from this point of view could be desired than is provided by the fact that the proceedings of conferences of all kinds held by Indians from all parts of the continent are conducted as a matter of course in English. Whatever significance may attach to the favourite catch-cry of the Indian politician of to-day—"India a nation"—is derived from the genius which the British have shown for breaking down the barriers with which the many fragments—racial, religious, linguistic, and cultural—of which the population is composed are hedged around. From the point of view from which the people of this country will now be called upon to examine and pass judgment upon the future relations between the two countries this is by no means the least of the achievements which stand to the credit of Great Britain in India.

THE HISTORY OF NATIONS

Chapter 3

Independence and Partition

The Raj and the Nationalist Movement

BY FRANCIS ROBINSON

By the early twentieth century, English-educated elite members of the Indian National Congress and the Muslim League felt the injustices and inequality in their relationship with the British Raj. While they began to pressure the British for more influence in their own affairs, their methods were those of loyal subjects petitioning the government for greater representation. The events of World War I transformed this dynamic. Intent that India should be rewarded for her contribution to the war effort, by 1918 the Indian National Congress began to take the political initiative. This received a tremendous boost when Mohandas Gandhi joined the protest movement and enlarged its support base. The Muslim League similarly extended its appeal beyond a small elite group to rank and file Muslims. The cause of independence was further advanced during World War II when the British government, desperate for support, promised India her freedom in exchange for her involvement. In the following extract, historian Francis Robinson traces the changes in the relationship between the British Raj and leaders of India's nationalist movement from 1911 to 1947.

Loyalty to King-Emperor [George V] had a special force in Britain's system of political control [under the Raj]. It had been especially fostered in the cult of Queen Victoria, while the Indian Princes, who controlled two-fifths of the subcontinent and nearly a quarter of its people, were well aware of the importance of conspicuous support for an Imperial royalty. In those areas which the British controlled directly they formed alliances with rural élites, proprietary farmers for instance in the

Francis Robinson, "The Raj and the Nationalist Movement," *The Raj: India and the British 1600–1947*, edited by C.A. Bayly. London: National Portrait Gallery Publications, 1990.

Deccan and the Punjab, or large landowners in northern India. These élites were kept happy with favourable arrangements of land tax, while extra inducements could always be offered through the Raj's elaborate system of honours. As time had gone on the British had created structures for the formal consultation of these allies. By 1911 there was a widespread framework of elected municipal and district boards, as well as provincial legislative councils in which Indians made up just under half the numbers.

Hindus and Muslims as Humble Petitioners

Not all Indians were happy to receive only what the British chose to give them. Notably, the new class of those educated in government colleges, and sometimes in British universities, felt keenly the injustices of their situation in particular and that of India in general. They wanted a larger voice in the provincial councils, greater access to the higher ranks of the Civil Service, the raising of tariff barriers against British cotton goods, an end to the colonial status of India's economy, and respect rather than assertion of racial superiority from the British. For more than a quarter of a century these men had come together each Christmas week to debate these issues in the Indian National Congress. The annual sessions had come to be a celebration of India's growing sense of nationhood. Nevertheless, their stance was one of conspicuous loyalty, their approach to government one of humble petitioning; little happened during the rest of the year. Major figures in the movement were S.N. Banerjee, the 'Lion of Bengal'; Pherozeshah Mehta and Dadabhai Naoroji (India's first Member of Parliament) from Bombay; and the Maharashtrian adversaries B.G. Tilak and G.N. Gokhale, the latter being a member of the Viceroy's Council and widely admired for his statesmanlike qualities.

Muslims, rather more than one-fifth of India's population, were not well represented in the Congress. Under the guidance of their outstanding leader in the nineteenth century, Sayyid Ahmad Khan, the founder of Aligarh College, many, particularly from northern India, had avoided the Congress and overt political activity. By 1906, however, they had come to realize that this would not be enough to protect their interests and had founded their own political organization, the All-India Muslim League. This League, moreover, had been notably successful in winning separate electorates for Muslims in the reforms to the legislative councils which had been pushed through by Viceroy Minto and Secretary of State Morley in 1909. Despite this it was an even more humble petitioner to government than the Congress.

Some Indians no longer accepted these methods. Since 1905 small groups of educated Indians had emerged in Bengal, in western India and in the Punjab who favoured direct action against the Raj. Connected as they were with the cult of Kali, the goddess of destruction, in Bengal and with the Hindu revivalist celebrations of Shivaji and Ganpati in western India, they were much less receptive to the cultural, economic and political offerings of Western civilization. Their most notable actions were the *Swadeshi* movement, calling for the boycott of foreign cloth; and, particularly in Bengal, the use of the gun and the bomb. Tilak was their leading supporter in the Congress, which in 1907 split into 'extremist' and 'moderate' factions; in 1909 he was gaoled [jailed] for incitement to murder. Terrorism certainly alarmed the British—the Viceroy himself was injured by a bomb in 1912—but it had little support in political India as a whole. Representative of the politics of the vast majority was the Congress session of 1910, which proclaimed its loyalty to the King-Emperor and chose an Englishman, Sir William Wedderburn, to be its president.

The Impact of World War One

This situation was transformed by World War One. 'Before 1914 the Government of India on the whole held the initiative,' writes Percival Spear; 'after 1918 it was grasped by the Congress.' One reason was the enormous contribution Indians made to the war effort; almost all were keen to support the Empire, the Princes in the forefront and even Tilak toured the countryside in 1918 to raise more men and material. By these means 1,200,000 men were recruited, over £100 million was given outright to Britain and a further £20 to £30 million raised each year. Indian troops served with distinction on the Western Front and in Mesopotamia, although the latter campaign was managed so badly that the Secretary of State for India had to resign. Among the economic consequences were sharp rises in taxes, a doubling of prices between 1913 and 1920, falling living standards, bottlenecks and disturbances. Indians felt that government should reward them for their loyalty; the conditions favoured mass political action.

The war changed the way the Indians felt about their place in the world. The British were no longer seen, along with Russia, as one of the two superpowers, but to be merely one of several roughly equal powers; their aura of mastery was diminished. The decade before the war had seen revolutions in the despotic regimes of Persia, Turkey and China, while the war itself saw one in Russia; change in the most inflexible political structures now seemed possible. By 1916 the Congress and the League had come together to make a joint demand to establish Indian majorities in the legislative councils, the League exacting as its price Congress support for separate Muslim electorates. This demand, moreover, was strengthened by the return of Tilak to the Congress and the formation of Home Rule leagues by him and by the Irish theosophist Annie Besant. By 1917 these leagues were pulling many new groups into politics.

British intentions as to India's future also began to change, although not always fast enough to match Indian aspirations. Nevertheless, when the British made their political move it was a radical one. On 20 August 1917 the Secretary of State, Edwin Montagu, promised Indians the same kind of government as the white dominions:

> The policy of His Majesty's Government, with which the Government of India are in complete accord, is that of the increasing association of Indians in every branch of the administration and the gradual development of self-governing institutions with a view to the progressive realisation of responsible government in India as an integral part of the British Empire.

This was followed by reforms to the legislative councils in 1919, which bear the names of Montagu and Viscount Chelmsford, the Viceroy, in which Indians were given a substantial majority of the seats. Through the power-sharing mechanism of 'dyarchy' they gained complete control over the development areas of government, and the way was prepared for a federal political system.

Gandhi and Muslim Elites Join the Protest

The war and its aftermath was also the context in which Mohandas Karamchand Gandhi came to the leadership of the nationalist movement. The Mahatma ('great soul'), as he came to be known after being given the title by Rabindranath Tagore, spent more than twenty years struggling against racial discrimination in South Africa. During this time he developed a religious vision of India's freedom (*Swaraj*), which he saw not just as a political goal but also as a moral one involving a complete transformation of the relationship between Indians and the world in which they moved. It was, moreover, to be pursued by non-violent resistance to injustice (*Satyagraha* or 'truth-force'), which he regarded as the appropriate method because it actually helped forward his goal of moral transformation. After returning to India in 1915 he did not involve himself in politics, but toured the country making several experiments with non-violent resistance. Then, when the British demonstrated in their Rowlatt Bills of 1919 that they were going to maintain in peacetime the emergency measures they had used against 'sedition' in wartime, he found his issue. He led a nationwide protest in the form of a complete cessation of activity for one day. Unfortunately the protest sparked off disturbances in the Punjab, the province most severely affected by wartime demands, which led to a massacre at Amritsar in which troops fired without warning on crowds in the enclosed Jallianwala Bagh, killing 379 and wounding 1,200.

Finally, the war created the circumstances in which several of India's Muslim élites moved from a largely passive acquiescence in British rule to large-scale protest against it. The spur was the final decline of the Ottoman empire and the consequent reduction in the power of the Turkish Caliph (*Khalifa*) as the leader in succession to the Prophet of the Islamic community, a process which mirrored in the world at large the growing powerlessness of Muslims in the subcontinent in particular. Before and during the war growing concern about this development brought together young Western-educated Muslims, such as Muhammad and Shaukat Ali, and traditionally educated Muslim scholars (the *ulama*), like Abul Kalam Azad and Abdul Bari Firangi Mahali, in protests against their British rulers. After the war, as the very Ottoman heartland came to be dismembered, these men came to lead an enormous protest through a Khilafat organization, founded to defend the Turkish Caliphate. This was powerful because it united the skills in modern politics of the Western-educated Muslims with the mass-mobilizing abilities of the *ulama*.

In the summer of 1920 Gandhi and these Muslims came together to protest over their grievances in the Punjab—the Amritsar Massacre—and their concern over the Turkish Khilafat.

They led the Khilafat and Congress organizations in a campaign of non-violent non-cooperation with government (*Swadeshi*), which meant among other things not participating in elections to the Montagu-Chelmsford legislative councils, withdrawing from government law courts and schools, and making a point of using goods made in India. Many Congressmen were drawn into this action, some of them because they saw that the Montagu-Chelmsford franchise was so weighted towards the rural areas that they were unlikely to win council seats. Nevertheless, there was mass support for the movement throughout India, and although it was not enough to bring government to a halt, it was enough for numbers of pupils to fall in schools, excise revenue to dry up in some areas and imports of cloth to decline. When Gandhi, worried by rising violence in February 1922, called off the movement, some were calling for complete freedom from the Raj.

The Nationalist Movement Transformed

By this time the nationalist movement was utterly changed from that which existed before World War One. Now it was truly national, supported by men and women from all regions, all cultures and all social backgrounds. It was no longer just a movement supported by the speeches of an educated élite, but now one carried forward by the strikes of factory workers, the walkouts of tea-garden coolies, and the tax boycotts of peasants. In 1920 Gandhi reorganized the Congress so that it reached down to the Indian masses. In consequence its local branches were no longer based on the administrative divisions of government, but on the linguistic divisions of Indians. It no longer reflected the Raj but Indian society. The former shaping force of the colonial power was now denied, and the colonial mentality was cast off. The watchwords of nineteenth-century British liberalism came to be discarded by many in favour of indigenous symbols: for Muslims the crescent, which spoke of over a thousand years of successful Islamic history, for the Hindus the spinning wheel (*charkha*) which spoke of self-help against the foreigner. In his autobiographical fragment Muhammad Ali tells of the precise moment when his brother gave up his taste for fancy English shirts in favour of Muslim dress. The Nehrus, too, who were once conspicuous consumers of the finest British goods, now wore homespun clothes (*khaddar*) with pride. However, for all that the nationalist movement came to present itself in self-consciously

Indian form, it must not be forgotten that its dialogue with the Raj took place primarily within structures of power created by the British.

Between the Wars

In the years between the world wars India came to look a rather less promising item on Britain's balance sheet. With the decline of Britain's cotton industry and the shift in the British economy towards services and the production of consumer goods, India became less attractive as a market for British exports; by the 1930s the balance of trade had turned in India's favour. India also became less attractive as a focus for British investment; indigenous firms such as the Birlas and the Tatas were increasingly beginning to outstrip their British rivals. Most important, however, the Government of India was no longer able to maintain the armaments of its army at modern levels; Indian politicians had far more important things on which to spend the country's resources. By the late 1930s it was clear that, if the army was to be used for Imperial purposes, the British taxpayer would have to bear a substantial amount of its cost. Such a decline in India's value to Britain made the matter of how long Britain's constitutional connection with India should continue one of growing importance.

Over the same period mass support for the nationalist movement, which had first emerged in the Khilafat-non-cooperation period, broadened and deepened; Indians from all regions and from all classes increasingly came to sport the symbols of national identity: homespun clothes, the Gandhi cap and the Congress colours of saffron, white and green. As a whole this movement of peoples enormously diverse in language, in religion and in material interest was held together by the Congress organization, accessible to most, with a hierarchy of committees that mounted from the district through the provincial to the all-India level. Policy making and day-to-day decision making was in the hands of the 'Working Committee', a body often under the influence of Gandhi even though he was usually not a member of it. Alongside the Congress, and finding varying degrees of sympathy with it, ran other parties: the Muslim League, the nationalist movement's main rival for the Muslim vote; the Hindu Mahasabha, which represented conservative Hindus' interests; several socialist groups which flourished in the favourable atmosphere of the 1930s; and the Communist Party of India. There were also regional parties, such as the Unionist Party, which resisted Congress and League attempts to establish themselves in the Punjab until the 1940s. Political activity also took place outside the framework of parties: in organizations of writers, factory workers and peasants; movements for social uplift such as that to improve the lot of India's 50 million Untouchables; and movements of terrorist action such as that led by the Hindustan Socialist Republican Army.

Considerable political skills were required to navigate in these waters: arguably, political leadership was the greatest expression of Indian genius at this time. By the 1930s the leaders who were

From Gentle Petitioning to Demand for Home Rule

The tone of Dadabhai Naoroji's presidential speech to the second Indian National Congress in 1886 differs substantially from that of Annie Besant's presidential address to the 32nd National Congress in 1917.

Dadabhai Naoroji's Report to the 2nd Indian National Congress, 27 December 1886

Well, then what is it for which we are now met on this occasion? We have assembled to consider questions upon which depend our future, whether glorious or inglorious. It is our good fortune that we are under a rule which makes it possible for us to meet in this manner. (*Cheers*) It is under the civilizing rule of the Queen and people of England that we meet here together, hindered by none, and are freely allowed to speak our minds without the least fear and without the least hesitation. Such a thing is possible under British rule and British rule only. (*Loud cheers*) Then I put the *question* plainly: Is this Congress a nursery for sedition and rebellion against the British Government (*cries of no, no*); or is it another stone in the foundation of the stability of that Government (*cries of yes, yes*)? There could be but one answer, and that you have already given, because we are thor-

to take the nationalist movement to independence were in place. In addition to Gandhi, there was Jawaharlal Nehru from the United Provinces, who was regarded as the Mahatma's heir as the man best able to hold the nationalist movement together; Vallabhbhai Patel from Gujarat, who had great organizing skills; Abul Kalam Azad from Bengal, a profound theologian whose leading political role gave heart to nationalist Muslims; Rajendra Prasad from Bihar; and Rajagopalachariar from Madras. S.C. Bose was also part of this group, but fell out with Gandhi and in World War Two sought with German and Japanese help a military so-

oughly sensible of the numberless blessings conferred upon us, of which the very existence of this Congress is a proof in a nutshell.

Annie Besant's Report to the 32nd Indian National Congress, 26 December 1917

For long years Indians have been chafing over the many breaches of promises and pledges to them that remain unredeemed. The maintenance here of a system of political repression, of coercive measures increased in number and more harshly applied since 1905, the carrying of the system to a wider extent since the War . . . has deepened the mistrust. . . . The time for political tinkering is past; the time for wise and definite changes is here. . . .

India demands Home Rule for two reasons, one essential and vital, the other less important but weighty: First, because Freedom is the birthright of every Nation; secondly, because her most important interests are now made subservient to the interests of the British Empire without her consent, and her resources are not utilised for her greatest needs. It is enough only to mention the money spent on her Army, not for local defence but for Imperial purposes, as compared with that spent on primary education.

Dadabhai Naoroji and Annie Besant quoted in C.H. Philips, ed., *The Evolution of India and Pakistan 1858–1947. Select Documents*. London: Oxford University Press, 1964, pp. 201, 205.

lution to ending British rule. Outside the Congress Muhammad Ali Jinnah, a gifted lawyer from Bombay, had already come to dominate the Muslim League.

Gandhi's Civil Disobedience Campaign

The year 1927 saw the beginning of the next great contest between the nationalist movement and the Raj. Under the Government of India Act of 1919 the working of the Montagu-Chelmsford constitution was to be reviewed after ten years. In 1927, two years early, Parliament appointed a Commission of Inquiry under Sir John Simon. Unfortunately all its members were British. Indians were infuriated that their future was to be decided without participation. Congress responded by boycotting the Commission throughout India and by leading an all-parties conference to produce its own constitutional proposals, in the name of Motilal Nehru, the father of Jawaharlal, of which the most important was the achievement of full Dominion status by December 1929. The Viceroy, Lord Irwin, was prepared to discuss matters, but no satisfactory solution could be found. So Gandhi launched a campaign of civil disobedience in 1930 by marching from Ahmedabad to Dandi on the Gujarat coast to challenge the government monopoly on salt by making salt from the sea. For the next four years Congress and the government were in deadlock. Round Table Conference followed Round Table Conference in London. One civil disobedience campaign followed another in India, winning unprecedented support as the impact of the great depression brought a sharp fall in agrarian prices and standards of living. Such agreement as was eventually reached between the two sides was represented in the Government of India Act of 1935, in which the British retreated to the centre of India's federal system, leaving the eleven provinces to be governed by Indians on a franchise which produced 30 million voters. . . .

In India itself the interdependence of British and Indian lives remained as always, although in almost every field Indians were pressing forward into positions once held by their masters. This was taking place in the army officer corps, in the Civil Service and in the police; after World War Two only 500 senior civil servants and only 200 senior policemen were British. Similar changes were also under way in the universities, businesses, plantations and clubs. In other areas, most notably the game of cricket, the abilities of players such as Ranjitsinhji, C.K. Naidoo and the Nawab of Pataudi were suggesting that it would not be long before Indians would be the equals, if not the betters, of their rulers. . . .

The Declining Years of British Rule

In the last twelve years of British rule from 1935 to 1947 most British accepted that they were going to leave India. The main problems were how they were going to do it and when. Certainly the Raj demonstrated in World War Two that it still had considerable power. Two million Indians were recruited to the army, vast quantities of material were raised for the war effort, and a concerted attempt by the Congress in the Quit India movement of 1942 was stopped with ease. Yet it was clear that the British no longer needed to rule to win what benefits India still held for them. Moreover, they had already transferred too much power to Indians to be sure of being able to rule for any length of time. For the Congress, on the other hand, the main problems were how to get rid of the British in the quickest possible time, and how to do so in a way which enabled them to take over the strong centre of the federal system which the British had created. As a step in this direction, although with some reservations about British intentions, the Congress took office after victories in the general elections of 1937 in seven out of eleven provinces.

Two substantial unresolved problems loomed over the plans of the British and the Congress. One was the fate of the Princes. In 1921 these controllers of two-fifths of British India had been given a Chamber of their own to advise government on their interests. The 1935 Government of India Act created a federal framework into which they could be absorbed. But the Princes were incapable of agreeing on any scheme for federation. By 1939 they had lost their chance and these conservative Indian potentates, despite their special relationship with the British Crown, were bundled to one side by events. After independence they had no choice but to accept the few pitiful crumbs on offer in exchange for their territories.

The second problem was that of the Muslims. Throughout the 1920s and 1930s this had not seemed overwhelming. Muslim politicians, most notably in the important Muslim majority provinces of the Punjab and Bengal, had participated in political alliances with non-Muslims. The Muslim League, the organization of Muslim separatism, was virtually moribund from 1931 to 1934; its performance at the 1937 elections was unimpressive, winning only 22 per cent of the seats reserved for Muslims. The Muslims of the majority provinces seemed to feel that they were secure with provincial autonomy. In the late 1930s there seemed no reason to believe that Muslim separatism would lead to the division of India.

The Impact of World War Two

World War Two transformed Indian politics as the previous war had done. First, the Congress let slip its normally tight grip on the political scene. Straight after the Viceroy, the Marquess of Linlithgow, had declared war on behalf of Britain without discussing the matter with the nationalist leadership, the Congress instructed its ministries in the provinces to resign. The immediate consequence of its Quit India movement of 1942 was the imprisonment of the nationalist leadership and 60,000 party activists. For the whole of the war Congress hands were off the levers of power; for half of that time it was an enfeebled organization. Second, the British needed all the allies they could find in India to fight the war. On the very day after war was declared, Linlithgow invited Jinnah, the leader of the Muslim League, for talks on an equal footing with Gandhi; the man whom, before the war, government had been able to ignore, was now sought after as the most important representative of the Muslims. Less than three years later, the need for Indian support was so desperate that Sir Stafford Cripps made on behalf of the British Government his offer of independence after the war in exchange for the co-operation of the political parties for its duration. Indians now knew that independence was a real possibility in the near future. Thirdly, Jinnah made full use of the opportunities provided to improve the Muslim League's position. Within seven months of the declaration of war the League had laid down its terms for independence; in what is known as the Lahore or Pakistan Resolution it demanded the grouping of provinces in which Muslims were numerically in a majority into 'Independent States'. Precisely what the relationship was to be between these states and the rest of India was left unclear. These terms were both a bargaining counter to get the best possible results for Muslims at independence and a stick to persuade Muslim leaders in the majority provinces to support the League. By the end of the war

Jinnah had been successful in achieving the latter, and he had also built the League into an effective organization for mass political mobilization. The results were seen in the League's overwhelming victory in the general elections of 1945–6, in which it won nearly 90 per cent of the seats reserved for Muslims. The war did much to create the circumstances in which, whatever claims the Princes were able to make, and also towards the end the Sikhs, there were only two players that mattered alongside the British in the endgame, the Congress and the League.

Partition of India

In the first half of 1946 the British were still hoping to hand on their Raj to a single successor state. To this end the home government intervened directly, sending a delegation of Cabinet ministers to India who, in May, proposed an ingenious solution involving three tiers of government. The first was represented by the existing provinces; the second was to be formed out of separate Hindu and Muslim federations of provinces, to which the princely states could accede; and in the third—the central government—representatives of these federations would come together on an equal basis to deal with defence, foreign affairs and communications. For a few weeks both sides accepted the plan; indeed, recent scholarship has made an excellent case for this being the solution that Jinnah sought, but then agreement broke down. There was deadlock. Civil disorders grew. Partition became inevitable.

In February 1947 the home government intervened once more. Viscount Wavell was replaced as Viceroy by Lord Mountbatten, and Prime Minister Clement Attlee announced that the British intended to hand over power in India no later than June 1948. The politicians were to be pressured into agreement. Able and energetic, Mountbatten quickly saw that Britain could only withdraw by transferring power not to one government but to two. He also saw that it would not be possible to leave the large Hindu and Sikh minorities of the Punjab and the Hindu minority of Bengal under Muslim rule. The partition of India also meant the partition of Bengal and the Punjab. Congress accepted partition as the price it would have to pay to take over the strong centre which the British had created. The League was eventually forced to accept a 'truncated' Pakistan. To try to limit the growing problems of disorder, Mountbatten brought forward the date of withdrawal to August 1947. On the 14th, Pakistan inherited its share of the British Raj, and on the 15th so did India.

The last rites of the Raj were performed in the great new capital which some thirty-five years before the King-Emperor George V had proclaimed would be built by the British for their Indian Empire. Here, amid the magnificent symbols of central power, the Viceroy's palace—larger than Versailles and approached down the two-mile-long processional route of King's Way—Nehru announced to the Indian people that they had redeemed the pledge they had made in their tryst with destiny long years ago. Here, too, Nehru was sworn in by Lord Mountbatten as the first prime minister of the new Dominion. The former Viceroy stayed on for a year as Governor-General; some Britons stayed on for very much longer in industry and commerce, the army and the Civil Service. The lack of a sharp break in personnel emphasizes how much of a joint project it had been to build the new India, despite all the conflicts and sorrows there had been.

The Power of Nonviolent Noncooperation

By Mohandas K. Gandhi

Mohandas K. Gandhi was arrested on March 10, 1921, for writing four articles published in his newspaper Young India *that expressed dissatisfaction with the British Raj. Aware of his impending arrest, Gandhi issued a pretrial statement urging the Indian people to a course of nonviolent noncooperation. At his trial Gandhi pleaded guilty to "disaffection with the Government." In his courtroom statement, excerpted below, he describes how and why he turned from being a loyal adherent to British law to an ardent noncooperator. Gandhi was sentenced to six years in prison for the seditious articles, but was released after serving two years.*

I have been constantly thinking of what the people would do in case I am arrested. My co-workers also have been putting this question to me. What would be the plight of India if the people took to the wrong path through love run mad? What would be my own plight in such a case?

Rivers of blood shed by the Government cannot frighten me, but I would be deeply pained even if the people did so much as abuse the Government for my sake or in my name. It would be disgracing me if the people lost their equilibrium on my arrest. The nation can achieve no progress merely by depending upon me. Progress is possible only by their understanding and following the path suggested by me. For this reason I desire that the people should maintain perfect self-control and consider the day of my arrest as a day of rejoicing. I desire that even the weakness existing today should disappear at that time.

What can be the motive of the Government in arresting me?

Mahatma Gandhi, "The Arrest and Trial of Mahatma Gandhi," *India Emerges: A Concise History of India from Its Origin to the Present,* edited by Steven Warshaw and C. David Bromwell. Berkeley, CA: The Diablo Press, 1974.

The Government are not my enemy; for I have not a grain of enmity towards them. But they believe that I am the soul of all this agitation, that if I am removed, the ruled and the ruler would be left in peace, that the people are blindly following me. Not only the Government but some of our leaders also share this belief. How then can the Government put the people to the test? How can the Government ascertain whether the people do understand my advice or are simply dazzled by my utterances?

The only way left to them is to arrest me. Of course there still remains an alternative for them and that lies in the removal of the causes which have led me to offer this advice. But intoxicated as they are with power, the Government will not see their own fault and even if they do, they will not admit it. The only way then that remains for them is to measure the strength of the people. They can do this by arresting me. If the people are thus terrorized into submission, they can be said to deserve the Punjab and the Khilafat wrongs.

If, on the other hand, the people resort to violence, they will merely be playing into the hands of the Government. Their airplanes will then bomb the people, their (General) Dyers will shoot them, and their (Governor) Smiths will uncover the veils of our women. There will be other officers to make the people rub their noses against the ground, crawl on their bellies and undergo the scourge of whipping. Both these results will be equally bad and unfortunate. They will not lead to *Swaraj*. In other countries Government have been overthrown by sheer brute force, but I have often shown that India cannot attain *Swaraj* by that force. What then should the people do if I am arrested.

Gandhi Urges Noncooperation

The answer now is simple. The people 1) should preserve peace and calmness; 2) should not observe *Hartal;* 3) should not hold meetings, but 4) should be fully awake.

I should certainly expect 5) all the Government Schools to be vacated and shut down; 6) lawyers to withdraw from practice in greater numbers; 7) settlement by private arbitration of cases pending before the Courts; 8) opening of numerous national schools and colleges; 9) renunciation of all foreign cloth in favor of the exclusive use of hand-spun and hand-woven garments by lakhs of men and women, and selling or burning of any foreign cloth in stock; 10) none to enlist in the army or in any other

Government service; 11) those able to earn their livelihood by other means to give up Government service; 12) contribution of as much as is wanted towards national funds; 13) title holders to surrender titles in greater numbers; 14) candidates to withdraw from elections, or if already elected, to resign their seats; 15) voters who have not yet made up their minds, to resolve that it is sin to send any representative to the Councils.

If the people resolve and carry this out, they would not have to wait for *Swaraj* even for a year. If they exhibit this much strength we shall have attained *Swaraj*.

I shall then be set free under the nation's seal. That will please me. My freedom today is like a prison to me.

It will only prove the peoples' incompetence if they use violence to release me and then depend upon my help to attain *Swaraj* for them. Neither I nor any one else can get *Swaraj* for the Nation. It will be got on the Nation proving its own fitness.

In conclusion, it is useless to find fault with the Government. We get what government we deserve. When we improve, the Government is also bound to improve. Only when we improve can we attain *Swaraj*. Noncooperation is the Nation's determination to improve. Will the Nation abandon the resolve and begin to cooperate after my arrest? If the people become mad and take to violence and as a result of it crawl on their bellies, rub their noses on the ground, salute the Union Jack and walk eighteen miles to do it, what else is that but cooperation? It is better to die than to submit to crawling. In fine, consider it from any point of view, the course suggested by me is the right one for the people to take. . . .

Gandhi's Courtroom Statement

I owe it perhaps to the Indian public and to the public in England to placate which this prosecution is mainly taken up that I should explain why from a staunch loyalist and cooperator I have become an uncompromising disaffectionist and noncooperator. To the Court too I should say why I plead guilty to the charge of promoting disaffection towards the Government established by law in India.

My public life began in 1893 in South Africa in troubled weather. My first contact with British authority in that country was not of a happy character. I discovered that as a man and as an Indian I had no rights. On the contrary I discovered that I had no rights as a man because I was an Indian.

But I was not baffled. I thought this treatment of Indians was an excrescence upon a system that was intrinsically and mainly good. I gave the Government my voluntary and hearty cooperation, criticizing it fully where I felt it was faulty, but never wishing its destruction.

Consequently when the existence of the Empire was threatened in 1899 by the Boer challenge, I offered my services to it, raised a volunteer ambulance corps and served at several actions that took place for the relief of Ladysmith. Similarly in 1906, at the time of the Zulu revolt, I raised a stretcher-bearer party and

The Judge's Ruling at Gandhi's Trial

After Gandhi's statement, C.N. Broomfield, Session Judge, pronounced the following judgment:

"Mr. Gandhi, you have made my task easy one way by pleading guilty to the charge. Nevertheless what remains, namely, the determination of a just sentence is perhaps as difficult a proposition as a Judge in this country could have to face. The law is no respector of persons. Nevertheless it will be impossible to ignore the fact that you are in a different category from any person I have ever tried or am likely to have to try. It would be impossible to ignore the fact that in the eyes of millions of your countrymen you are a great patriot and a great leader. Even those who differ from you in politics, look upon you as a man of high ideals and of noble and even saintly life. I have to deal with you in one character only. It is not my duty and I do not presume to judge or criticize you in any other character. It is my duty to judge you as a man subject to the law who has by his own admission broken the law and committed, what to an ordinary man must appear to be, grave offenses against the State. I do not forget that you have consistently preached against violence and that you have on many occasions, as I am willing to believe, done much to prevent

served till the end of the rebellion. On both these occasions I received medals and was even mentioned in despatches. For my work in South Africa I was given by Lord Hardinge a Kaiser-i-Hind Gold Medal. When the War broke out in 1914 between England and Germany, I raised a volunteer ambulance corps in London consisting of the then resident Indians in London, chiefly students. Its work was acknowledged by the authorities to be valuable. Lastly in India when a special appeal was made at the War Conference in Delhi in 1917 by Lord Chelmsford for recruits, I struggled at the cost of my health to raise a corps in Kheda and the response was being made when the hostilities

violence. But having regard to the nature of political teaching and the nature of many of those to whom it was addressed how you could have continued to believe that violence would not be the inevitable consequence, it passes my capacity to understand. There are probably few people in India who do not sincerely regret that you should have made it impossible for any Government to leave you at liberty. But it is so. I am trying to balance what is due to you against what appears to me to be necessary in the interest of the public, and I propose in passing sentence to follow the precedent of a case in many respects similar to this case that was decided some twelve years ago. I mean the case against Mr. Bal Gangadhar Tilak under the same section. The sentence that was passed upon him as it finally stood was a sentence of simple imprisonment for six years. You will not consider it unreasonable I think that you should be classed with Mr. Tilak. That is a sentence of two years' simple imprisonment on each count of the charges, six years in all which I feel it my duty to pass upon you; and I should like to say in doing so that if the course of events in India should make it possible for the Government to reduce the period and release you no one will be better pleased than I."

Steven Warshaw and C. David Bromwell, *India Emerges: A Concise History of India from Its Origin to the Present*. Berkeley, CA: Diablo Press, 1974, p. 198.

ceased and orders were received that no more recruits were wanted. In all these efforts at service, I was actuated by the belief that it was possible by such services to gain a status of full equality in the Empire for my countrymen.

The first shock came in the shape of the Rowlatt Act, a law designed to rob the people of all real freedom. I felt called upon to lead an intensive agitation against it. Then followed the Punjab horrors beginning with the massacre at Jallianwala Bagh and culminating in crawling orders, public floggings and other indescribable humiliations. I discovered too that the plighted word of the prime Minister to the Mussulmans of India regarding the integrity of Turkey and the holy places of Islam was not likely to be fulfilled. But in spite of the foreboding and the grave warnings of friends at the Amritsar Congress in 1919, I fought for co-operation and working the Montagu-Chalmsford reforms, hoping that the Prime Minister would redeem his promise to the Indian Mussulmans, that the Punjab wound would be healed, and that the reforms, inadequate and unsatisfactory though they were, marked a new era of hope in the life of India.

Exploitation of the Masses

But all that hope was shattered. The Khilafat promise was not to be redeemed. The Punjab crime was whitewashed, and most culprits went not only unpunished but remained in service and some continued to draw pensions from the Indian revenue and in some cases were even rewarded. I saw too that not only did the reforms not mark a change of heart, but they were only a method of further draining India of her wealth and of prolonging her servitude.

I came reluctantly to the conclusion that the British connection had made India more helpless than she ever was before, politically and economically. A disarmed India has no power of resistance against any aggressor if she wanted to engage in an armed conflict with him. So much is this the case that some of our best men consider that India must take generations before she can achieve the Dominion Status. She has become so poor that she has little power of resisting famines. Before the British advent, India spun and wove in her millions of cottages just the supplement she needed for adding to her meager agricultural resources. The cottage industry, so vital for India's existence, has been ruined by incredibly heartless and inhuman processes as described by English witnesses. Little do town-dwellers know how the semi-starved masses of Indians are slowly sinking to lifelessness. Little do they know that their miserable comfort represents the brokerage they get for the work they do for the foreign exploiter, that the profits and the brokerage are sucked from the masses. Little do they realize that the Government established by law in British India is carried on for this exploitation of the masses. No sophistry, no jugglery in figures can explain away the evidence the skeletons in many villages present to the naked eye. I have no doubt whatsoever that both England and the town-dwellers of India will have to answer, if there is a God above, for this crime against humanity which is perhaps unequalled in history. The law itself in this country has been used to serve the foreign exploiter. My unbiased examination of the Punjab Martial Law cases has led me to believe that at least ninety-five percent of convictions were wholly bad. My experience of political cases in India leads me to the conclusion that in nine out of every ten the condemned men were totally innocent. Their crime consisted in love of their country. In ninety-nine cases out of a hundred, justice has been denied to Indians as against Europeans in the Courts of India. This is not an exaggerated picture. It is the experience of almost every Indian who has had anything to do with such cases. In my opinion the administration of the law is thus prostituted consciously or unconsciously for the benefit of the exploiter.

Freedom of Speech

The greatest misfortune is that Englishmen and their Indian associates in the administration of the country do not know that they are engaged in the crime I have attempted to describe. I am satisfied that many English and Indian officials honestly believe that they are administering one of the best systems devised in the world and that India is making steady though slow progress. They do not know that a subtle but effective system of terrorism and an organized display of force on the one hand, and the deprivation of all powers of retaliation or self-defense on the other, have emasculated the people and induced in them the habit of simulation. This awful habit has added to the ignorance and the self-deception of the administrators. Section 124-A under which I am happily charged is perhaps the prince among the political sections of the Indian Penal Code designed to suppress the liberty of the citizen. Affection cannot be manufactured or regulated by law. If one has no affection for a person or thing, one should be free to give the fullest expression to his disaffection so long as he does not contemplate, promote or incite to violence. But the Section under which I am charged is one under which mere promotion of disaffection is a crime. I have studied some of the cases tried under it and I know that some of the most loved of India's patriots have been convicted under it. I consider it a privilege therefore to be charged under it. I have endeavored to give in their briefest outline the reasons for my disaffection. I have no personal illwill against any single administrator, much less can I have any disaffection towards the King's person. But I hold it to be a virtue to be disaffected towards a Government which, in its totality, has done more harm to India than any previous system. India is less manly under the British rule than she ever was before. Holding such a belief I consider it to be a sin to have affection for the system. And it has been a precious privilege for me to be able to write what I have in the various articles tendered in evidence against me.

In fact I believe that I have rendered a service to India and England by showing in noncooperation the way out of the unnatural state in which both are living. In my humble opinion, noncooperation with evil is as much a duty as is cooperation with good. But in the past, noncooperation has been deliberately expressed in violence to the evil doer. I am endeavoring to show to my countrymen that violent noncooperation only multiplies evil and that as evil can only be sustained by violence, withdrawal of support of evil requires complete abstention from violence. Nonviolence implies voluntary submission to the penalty for noncooperation with evil. I am here therefore to invite and submit cheerfully to the highest penalty that can be inflicted upon me for what in law is deliberate crime and what appears to me to be the highest duty of a citizen. The only course open to you, the Judge and the Assessors, is either to resign your posts and thus dissociate yourselves from evil, if you feel that the law you are called upon to administer is an evil and that in reality I am innocent, or to inflict on me the severest penalty if you believe that the system and the law you are assisting to administer are good for the people of this country and that any activity is therefore injurious to the public weal.

A Critical Assessment of Gandhi

By Judith M. Brown

According to historian of India Judith M. Brown, contrary to popular conception, Mohandas Gandhi was not the driving force of India's struggle for independence. While he shaped the unique character of the Indian nationalist movement, restored Indian pride, and unified Indian society through his strategy of nonviolence, Gandhi failed to achieve his main objectives. Contemporary India shows little evidence of his social, economic, and political ideals. While he found no solutions to many of the issues he pondered, in Gandhi—Prisoner of Hope, *from which the following extract is drawn, Brown says he was a man of vision and action with wide-ranging concerns and deep humanity.*

When India achieved independence in August 1947 the president of Congress hailed Gandhi as the father of the Indian nation. But that was too easy an epigram on his life, and is too simple an epitaph after his death. Certainly Gandhi was and is the individual who most clearly personifies free India for Indians and foreigners alike. The frail man with his long walking-staff, his round spectacles and his spinning-wheel is the symbol of India's movement for freedom from imperialism; and the hagiography of the early historians of Indian nationalism has been confirmed vividly in the eyes of a later generation by Richard Attenborough's film of Gandhi's life which was widely shown in the 1980s. Yet India's nationalist movement existed before Gandhi and would have attained its goal without him. For far deeper economic and political forces than the leadership of one man were at work loosening the links between

Judith M. Brown, *Gandhi: Prisoner of Hope*. New Haven, CT: Yale University Press, 1989.

Britain and India—forces that had their origins in India, in Britain, and in the wider world economy and balance of power. Yet his skills and his particular genius marked the nationalist movement and gave it a character unlike that of any other anti-imperial nationalism of the century.

An Indian Identity

Gandhi was an ingenious and sensitive artist in symbols. In his own person as a self-denying holy man, by his speeches full of pictorial images and references to the great Hindu myths, by his emphasis on the *charkha* and on the wearing of *khadi* as a uniform to obliterate distinctions of region and caste, he portrayed and publicized in a world with few mass communications and low literacy, an ideal of an Indian nation which was accessible even to the poor and unpoliticized. For many, at least for a time, the ideal of the nation and a sense of national identity were lifted out of the rough and often sordid world of politics, although the inevitable struggles and intrigues accompanying any shifts of power in a complex polity jostled uneasily with the vision of nationhood and often threatened to engulf it. A new nation had to be fashioned out of the numerous loyalties and contests for dominance which were the stuff of Indian politics. Gandhi knew this full well as he agonized over political strategies, as he attempted to minimize conflict among Indians and generate a moral community which encompassed and purified old loyalties. His long march to Dandi to make salt in 1930, his fasts in Poona in 1932 and in Delhi in 1948 were not personal idiosyncracies but a careful understanding and weighing of some of the realities of Indian society and politics that militated against nationhood. Those who clustered round him and formed the central Congress leadership realized that in the Mahatma they had a living symbol and a man of considerable political creativity, whose background and beliefs particularly suited him for this role of popularizing a new Indian identity, whereas the early Congress leaders, inhibited by their backgrounds and ideals, had failed to create more than a minority political movement in the name of the nation.

Many ideological and political struggles are watered with the blood of martyrs. Under Gandhi's presiding genius India's campaign for political identity and freedom was sealed with common experiences of conscious and conscientious law-breaking, of feeling the blows of police *lathis*, and of going to gaol. Where once such experiences would have been considered demeaning and insulting, Gandhi helped to turn them into badges of high moral and emotional commitment. British imperial administrators had long emphasized the importance of *izzat*, of the prestige of place and power in their imperial regime; now Gandhi turned *izzat* on its head, making ignominy and pain the hallmarks of a new and greater esteem according to the logic of nationalism. Where once so many Indians had felt alienated from their roots, living in a no man's land between their own and Western civilization, Gandhi helped to rekindle a proper pride and a new courage deeply embedded in Indian culture. Yet this powerful manipulation of symbol in the national cause had its grave drawbacks: chief among them was the growing disquiet of many Muslims at the Hindu tenor of Congress politics as it broadened its appeal; as Gandhi, a Hindu Mahatma, became its leader, preaching in revivalist tones the coming of a new kingdom of God on earth when swaraj was attained. Increasingly for Muslims such a vision meant the coming of Ram rather than Allah, and in concrete terms the dominance of Ram's devotees, the Hindu majority.

Non-Violence

Gandhi's other great contribution to India's national movement was his technique of non-violent protest. It was such a contrast to the politics of petitioning or the terrorist tactics that had preceded it that it was little wonder that the rulers were perplexed by it, Indians were sceptical of it, and later observers have seen it as the Gandhian hallmark. Yet . . . when the myth and exaggerations are stripped away, it becomes clear that non-violent forms of opposition to the British raj rarely achieved major or immediate political concessions; and satyagraha on a national scale certainly did not evict the British from the sub-continent. Satyagraha worked, in the ordinary political sense of procuring a remedy for a complaint or making a substantial demonstration (rather than in the peculiar Gandhian sense of inevitably purifying its true adherents and their opponents), when it was deployed on a limited and clearly demarcated issue, by a small number of highly committed and disciplined adherents, against an opponent who was particularly vulnerable, either to pressure from a higher authority which had different priorities (as in Champaran in 1917) or to public opinion at home and abroad.

However, the British raj was in the long term a vulnerable superstructure raised over a complex and ancient society over which it had little control. As its civil servants and military officers alike realized, it remained stable and functioning as long as it retained the formal or informal collaboration of certain key groups of Indians, and the acquiescence of the vast majority. Dislodging the imperial power was in large part a battle for the mind, both of Indians and the British rulers and electorate, and their foreign allies. In this, satyagraha and Gandhi's preaching of its meaning proved highly significant because it encouraged Indians to shed their ingrained fear and acceptance of the raj, and to realize their own strength. It also alienated from the imperial regime many moderate men and those who were educated yet did not play an active political role, not least because of the treatment its exponents suffered at the hands of the raj, and it cast the British in the role of moral villain in the eyes of her essential allies across the Atlantic. Increasingly the British realized that smashing such a movement on a large scale would be too costly in moral and material terms for what it could achieve. In the economic and political world order from the 1930s, and increasingly after the second world war, a contented ally and trading partner within the Commonwealth was a much better proposition than a restless dependency, held down by unconvinced soldiers and civil servants, which was anyway far less significant in terms of jobs, investment, trade and strategic protection of British world interests than it had been in the later nineteenth century when the raj was at its most secure and most profitable to its British rulers.

Non-Co-Operation

Non-co-operation also played a politically significant educative and incorporative role in the development of Indian nationalism. It could be adapted to suit the immediate and local needs of a wide range of people, in stark contrast to the politics of the early Congress which were accessible only to the highly educated and the English-speaking. Gandhi's campaigns offered modes of opposition to the old and young, to men and women, to the educated as well as the poor and illiterate. Children could sing patriotic songs in procession, students could leave their desks and take part in demonstrations, women could picket liquor and foreign cloth shops and visualize themselves as latter-day Sitas, peasants could cut grass and graze their cattle in prohibited places, owner-cultivators could withhold their land revenue, townsmen could enjoy a good bonfire of foreign cloth, while professional people could ostentatiously boycott the legislatures and the courts. Yet this very inclusiveness, incorporating different and often pre-existing struggles into one national movement and reinterpreting them as facets of nationalism, had its dangers. Mass movements very easily slipped from central control and an apparently national campaign could rapidly disintegrate into its disparate and often conflicting parts, and into violence which was the negation of everything for which Gandhi claimed to stand.

In the end after many attempts to organize, lead and control a broadly based campaign, Gandhi recognized that he had failed to find the right formula; he ended his life trying to exert non-violence as a lone individual who could at least control his own actions and try to purify his own intentions. Furthermore, Gandhi never converted more than a handful into true believers in *ahimsa*. For the vast majority of politicial activists, even among his closest and most influential political colleagues, non-violence was a desirable and often very useful political strategy in a specific situation rather than a total moral commitment as it was for him. Consequently satyagraha could easily degenerate into violence among some on the radical wing of Congress, as in 1942, or shade off into constitutional co-operation among other Congressmen who always intended eventually to use the established political structures and saw in non-co-operation a way of extending those structures and generating a political following which would ultimately elect them to positions of power.

Strengths and Limitations

The experience of participating in non-co-operation undoubtedly also helped to bond several generations of Indians, to recruit, train and incorporate many who might have become angry and uncontrollable young men, and to unite Indians across regional and language boundaries in one national movement. Furthermore, Gandhi's passion for order and organization, his vision of a disciplined body of national servants and his eye for minute detail also played a part in binding together a national Congress. It was not for nothing that Gandhi was a *bania* by caste; he sometimes laughingly used and played on this image of the careful businessman, keeping his books, watching his finances and minding his stock. The zeal that prompted him to send G.D. Birla meticulous accounts of the way he spent all his benefactor's munificent donations took another form in his repeated attempts to reform the Congress organization into a body able to receive and act on national commands, which spanned every province and reached down to every village. His ideal of a fully functional popular body never materialized, nor did his vision of a dedicated body of public servants. But in considerable part because of his emphasis on effective organization, shared by Nehru and Patel, the Congress particularly from the 1930s onwards became a far more streamlined and broadly based party than the ramshackle affair he had attended on his return from South Africa. In the long term the range and experience of the Congress as an organization for protest stood it in good stead when it became the party of government: it was one of the institutions that helped to keep the Indian union intact in the first difficult years after independence and partition. In contrast, the fact that the Muslim League had so comparatively little time to organize its supporters, to become a natural arena for Muslim politics, and to put down real roots in the social soil of the areas which became Pakistan, accounts in part for the instability of democracy in Pakistan and the ultimate disintegration of Jinnah's Pakistan with the creation of Bangladesh.

Yet it would be wrong to see Gandhi, for all his skills of organization, publicity and strategy, as the great driving force of Indian nationalism. He was used by India's politicians, followed for his skills and potential and at times tactfully ignored by them when his priorities and practices seemed unproductive or divisive. He recognized this with a cheerful realism, and was content to be put on the shelf in ordinary political terms, provided that he was permitted to get on with what he perceived as his life's work—the construction of a new Indian polity and society infused with non-violence and godliness—by other means. Ironically it was precisely because he was not a career politician that he had such a long career in politics, survived what to others would have been political retirement or even suicide, and was able to come back again and again to play a formidable political role when events made him a valuable resource to a significant number of his compatriots. He did indeed have a charismatic effect on individuals and on vast crowds; but it was utility rather than charisma or mass conversion to his ideals which gave him at times such influence in national politics. Once this is understood it becomes clear why his influence in independent India was so limited. He himself sensed this would be so in the closing months of his life: that there would be no place for his ideals of self-denial and service when power was within the politicians' grasp, that there would be no scope for his modes of action once Congress was the government rather than opposing the established regime.

Limited Influence Today

Most Indian towns indeed have their statues of Gandhi, there are many roads named after him, and many institutions trade under his name. Yet on the issues that deeply concerned him there is little evidence that Gandhi is the father of contemporary India. During his life he confronted many of the real problems of India in a basic and forthright way which contrasted strongly with the intellectual nationalism of so many of his generation of politicians and even earlier Congressmen. [He dealt] not only with 'high politics' but with the varied concerns of ordinary people—health, food, agriculture, education, caste, marriage customs, women's role (even their jewellery), public cleanliness, the meaning of religion and the best way to pray, to name but a few. . . .

Yet in contemporary India so much that he strove to change in order to achieve real swaraj has remained or indeed has developed in directions alien to Gandhi's thinking. Although he accepted that a Western style of democratic state was probably necessary in India, at least in the short term, his ideal was the diffusion of power down to local level so that village communities could organize their own affairs as far as possible. In modern India the state has increased massively in power since the days of imperial rule. The British raj was a light-handed, amateur affair compared to the Indian state of the later twentieth century, with its greatly increased numbers of employees and functionaries, its bigger revenues, higher expenditure on the army and the police, its economic planning and control of the economy through directives and a pervasive system of licences. It is also far more intrusive into personal life with its policies for development, education, welfare, and family planning. Even the new structures of village-based local government bear no resemblance to Gandhi's ideals, but are the instruments of government control and often the arenas for local factional struggles and the exercise of power rather than service of the community.

Gandhi's economic ideals have similarly been shelved. Whereas he had envisaged a very small role for modern-style industry and a dominant place in the economy for small-scale, rural industry complementing agriculture, India has become one of the world's most highly industrialized nations, its range of products and its development of a consumer-orientated economy a far cry from the austere economy of sufficiency advocated by Gandhi. Handicrafts are an aspect of tourism and interior decor rather than a local supplying of basic needs of clothing, and domestic and agricultural equipment; those village-based industries that have developed have tended to eliminate jobs and line the pockets of those who have the capital to invest in plant and machinery, whereas he had advocated them as a means of alleviating rural unemployment and giving the poorest an additional source of income to ensure their dignity of life. India is still a land of villages and villagers—only about 20% of Indians live in towns. Yet percentages belie numbers. Because the population has risen so steeply in the last half of the century, as a result of greatly improved health and nutrition, and a falling death-rate, millions more Indians now actually experience what Gandhi felt were the degrading and de-Indianizing influences of urban life than ever did in his day.

In social relations, too, there are few signs of change as a direct reflection of Gandhi's work. Certainly his growing hostility to caste as he found it in India and his abhorrence of untouchability were significant in moulding the Congress mind; and when an independent government, freed from the inhibitions of an alien, imperial regime, took power it rapidly and robustly legislated against the public observance of untouchability and proclaimed the equality of all citizens, regardless of caste. But as Gandhi knew full well, laws need public support, and he was realistic in his assertion that the critical change needed was one of attitudes. Many of India's apparently radical legislative reforms of social customs have been honoured in the breach rather than in observance. Untouchability, for example, persists with its degradation; it rests on unchanged attitudes and the harsh facts of economic life which prevent most untouchables from gaining access to essential credit, to new employment and to new wealth. As change does slowly occur in caste perceptions and relationships it is the result of new values inculcated through mass education, which in form and content reflects Western values and practices in a way which would have horrified Gandhi who had formulated such distinctive and Indian plans for Basic Education. . . .

It would be possible to go on demonstrating the facets of modern Indian life that would have distressed Gandhi. Not the least would be the tragic evidence of continuing violence in public life, often stemming from persisting communal loyalties and hostilities, Muslim set against Hindu, Sikh in conflict with Hindu, as a plural society searches for appropriate political forms to contain its tensions and channel its ambitions.

Deeper Moral Issues

This bleak assessment of contemporary India in the light of Gandhi's vision of true swaraj as distinct from mere Indian assumption of political power in an unreformed polity suggests how strong and pervasive were many of the social and political forces that constrained Gandhi in his life. In recognizing them one is more able to perceive the true stature of the man and to see the depth of his struggle to create a new order free from what he saw as the evil effects of imperialism and tradition alike. It is in his struggles with himself and his society that some of his most powerful and lasting contributions to this century lie. He was not a trained philosopher or interested in producing a coherent body of thought. Rather, he was inspired by a powerful religious vision which prompted him to grow through experience, to be courageous enough to be pragmatic, and to refine his views in the light of reality. Consequently his lines of thought are sometimes hard to follow, and the British thought him a slippery customer. But in his strivings, his set-backs and even his self-contradictions he faced crucial human questions which find resonances in almost any time and place. It is because of his confrontations with fundamental religious, philosophical and moral questions in the context of an active public life that he still exercises such a fascination, can still inspire hostility as well as hope.

In Gandhi's eyes men and women were human in virtue of their capacity for religious vision. It was this which distinguished them from the rest of creation; if this was stifled by the individual or by political and economic structures then people were degraded and dehumanized. This was as strong and striking an attack on secular materialism as could be made. Yet he was equally pungent in his criticism of much that passed for religion in many of the world's major traditions, though inevitably his main criticisms were of his own. Observance of religious forms, belonging to organized religious bodies were of themselves, nothing to him; true religion lay in the deepest places of the heart, when and where a man strove to realize his origins and true being. It was a search for fundamental truth, for an undergirding reality which, if genuine, would overflow into love for others and a life of service. It was from this understanding of the true nature of humanity and personhood that Gandhi developed his increasingly radical conception of the equality of people across boundaries of creed, sex, race and social or economic background. Given this underlying sense of equality, Gandhi's sense of fraternity also flowered, ultimately into a passionate identification with the poor and despised. His glorification of poverty and his difficult phrases about finding God in the poor jarred on the ears of men like Nehru who thought poverty a shameful curse and rebelled at the idea of giving it any aroma of sanctity rather than working to obliterate it; just as Gandhi's sentiments still alienate those who feel that such an attitude only serves to reinforce the status quo and to generate charity rather than equality.

As an avowed and genuine religious seeker and visionary who felt compelled by his vision to participate in a wide range of public activity rather than retire to a contemplative seclusion, Gandhi not only rejected religious quietism and a purely private piety. He also confronted the problem of means and ends, from which none can escape, particularly those who handle public power and influence the minds and destinies of many. Gandhi's response to this age-old dilemma was first a strong affirmation that there could be no distinction between public and private life; that public life did not permit a different and more utilitarian moral stance. In his own mind there was then only one unfailing solution to the problem—to adopt a means which was in a sense itself the end, which would generate the qualities that would effectively transform any situation. Non-violent striving after truth, satyagraha, was just such a means. It recognized that no person or group had a total grasp of truth, and ensured that in conflict none was coerced beyond the dictates of conscience. (In practice, of course, 'non-violence' could be very different from Gandhi's ideal, and even his fasts exerted a moral pressure for which non-violence was a dubious description.) What he discovered to his cost—but not at the expense of continuing hope and action—was that all men of vision find that life is full of unavoidable contradictions, constraints and compromises. There is rarely a choice between absolute good and evil, clear truth and falsehood, but generally between lesser and greater evil, a further or nearer approximation to a vision of truth. . . .

Search for Truth

Contemporary and later observers criticized Gandhi's asceticism, his attitude to sexuality, his negation of the body as harsh and joyless, and have traced its roots to deep tensions within his own personality. There is considerable truth in this. His was not a personality at peace with itself. Often he was tormented with self-questioning, anger and frustration; yet it is only out of tension, stress and conflict that lasting resolutions of fundamental problems are born. Further, against the harshness and self-distrust, against the demands he made on others and himself, must be set the evidence of humour and tenderness which did so much to attract men and women to him, the personal concern for the individual which made so many feel at his death a personal bereavement and the extinguishing of a guiding light. Gandhi's experiments with simple, communal living and with health for villagers which did not rely on expensive drugs, even led him to consideration of mankind's relations with the environment, human obligations towards animals, and use of air, water and soil. Unlike most politicians of his day, his breadth of concern again led him to ask fundamental questions about life. They make him sound distinctly modern as his ideals of simplicity and smallness of scale echo the fears of people in the later part of the century who have glimpsed some of the darker aspects and unsuspected repercussions of industrialization, the driving force of the Western civilization he so condemned.

Gandhi was no plaster saint. Nor did he find lasting and real solutions to many of the problems he encountered. Possibly he did not even see the implications of some of them. He was a man of his time and place, with a particular philosophical and religious background, facing a specific political and social situation. He was also deeply human, capable of heights and depths of sensation and vision, of great enlightenment and dire doubt, and the roots of his attitudes and actions were deep and tangled, as are most people's. He made good and bad choices. He hurt some, yet consoled and sustained many. He was caught in compromises inevitable in public life. But fundamentally he was a man of vision and action, who asked many of the profoundest questions that face humankind as it struggles to live in community. It was this confrontation out of a real humanity which marks his true stature and which makes his struggles and glimpses of truth of enduring significance. As a man of his time who asked the deepest questions, even though he could not answer them, he became a man for all times and all places.

Muhammed Ali Jinnah and the Creation of Pakistan

By Akbar S. Ahmed

While Gandhi was a force of unity and identity formation for Hindu India, Muhammed Ali Jinnah was his counterpart among the Muslim community of the subcontinent. In the following article, Muslim spokesman Akbar S. Ahmed explores the motives behind Jinnah's demand for the creation of Pakistan. He says changes in the cultural and political climate in India after 1920 account for Jinnah's actions. Formerly a secular politician who supported a united Hindu-Muslim India, Jinnah changed his position in the face of growing militant Hindu extremists, the unresponsiveness of the Indian National Congress to Muslim interests, and political demands from grass-roots Muslim groups. These factors propelled Jinnah to unite the Muslims of India and demand a separate homeland. Akbar Ahmed is an associate member of the Centre of South Asian Studies in Cambridge, and presenter of a BBC series on "Living Islam."

The understanding of why Muhammad Ali Jinnah wanted Pakistan, the nation he created, is crucial to an understanding of the nature of South Asian politics even today. . . .

What continues to baffle people is the conversion of Jinnah from a liberal, Anglicised, seemingly secular politician, whose proudest title was Ambassador of Hindu-Muslim Unity and whose early political life was spent fighting for a united India, to the champion of an exclusive Muslim identity. It is one of the most intriguing yet least explored areas of modern South Asian history.

In exploring it I do not suggest a Damascene conversion in Jinnah. I shall, however, point to the cultural and political changes taking place around him, and personally within him after 1920 which help to explain the conversion. In December that year his position is clearly expressed in a conversation with Durga Das, a prominent writer, after rejecting Gandhi's non-co-operation call:

> Well, young man—I will have nothing to do with this pseudo-religious approach to politics. I part company with the Congress and Gandhi. I do not believe in working up mob hysteria. Politics is a gentleman's game.

Yet just over a decade later Jinnah would have changed his position.

The Cultural and Political Climate

Although some of the developments which explain Jinnah's conversion (and that of other Muslims as well) and the eventual creation of Pakistan do not relate directly to Jinnah they assisted in creating a cultural and political climate which influenced his decision. First, the Anglicised, liberal, humanist politics based on a few wealthy individuals which prevailed until the First World War had become obsolete. A different kind of politics drawing in the masses began to take shape which would sharpen communal confrontation.

The vacuum formed by the deaths within a few years of each other of Gokhale, Mehta and Tilak, influential figures of the earlier kind of politics, was filled spectacularly by Gandhi after he captured the Congress in 1920 (the year Tilak died). The most dramatic manifestation of the new mass politics was Gandhi himself who directly appealed to those previously neglected the villagers, the untouchables, the poor. It was a radical strategy and would lead to freedom from the British. The colonial masters would never again be able fully to take the initiative or be entirely in control.

Secondly, the Montagu-Chelmsford Report of 1918 led to significant political shifts in British India. The emphasis moved from urban based politicians to those backed by large rural populations. from the United Provinces and Bombay to the Punjab and Bengal in terms of Muslim politics. New groups began to emerge with long-reaching consequences for political leadership.

The Arains, traditionally lower-class Punjabi agriculturalists, emerged socially and economically to articulate their demands and identity in specifically Islamic terms. In time they would be ardent supports of Jinnah and the Pakistan movement. One of them—General Zia-ul-Haq—would become president of Pakistan. Without the Punjab, the biggest and most powerful province of Pakistan, there would have been no Pakistan.

Thirdly, Muslims responded to the punishment of the vanquished Turks and humbling of the Caliphate/Khilafat (from the Islamic notion of the Caliph; the head of the Ottoman empire) at the Treaty of Sevres in 1920 with what became known as the Khilafat movement. The Khilafat was abolished in Turkey by the Turks themselves wishing for a modern identity. The Muslims of India, however, saw this as yet another British plot to undermine Islam and protested. Their leaders advised them to march out of British India and migrate to Afghanistan and other Muslim countries as a protest. Gandhi championed the Khilafat movement but Jinnah, though sympathetic to the Turks, was not convinced. The movement caused a flutter of excitement in the community but also great hardship and in the end led to nowhere. The movement illustrated that the Muslims of India were leaderless and devoid of a viable objective. Jinnah and the idea of Pakistan would give them both in the next decade.

Hindu Extremists

Fourthly, Hindu fundamentalist organisations came into being in the 1920s with a specific in-built bias against the minorities (especially Muslims). Hindu communalism would grow rapidly from the 1920s onwards. Leaders like Hedgewar were angry at the Khilafat movement which, to them, expressed Muslim disloyalty to India. The 1923 major Hindu-Muslim riot in Nagpur was not the first of its kind but it helped to start organised and regular communal rioting.

Nagpur was followed by the setting up of the RSS (Rashtriya Seva Sangh) organisation, a Hindu fundamentalist party, which in time would influence parties like the BJP (Bhatativa Janata Party). Physical exercises, cabalistic oath ceremonies, flags, secret funds and disciplined cadres soon characterised it. A militant Hindu philosophy motivated the RSS. A member of this group would

Jinnah's Demand for the Partition of India

Following Jinnah's presidential address to the Muslim League in March 1940, an extract of which appears below, the League adopted the famous Lahore resolution demanding the partition of India and creation of a separate Islamic state.

The problem in India is not of an inter-communal character but manifestly of an international one, and it must be treated as such. So long as this basic and fundamental truth is not realised, any constitution that may be built will result in disaster and will prove destructive and harmful not only to the Musalmans [Muslims] but to the British and Hindus also. If the British Government are really in earnest and sincere to secure peace and happiness of the people of the subcontinent, the only course open to us all is to allow the major nations separate homelands by dividing India into 'autonomous national states'. There is no reason why these states should be antagonistic to each other. On the other hand, the rivalry and the natural desire and efforts on the part of one to dominate the social order and establish political supremacy over the other in the government of the country will disappear. It will lead more towards natural goodwill by international pacts between them, and they can live in complete harmony with their neighbours. This will lead further to a friendly settlement all the more easily with regard to minorities by reciprocal arrangements and adjustments between Muslim India and Hindu India, which will far more adequately and effectively safeguard the rights and interests of Muslims and various other minorities.

It is extremely difficult to appreciate why our Hindu friends fail to understand the real nature of Islam and Hinduism. They are not religions in the strict sense of the word, but are, in fact, different and distinct social orders, and it is a dream that the Hindus and Muslims can ever evolve a common nationality, and this misconception of one Indian nation has gone far beyond the limits and is the cause of most of your troubles and will lead India to destruction if we fail to revise our notions in time.

The Hindus and Muslims belong to two different religious philosophies, social customs, literatures. They neither intermarry nor interdine together and, indeed, they belong to two different civilisations which are based mainly on conflicting ideas and conceptions. Their outlooks on life and of life are different. It is quite clear that Hindus and Musalmans derive their inspiration from different sources of history. They have different epics, different heroes, and different episodes. Very often the hero of one is a foe of the other and, likewise, their victories and defeats overlap. To yoke together two such nations under a single state, one as a numerical minority and the other as a majority, must lead to growing discontent and final destruction of any fabric that may be so built up for the government of such a state. . . .

The present artificial unity of India dates back only to the British conquest and is maintained by the British bayonet, but termination of the British regime, which is implicit in the recent declaration of his Majesty's Government, will be the herald of the entire break-up with worse disaster than has ever taken place during the last one thousand years under Muslims. Surely that is not the legacy which Britain would bequeath to India after 150 years of her rule, nor would Hindu and Muslim India risk such a sure catastrophe.

Muslim India cannot accept any constitution which must necessarily result in a Hindu majority government. Hindus and Muslims brought together under a democratic system forced upon the minorities can only mean Hindu raj. Democracy of the kind with which the Congress High Command is enamoured would mean the complete destruction of what is most precious in Islam. We have had ample experience of the working of the provincial constitutions during the last two and a half years and any repetition of such a government must lead to civil war.

C.H. Philips, ed., *The Evolution of India and Pakistan 1858–1947. Select Documents*. London: Oxford University Press, 1964, pp. 353–54.

assassinate Gandhi for being too sympathetic to the Muslims.

Golwalkar, who followed Hedgewar to become one of the major ideologues of this form of Hinduism, compared the situation of the Muslims of India to the Jews in Germany in *We or our Nationhood Defined* (1938). If, he argued, the German Jews could be exterminated by Hitler so could the Indian Muslims by the Hindus. Hitler's attempt at 'purity' was 'a good lesson for us in Hindustan to learn and profit by', he wrote. Jinnah, living in Bombay, the main RSS centre, understood and commented on the implications of treating Muslims 'like Jews in Germany'. . . .

Since the 1920s, therefore, those Hindus who wished to preserve Hinduism as peaceful, universal and nonviolent, faced a growing challenge within their own house. This internal crisis informed an increasingly bitter confrontation which reached a climax in the 1990s. Figures like Gandhi and Nehru, in retrospect, are openly criticised; they were too soft on the minorities (especially the Muslims); they ultimately betrayed Hinduism for advocating a secular India.

Jinnah recognised that while Hindu leaders like Gandhi and Nehru were not enemies of the Muslims (on the death of the former he would say the Muslims of India had lost their best friend) Hindu extremists would make life difficult if not impossible for Muslims. He voiced Muslim sentiment, alarmed at the growing Hindu communalism, when he declared that British Raj would be succeeded by Hindu, or Ram Raj. Jinnah's prediction would echo in the slogan of the BJP, a party that commands 119 seats in parliament.

Congress Dismisses Muslim Demands

Fifthly, it was becoming clear in the 1920s that the British would be sharing power with Indians, sooner rather than later. The Congress was emerging as the authentic voice of India after Gandhi gave it fresh confidence through his high media profile and wide, popular appeal. It was already planning for a strongly centralised India. Its leadership—which would take India to independence—was beginning to fall into place: Gandhi the saintly politician, the personification of renascent India; Nehru the cultivated, charismatic spokesman for, and one of the main figures of, the Congress; Patel, the committed Hindu nationalist, always a strong contender for Nehru's position; Azad, the scholarly and gentle Muslim presence in the Congress (Muslims like Jinnah dismissed Congress Muslims; to Jinnah, Azad was a mere 'show-boy').

Muslims complained that Congress, sensing power in the 1920s, was becoming arrogant. It dismissed their demands, ignored their sense of insecurity and preferred to speak on their behalf. Many Muslims felt that they would become second-class citizens with not only their religion but also their culture under threat. For instance, the Urdu language, generally, though not exclusively, associated with Muslims, was increasingly the target of groups like the RSS as being 'foreign'. In time its script would be changed and in many places it would cease to be taught altogether.

Finally, and from a personal point of view, while the India Jinnah knew and loved was changing so dramatically, after 1920 Jinnah's own life was also changing. He was over forty years old, the age Muslims, following the tradition of the Prophet, believe is a turning point in life. His married life had turned sour in the 1920s, though in a rare exhibition of public emotion Jinnah wept like a child as his wife was buried following her death in 1929.

Still a successful lawyer, he withdrew the next year to London. Here he led a quiet and comfortable life in Hampstead. An English chauffeur drove his Bentley to chambers in the city. He had retreated from an active role in political life in India.

But many Muslims in India, becoming aware of the mounting threat they faced without a leader of stature in the changing political climate, appealed to him to return. Some, like Liaqat, who would become Pakistan's first prime minister, and the great poet, Allama Iqbal, visited him in London with the invitation. By accepting the leadership of the Muslim League and returning to India in 1934 he crossed the Rubicon.

Jinnah's family life was over and this essentially private man now poured his energy and his commitment into championing the Muslims. It led him to the quest for Muslim identity and destiny, the embodiment of which would be Pakistan. Within a decade from the poor showing in 1937 of his party, the Muslim League, the demand for Pakistan would become an irresistible flood.

Although there were compelling factors in the 1920s for Muslims to think of their identity and their future, the idea of India divided into two nations, Hindu and Muslim, had been around, however ill-defined, for half a century. The great poets and scholars of Muslim India—Sir Sayyed, Hali, Iqbal—reflected on the themes of loss of power, crisis of identity and the search for destiny which fed into the idea of a separate Muslim nation. In Jinnah the Muslim intellectuals had found their leader. Iqbal summed it up in one of the several letters he wrote to 'the only Muslim in India today to whom the community has a right to look to for safe guidance through the storm which is coming'.

THE HISTORY OF NATIONS

Chapter 4

Post-Independence India

A Tryst with Destiny: The Future of Independent India

By Jawaharlal Nehru

On August 14, 1947, the eve of India's independence, Jawaharlal Nehru, India's first prime minister, addressed India's Constituent Assembly with his famous speech "A Tryst with Destiny." In the address Nehru sets the tone and direction for an independent India, laying emphasis on the need to tackle poverty and inequality and for India to assume a leadership role in world affairs. In his radio address to the nation the following day, he urges his people to end their conflict with the newly created Pakistan and with Muslims in general, and instead work together to address the needs of India's poor through planned industrial development programs and more equitable distribution of resources. Both speeches are excerpted below.

Address to the Constituent Assembly, August 14, 1947: Long years ago we made a tryst with destiny, and now the time comes when we shall redeem our pledge, not wholly or in full measure, but very substantially. At the stroke of the midnight hour, when the world sleeps, India will awake to life and freedom. A moment comes, which comes but rarely in history, when we step out from the old to the new, when an age ends, and when the soul of a nation, long suppressed, finds utterance. It is fitting that at this solemn moment we take the pledge of dedication to the service of India and her people and to the still larger cause of humanity.

At the dawn of history India started on her unending quest,

Jawaharlal Nehru, *Independence and After: A Collection of Speeches 1946–1949.* New York: The John Day Company, 1950.

and trackless centuries are filled with her striving and the grandeur of her success and her failures. Through good and ill fortune alike she has never lost sight of that quest or forgotten the ideals which gave her strength. We end today a period of ill fortune and India discovers herself again. The achievement we celebrate today is but a step, an opening of opportunity, to the greater triumphs and achievements that await us. Are we brave enough and wise enough to grasp this opportunity and accept the challenge of the future?

Freedom and power bring responsibility. That responsibility rests upon this Assembly, a sovereign body representing the sovereign people of India. Before the birth of freedom we have endured all the pains of labour and our hearts are heavy with the memory of this sorrow. Some of those pains continue even now. Nevertheless, the past is over and it is the future that beckons to us now.

The Work Ahead

That future is not one of ease or resting but of incessant striving so that we may fulfil the pledges we have so often taken and the one we shall take today. The service of India means the service of the millions who suffer. It means the ending of poverty and ignorance and disease and inequality of opportunity. The ambition of the greatest man of our generation has been to wipe every tear from every eye. That may be beyond us, but as long as there are tears and suffering, so long our work will not be over.

And so we have to labour and to work, and work hard, to give reality to our dreams. Those dreams are for India, but they are also for the world, for all the nations and peoples are too closely knit together today for any one of them to imagine that it can live apart. Peace has been said to be indivisible; so is freedom, so is prosperity now, and so also is disaster in this One World that can no longer be split into isolated fragments.

To the people of India, whose representatives we are, we make an appeal to join us with faith and confidence in this great adventure. This is no time for petty and destructive criticism, no time for ill-will or blaming others. We have to build the noble mansion of free India where all her children may dwell.

I beg to move, Sir,

That it be resolved that:

After the last stroke of midnight, all members of the Constituent Assembly present on this occasion, do take the following pledge:

At this solemn moment when the people of India, through suffering and sacrifice, have secured freedom, I,. . . . . , a member of the Constituent Assembly of India, do dedicate myself in all humility to the service of India and her people to the end that this ancient land attain her rightful place in the world and make her full and willing contribution to the promotion of world peace and the welfare of mankind. . . .

Eyes on the Future

Address to the nation, August 15, 1947: Fellow countrymen, it has been my privilege to serve India and the cause of India's freedom for many years. Today I address you for the first time officially as the First Servant of the Indian people, pledged to their service and their betterment. I am here because you willed it so and I remain here so long as you choose to honour me with your confidence.

We are a free and sovereign people today and we have rid ourselves of the burden of the past. We look at the world with clear and friendly eyes and at the future with faith and confidence.

The burden of foreign domination is done away with, but freedom brings its own responsibilities and burdens, and they can only be shouldered in the spirit of a free people, self-disciplined, and determined to preserve and enlarge that freedom.

We have achieved much; we have to achieve much more. Let us then address ourselves to our new tasks with the determination and adherence to high principles which our great leader has taught us. Gandhiji is fortunately with us to guide and inspire and ever to point out to us the path of high endeavour. He taught us long ago that ideals and objectives can never be divorced from the methods adopted to realize them; that worthy ends can only be achieved through worthy means. If we aim at the big things of life, if we dream of India as a great nation giving her age-old message of peace and freedom to others, then we have to be big ourselves and worthy children of Mother India. The eyes of the world are upon us watching this birth of freedom in the East and wondering what it means.

An End to Violence and Suffering

Our first and immediate objective must be to put an end to all internal strife and violence, which disfigure and degrade us and injure the cause of freedom. They come in the way of consideration of the great economic problems of the masses of the people which so urgently demand attention.

Our long subjection and the World War and its aftermath have made us inherit an accumulation of vital problems, and today our people lack food and clothing and other necessaries, and we are caught in a spiral of inflation and rising prices. We cannot solve these problems suddenly, but we cannot also delay their solution. So we must plan wisely so that the burdens on the masses may grow less and their standards of living go up. We wish ill to none, but it must be clearly understood that the interests of our long-suffering masses must come first and every entrenched interest that comes in their way must yield to them. We have to change rapidly our antiquated land tenure system, and we have also to promote industrialization on a large and balanced scale, so as to add to the wealth of the country, and thus to the national dividend which can be equitably distributed.

Production today is the first priority, and every attempt to hamper or lessen production is injuring the nation, and more especially harmful to our labouring masses. But production by itself is not enough, for this may lead to an even greater concentration of wealth in a few hands, which comes in the way of progress and which, in the context of today, produces instability and conflict. Therefore, fair and equitable distribution is essential for any solution of the problem.

The Government of India have in hand at present several vast schemes for developing river valleys by controlling the flow of rivers, building dams and reservoirs and irrigation works and developing hydro-electric power. These will lead to greater food production and to the growth of industry and to all-round development. These schemes are thus basic to all planning and we intend to complete them as rapidly as possible so that the masses may profit.

All this requires peaceful conditions and the co-operation of all concerned, and hard and continuous work. Let us then address ourselves to these great and worthy tasks and forget our mutual wrangling and conflicts. There is a time for quarrelling and there is a time for co-operative endeavour. There is a time for work and there is a time for play. Today, there is no time for quarrelling or overmuch play, unless we prove false to our country and our people. Today, we must co-operate with one another and work together, and work with right goodwill.

Nehru's Legacy

By Michael Brecher

Jawaharlal Nehru, India's first prime minister, made crucial contributions to India's independence struggle and to the formation and character of the new republic. According to biographer Michael Brecher, Nehru's greatest achievements were in establishing an enduring parliamentary democracy, an independent judiciary, and the planning machinery to promote economic growth and industrial development in India. Nehru's record in international affairs was impressive, and he was a highly respected mediator in world conflicts. In socioeconomic reform, however, Nehru's achievements fell short of his goals, and his failure to resolve the dispute over Kashmir continues to plague Indo-Pakistan relations today.

[In the struggle for Indian independence, Nehru] was the indispensable link between Gandhi's traditionalism and the modern outlook of the new intelligentsia whom he mobilized to active service in the Congress cause. He was, too, the voice—and conscience—of the Indian nationalist movement in the conflict of the 1930s and beyond between liberal and progressive forces, on the one hand, and the Nazi-Fascist alliance, on the other. As the leader of the left-nationalists—within and outside Congress—he was . . . the hope for land reform among India's peasants, awakened by Gandhi but eager for material change after centuries of oppression by an entrenched landed gentry. He was, as well, the catalyst to pre-independence thought about economic planning, through the National Planning Committee of the Congress in 1938–39. Among the nationalist leaders, he was the most committed to a political system based upon universal participation in the political process through free elections at all levels of government. And in that system he was determined to enshrine the array of individual rights of classic liberalism. Through these roles Nehru made a crucial contribution, second only to Gandhi, to the attainment of independence. No less important, they created the foundations of the Republic of India.

Political Legacy

Nehru's legacy was even more striking in the domain of political institutions. While others, notably Ambedkar, drafted the new, impressive Constitution of the Republic, cumbersome and complex as it is, Nehru profoundly influenced its philosophy and thrust in the deliberations of the Constituent Assembly.

More important, the Indian National Congress, transformed by Gandhi into a mass party from 1920 to 1947, became, in the Nehru era, the primary instrument of political stability, national unity and institutional continuity. From 1951, when, in the aftermath of Patel's death, Nehru achieved effective control of the party machine, until 1964, he shaped the Congress to win all national and most state elections and to mobilize mass support for the new modernizing policies of economic planning, industrialization, limited land reform and social change, the reorganization of the states along linguistic lines, and the enlargement of the domain of science, through the creation of advanced institutes of technology and a critical mass of scientists in atomic energy and related fields. Congress *Raj* continued for twenty-five years after his death, following a brief interlude of opposition (1977–80), though its image was tarnished by his daughter's experiment in authoritarian rule (1975–77) and the decline of values, efficiency, elan and achievements under his grandson's tenure in the late 1980s. . . .

An independent judiciary, too, was fostered by Nehru. And the basic freedoms of a modern democratic society—of speech, faith, assembly, organization, etc.—were, in large measure, protected by the Indian courts, except in the days of the 'Emergency' (1975–77). Certainly they had a high value in the Nehru era, though even then the implementation of individual rights was not without blemish. There was, too, frequent resort to 'President's Rule' by the Centre over a State, sometimes for reasons other than good government; and this occurred under Nehru, as well as under his successors.

Commitment to Democracy

Overall, the record of parliamentary democracy in India since 1947 has been impressive, except for the brief lapse of the 'Emergency,' when Nehru's daughter betrayed his trust by trampling on one of his highest values. (Even in the darkest days of India's China debacle in November 1962 Nehru did not undermine the authority of Parliament; on the contrary, he used it to mobilize national resistance when India's territorial integrity was in peril.)

It is true that the political institutions of the Republic of India had deep roots in the British Raj, certainly since the Reforms of 1919. But that legacy was near-universal among British colonies, from neighbouring Pakistan to distant Guyana, from nearby Burma to far-off Rhodesia. And in most of the new states which emerged from British rule democracy faltered or languished—or was replaced for lengthy periods by an authoritarian regime, military or civilian. India was the great exception, certainly the most notable case of almost unbroken, genuine democracy in the post-colonial Third World.

While many factors help to explain this achievement, Nehru's

Nehru Failed Us

In the following excerpt from India Unbound, *published in 2002, author Gurcharan Das argues that Nehru's policies failed his people.*

Nehru was our chief modernizer. His elegant autobiography and his unique interpretation of India's past testified to his faith. For the first seventeen years of free India, he got the chance of a lifetime to practice these ideas and to transform India. He called his approach "a third way, which takes the best from all existing systems—the Russian, the American, and others—and seeks to create something suited to one's history and philosophy." The third way tried to combine the growth of capitalism with the equity of socialism without the violence of communism. In the end, the third way failed. Even before Nehru died in 1964, we had begun to despair. We were getting neither the dynamic growth of capitalism nor the equity of socialism. We were not making significant impact on mass poverty. We began to wonder whether India could modernize without a violent communist revolution. A modest growth in income was being virtually neutralized by a demographic explosion as population

commitment to free elections, parliamentary control over the executive, an independent judiciary, and individual rights was crucial to the flourishing of democracy, despite periodic crises and wars, economic dislocations, and ethnic, religious, regional and caste strife during the Nehru era and after. Not that he was unaware of an authoritarian strain in his personality:

> "Men like Jawaharlal . . . are unsafe in a democracy," he wrote about himself anonymously in 1937. "He calls himself a democrat and a socialist, and no doubt he does so in all earnestness . . . but a little twist and he might turn into a dictator. . . . he has all the makings of a dictator in him—vast popularity, a strong will, energy, pride . . . and with all his love of the crowd, an intolerance of others and a certain contempt for the weak and

---

growth began to rise from 1 percent in the first half century to 2.5 percent. Corruption had begun to grow and was becoming ubiquitous, and discipline in public life was plummeting. Reality had begun to catch up and facts began to diverge from our modernist ideals.

Nehru may have been a great modernizer, but he was a poor manager. He had no patience for organization, implementation, and detail. More than policies, it was their administration that failed us. It was all very well to proclaim the ideas of the French Revolution, but it was apparent to everyone that "liberty" was deteriorating into indiscipline, an all-powerful bureaucrat-political class was rising in the name of "equality" for the poor, and "fraternity" existed mainly between the giver and taker of bribes. The unions, especially in the public sector, were becoming invincible, and it was increasingly difficult to administer the country. . . . If care had been taken to monitor performance, periodically assess the impact of policies, remove roadblocks to effectiveness—all the things that a good manager does in the course of a working day—things might have been different.

Gurcharan Das, *India Unbound*. New York: Alfred A. Knopf, 2001, p. 295.

> inefficient. . . . His overwhelming desire to get things done . . . will hardly brook for long the slow processes of democracy."

Perhaps because of this self-insight or a belief that others so perceived him, perhaps because he sensed that democracy was a delicate plant that needed to be nourished, he did so throughout his tenure as Prime Minister. Even after the deterioration in his health, from 1961 onwards, and especially after 1963, he displayed his unswerving respect for Parliament by being actively present at least for the Question Period whenever possible. And, despite the comfortable Congress majority in both Houses, he listened to the views expressed by Opposition MPs: it was a conscious attempt to make the legislative process by elected members and the institution of Parliament sacrosanct. Although no political system is invulnerable, the judgment from the perspective of the centenary must be that Nehru's efforts to enshrine parliamentary democracy in India were exceptionally successful.

Economic Development

In the domain of economic development Nehru's legacy was no less enduring. It was he who shaped the model for industry, science and technology, on the basis of India's reality at the time of independence—mass poverty, underdevelopment and military weakness, along with India's potential for great power status. The goals were, therefore, higher living standards and rapid industrialization. As Nayar observed:

> Quite dramatically in contrast to Gandhi, Nehru stood for an industrial society, a strong central government, economic planning and socialism, with an accompanying distrust of private business, aversion to capitalism and abhorrence of the profit motive together with emphatic support for an expanding public sector. For Nehru socialism encompassed all that was good and desirable.

Moreover, Nehru was acutely conscious of the link between economic strategy, especially the creation of a heavy industry base, and the ensuring of political independence. Time and time again he declared: ". . . it is essential for our strength, for our military strength . . . to have an industrial base. . . . I say you cannot even remain free in India without an industrial base."

The entire thrust of economic planning in India must be credited to Nehru, for he presided over and infused the first three five-year plans from 1951 to 1965. While Indian planning changed direction and its centrality declined under his successors, the Nehru-instilled idea of planning as essential to economic growth and economic independence remained a permanent feature of India's public policy throughout the twenty-five years since his death. And the achievement of the decade of planning under Nehru was impressive: an annual growth rate in industrial production of 7% during the Second Plan, 42% from 1956 to 1960, and almost 8% annually in the Third Plan.

Closely related was Nehru's successful infusion of the scientific spirit into the consciousness of India's elites. His own belief in the importance of science dates to his Cambridge student period. And from the mid-thirties onward he urged his Congress colleagues and others to recognize the central role of science in modernization. In this he was assisted, during the years of independence, by a trio of distinguished Indian scientists—S.S. Bhatnagar, a chemist, H.J. Bhabha, a nuclear physicist, and P.C. Mahalonobis, a statistician. From their combined efforts India was to develop one of the largest reservoirs of qualified scientists and engineers in the world, a critical component in the continuing surge to economic development.

Socio-Economic and Political Shortcomings

There were, of course, serious shortcomings in the socio-economic domain: despite his ideological and emotional commitment to egalitarianism, basic land reform and communal harmony, performance did not always measure up to aspiration. The first was a chimera, far beyond the capacity of any democratic leader in the short time allotted to a Prime Minister of India confronting the cumulative legacy and hard shell of structural inequality in Indian society. Moreover, Nehru's failure to achieve the goal of a transformation in agrarian relations is not surprising: this was foredoomed by his higher commitment to non-violent, democratic means to achieve social and economic change. Nothing short of drastic, sustained authoritarian methods, including mass arrests, executions and exile, as practiced by Stalin in the thirties and Mao in the fifties, could have attained Nehru's goals in this domain—and he placed a higher value on consensual means than on revolutionary ends. Thus his persistent verbal assault on an encrusted, antiquated and entrenched system of land relations, with tens of millions of landless labourers, did not lead to substantive land reform in the Nehru era, a fate shared by Egyptian peasants in Nasser's Egypt in the fifties and sixties and, indeed, in most Third World states after independence. A revolutionary leader might have accomplished this in India, as Stalin and Mao did in the Soviet Union and China—but at an enormous price in terms of curtailed, in fact, extinguished individual freedom and civil rights. *Nehru was not prepared to pay that price: Gandhi's admonition on means and ends held sway.* For Nehru was a reformer, not a revolutionary leader.

In terms of the Nehru legacy, this failure was even more glaring because none of his successors—Shastri, Indira Gandhi, Morarji Desai, Rajiv Gandhi—placed land reform or the broader social goal of egalitarianism high on their political agenda, though Nehru's daughter paid lip service to these ideals, in her populist election slogan, 'remove poverty, remove unemployment;' and her son, Rajiv, revived the slogan in 1988. Thus India's system of agrarian relations is no more progressive twenty-five years after Nehru's death than it was in 1964, and very little more so than in the days of the British *Raj*.

There were political shortcomings, too, with a continuing legacy to the present: Nehru's failure to solve the persistent Punjab problem at the time of states reorganization in the mid-fifties and beyond, in order to satisfy Sikh aspirations without undermining the territorial integrity of India; the inability to meet the demands of tribal minorities on India's peripheries, in Nagaland, Tripura, and elsewhere; and a compromise over the national language issue which satisfied neither Hindi nor non-Hindi advocates. However, this negative legacy was hardly of the order of the positive Nehru legacy in the political domain—national unity amidst regional fissures, political stability, and sustained economic growth.

Foreign Policy Achievements

Nehru's achievements in foreign policy were more dramatic but less enduring. As noted, he was a founding father of the Non-Aligned Movement, through his pivotal role at the Delhi conferences in the late 1940s and Bandung in 1955. Acting through Krishna Menon, he was a visible and successful mediator in the

Korean War and the first Vietnam War. He was the role model for many leaders of new states in Asia and Africa. He was a voice of reason in support of arms control and non-violent conflict resolution throughout the Cold War, though his credibility in this respect was diminished by his use of force to expel the Portuguese from Goa in 1961 and, in the view of some, by a willingness to use force in order to assert India's claims in the territorial dispute with China. Nehru was also the catalyst to the transformation of the British Empire into a club of equals by his magnanimous decision to retain India's association with the former colonial power, even with the monarch as symbolic Head of the Commonwealth. And he was able to forge and sustain a profitable national interest relationship with the Soviet Union, reflected in military and economic assistance and, where necessary, as in the Kashmir dispute and, to a lesser extent, in the conflict with China, valuable diplomatic support. Indeed, Indo-Soviet friendship was probably the most substantive enduring legacy of Nehru's foreign policy.

Much of the halo surrounding Nehru's role in world politics vanished with the China debacle. (*Inter alia,* this shattered the *Panch Sheel,* the Five Principles of Peaceful Coexistence, which Nehru considered his most important contribution to world order.) It would have declined steadily in any event as the superpowers moved from Cold War confrontation to detente following the Cuban Missile Crisis; that is, the changing structure of world politics—from tight bipolarity to polycentrism—made India's non-alignment and Nehru's mediation role less relevant to East-West and US-Soviet relations. As that change became more visible in the post-Nehru era, non-alignment became superfluous, as the decline of the Non-Aligned Movement in the 1970s and 1980s amply demonstrates. In these respects, then, the Nehru foreign policy legacy did not endure.

International Conflicts

Much more damaging to Nehru's record in foreign affairs than this systemically-generated decline in India's stature and role in world politics was Nehru's failure to solve major territorial conflicts with India's most important neighbours. The Kashmir dispute, trigger to two Indo-Pakistani wars (1947–48, 1965–66), was a thorn for Nehru throughout his 17 years in power and caused more harsh criticism of his behaviour in foreign policy from friend and foe than any other single issue. His intense effort to find a solution, in the final months of his life, suggests that he too was unhappily aware of this negative legacy to his successors, none of whom, parenthetically, has moved the dispute closer to a settlement. Nehru alone was not responsible for the Kashmir impasse. Pakistani leaders, military and civilian, and Indian leaders since 1964 share the blame and demonstrate that the Kashmir dispute is not easily resolved. Nevertheless, great leaders are expected to rise above parochial interests and find a way through the morass; Nehru did not.

The India-China conflict is even more complex. China's leadership, as well as Nehru's senior colleagues, Pandit Pant and Morarji Desai, imposed severe restraints on his freedom of action, at the Delhi summit in April 1960 and after. Some scholars have claimed to find evidence that Nehru failed the test of leadership in this case by misperceiving China's intentions and capabilities, as well as its objectives in that conflict. Others have been more generous in their interpretation of perceptions and behaviour. Whichever view is correct, there appears to have been a basis for compromise at the Nehru-Chou summit in 1960: if accepted in principle, India and Nehru would have been spared a humiliating defeat on the battlefield in 1962, and Nehru's successors would have been freed from the danger of a hostile China ever-ready to take advantage of India's external problems, as it tried to do in the India-Pakistan wars of 1965–66 (over Kashmir) and 1971 (over Bangladesh). Nehru's inability to initiate or accept a compromise settlement of the border dispute with China profoundly undermined his image in India and the world, then and since his death. . . .

Despite his failure to realize his vision in full, his shortcomings, and the setbacks of his twilight years, Nehru's stature as humanist and leader seems to me to have grown over time. Nor is there any evidence on the eve of his centenary to alter an appraisal written at the height of his power: "If political greatness be measured by the capacity to direct events, to rise above the crest of the waves, to guide his people, and to serve as a catalyst of progress, then Nehru surely qualifies for greatness. Almost single-handed he has endeavoured to lift his people into the twentieth century. He is, indeed, India's nation-builder."

The Irony of Indira Gandhi's Rule

By James Manor

After a short interim period following Nehru's death, his daughter, Indira Gandhi, became prime minister and ruled India from 1967 to 1977 and 1980 to 1984. In the following selection, political scientist James Manor argues that despite Indira Gandhi's rhetoric for democracy, freedom, and equality, her rule was marked by autocratic excesses. In her efforts to maintain her position of power, she destroyed the democratic workings of the Congress Party. The most notorious of her attempts to centralize power came in 1975, when Mrs. Gandhi declared a 19-month state of emergency to root out dissidents within her own party. According to Manor, her heavy-handed measures produced results diametrically opposed to her intentions. Manor concludes that compared to her predecessors M.K. Gandhi and Nehru, who were alert to the undesirable consequences of their actions and could respond accordingly, Indira Gandhi was blind to the impact of her measures and thus had a largely negative impact on the country.

In 1967, within a few months of assuming the leadership, Mrs. Gandhi led the Congress party into India's fourth general election. The results were embarrassing. The party retained control of Parliament but with a much-reduced majority, and in a more serious development, it failed to gain legislative majorities in eight states. As the central figure in the failed election campaign, she suddenly found herself vulnerable. She concluded that if she followed routine patterns of Nehruvian leadership, her future and that of her party might be in grave jeopardy. If Congress remained a rather decentralized organization with major powers in the hands of regional bosses, they might eventually treat her as a scapegoat for the losses of 1967 and depose her. If she adhered to routine Congress election

James Manor, "Innovative Leadership in Modern India: M.K. Gandhi, Nehru and I. Gandhi," *Innovative Leaders in International Politics*, edited by Gabriel Sheffer. New York: State University of New York Press, 1993.

strategies that mainly sought support from dominant landed groups, and that offered voters only vague centrist policies with some empty references to "socialism," the growing impatience of poorer groups—which had begun to show itself in the 1967 election results—might eventually sweep Congress from power.

Mrs. Gandhi therefore began to make unprecedented use of progressive rhetoric, of calls for a redistribution of resources and for an end to unjustified privileges and inequalities. She implied that powerful regional barons in her party were stodgy conservatives and defenders of injustice, and then in 1969 she forced a split in the Congress party. She advertised this as an effort to drive out the corrupt and reactionary bosses in order to make Congress a party of the democratic left that appealed not to the totality of India's interest groups but to a poorer majority of voters who had once been docile and underinformed, but who were now increasingly aware and assertive. The split, the leftward tilt, and the new social base that she claimed to seek all represented significant departures from the old routine.

Bold Innovations

A careful examination of the lists of politicians that stayed with her and left her at the time of the split indicates that factional cleavages counted for far more than ideology in their decisions. But Mrs. Gandhi continued to stress the latter by enacting modestly reformist measures and by adopting the populist slogan *Garibi Hatao* ("Abolish poverty"). Because she had seized the initiative so dramatically, because her Congress party for the first time faced genuinely threatening opposition—from the new Congress party, formed by those with whom she had split in 1969—and because she had suspended intraparty democracy, power was for the time being at least radically centralized in the leader's hands. In what seemed an attempt to make her Congress into a genuine force for change, she assumed the role of one-woman vanguard in a manner distinctly reminiscent of M.K. Gandhi's role as crisis leader during civil-disobedience campaigns before independence.

In 1971, Mrs. Gandhi continued to play the audacious innovator by calling a surprise general election a year before it was due—another "first" for India. Her Congress party won a huge majority, for three main reasons. First, Mrs. Gandhi was able to gain votes both from those who sought continuity—since she was the incumbent prime minister and the heir to Nehru's legacy—and from poorer groups and others who sought change. Second, and despite her reformist rhetoric, her Congress party contained enough leaders from landed groups to continue to draw heavy backing from them. Finally, her party had a formidable array of talented machine politicians, so that in most states her organization was at least the equal of the opposition.

Once the landslide had been achieved, Mrs. Gandhi produced two further surprises, both of which led her into difficulty. She first failed to follow her promises of energetic reform with tangible programs. This created resentment among many whom she had mobilized in 1971, and by 1974 it helped to fuel protests against her. She also failed to resume the flow of political resources to her party, whose role in her 1971 victory she disregarded. Nor did she abandon her centralizing mode of crisis leadership within the Congress party, even though her landslide appeared to bring the crisis to an end. Intraparty democracy and accommodations with powerful regional and subregional leaders and groups—central elements of the routines of Congress under Gandhi and Nehru—were not restored.

In ways that are too complex to explain here, she used her enormous prestige to begin a drive for deinstitutionalization and personal dominance—within both the party and the formal institutions of state—that was the main theme in her career until her death in 1984. This caused deep dismay within the ranks of Congress, so that when protests, state-level election reverses, and legal troubles rendered her vulnerable in mid-1975, potent forces in her own party tried to force her out of power. To save herself in the face of what was very much a personal and not a national crisis, she brought in a state of emergency.

State of Emergency

It lasted for nineteen months and bore such an uncanny resemblance to the autocratic mode of crisis leadership and governance employed by the British that one historian has described it as "the last emergency of the Raj." The huge numbers of detentions without trial, the suspension of habeas corpus and other fundamental rights, the control of the press, and the like all mirrored draconian British measures to deal with [M.K. Gandhi's] *satyagraha*, and so did the manner in which the security forces and bureaucracy were mobilized to conduct this exercise. In several respects, however, Mrs. Gandhi's form of crisis governance went further than that which was seen in the late British period. A constitutional amendment—repealed under a later government—made it illegal, even when a state of emergency was not in force, to criticize the prime minister. Torture was used and in one state, police mounted a campaign of systematic murder against middle-level cadres of a Marxist party. No British regime ever allowed a mentally unbalanced person such as Mrs. Gandhi's ne'er-do-well son Sanjay a major policy-making role. His massive campaign of forced vasectomies left large areas of India terrorized and incensed, and set legitimate birth control efforts back for a generation or more.

Indira Gandhi's abandonment of intraparty democracy converted Congress into an organization of yes-men and destroyed a once formidable information-gathering instrument. She thought that this departure from the routine modes of the Nehru era would strengthen her hand, but instead it weakened her. In early 1977, believing inevitable but false reports from her party that the Emergency was hugely popular, she called for a general election. She was buried by a landslide vote in favor of a hastily assembled and variegated coalition of opposition groups. Its internal contradictions tore it apart after two and a half years of incompetent government, and a negative vote against it by a still more awakened and impatient electorate returned Mrs. Gandhi to power in the first week of 1980.

Last Term in Office

Her last premiership was marked by a resumption of efforts to centralize power and undermine the corporate substance of formal institutions and of her party (which was again denied the resources it needed to cultivate popular support) in the interests of personal and now dynastic rule. She worked relentlessly to secure the succession first of her wayward son Sanjay and, after his death, of her sane son, Rajiv. Loyalty to the leader and her heir was the dominant criterion governing political advancement, and although most of the autocratic excesses of the Emergency were not revived, this led to some bizarre results.

Consider just two examples. First, large numbers of "loyalists" who were also convicted criminals were admitted into the Congress party. Their influence varied greatly from state to state, but in India's largest state, Uttar Pradesh, 155 Congress members of the legislature—a solid majority of the party's delegation—were ex-convicts. Second, in her determination to insert a loyalist into the Indian presidency—since in a parliamentary or succession crisis, it is the president who decides what to do—Mrs. Gandhi called her own judgment and the presidency itself into disrepute. In 1982, she engineered the election of her home minister who, only a few weeks earlier, had commended the achievements of Adolf Hitler to the Indian Parliament. In Nehru's time, this would have discredited the minister and he would have been dismissed immediately. In 1982, it discredited him but—by the inverted logic that Indira Gandhi was using—it also earned him promotion to the highest office in the land since by raising him up from such abjection, she could be sure of his future loyalty. (Ironically, however, he would become a major problem for her son.)

Mrs. Gandhi also sought to increase her power at the expense of state-level governments and units of the Congress party. She thought that the accommodative approach that had been routine in Nehru's time had allowed state-level leaders to acquire too much power and had permitted the natural heterogeneity of India's states to get out of hand. Her efforts to rule more assertively and to homogenize the varied states produced ironic results. Two examples will illustrate the point.

In 1982, a political analyst traveled to two Indian states, both of which were ruled by the Congress party. They were being run in diametrically opposite ways. In one, British-style bureaucratic raj prevailed since the chief minister (the head) of the state government had so drastically centralized power and corruption in his own hands that elected legislators and even his ministers could not influence civil servants who took orders directly and only from the top. In the other state, bureaucrats were routinely harassed, publicly abused, and forced to commit illegal acts by Congress legislators who had a blank check from *their* chief minister to enrich themselves by whatever means they chose. The analyst asked a general secretary in the national headquarters of the Congress party whether this was not a serious inconsistency under Mrs. Gandhi's supposedly homogenizing rule. He agreed, but when asked why the prime minister did not act to correct the problem he said that she did not know of it. It then emerged that her habit of firing people who brought her unwelcome tidings prevented her from hearing of this and many other serious problems. Thus, her mode of centralizing had actually weakened her

Indira Gandhi Defends Her Emergency Measures

Pupul Jayakar, friend and confidante of Indira Gandhi, was Mrs. Gandhi's chosen biographer. In the following extract from Jayakar's book, the author talks about how she first learned of the 1975 declaration of a state of emergency and records Gandhi's memo to her justifying her decision. Gandhi's lack of awareness of the impact of these measures on popular opinion is clear from this document.

I arrived in New York on June 25, [1975]. Early the morning of the twenty-sixth, Dorothy Norman, a mutual friend at whose home I was staying, woke me to tell me that she had just heard that Indira had arrested a vast number of Opposition leaders.

People started telephoning to ask whether a civil war had broken out in India. . . . I phoned India's Ambassador in Washington; he too had no information. So I decided to phone Indira. I was told that it would be impossible to reach her, but to my surprise, in five minutes she was on the line. I asked her what had happened. I also told her of the rumors and the reports of civil war. She could feel from the tone of my voice that I was greatly disturbed, and said, "Don't be anxious, Pupul, no civil war has been declared. It is true I have imposed Emergency and a number of Opposition leaders have been arrested, including Jayaprakash Narayan and Morarji Desai. Jayaprakash addressed a meeting where he appealed to the army and police not to obey the orders of Government." I could sense that she was very tense. She said, "No Government can tolerate this." I told her of the atmosphere in New York. I did not know then that censorship was total. She said she would immediately dictate a note and send it to me so that I could reply to any queries made to me. By the next day a note reached me under the signature of N.K. Seshan, her Private Secretary, "as dictated for Pupul Jayakar by Prime Minister."

Message from Prime Minister:

- Atmosphere of violence was increasing. Opposition parties had planned a program of disruption, bandhs, gherao, etc. from twenty-ninth of this month. Jayaprakash especially once again strongly incited industrial workers, police and armed forces not to obey orders. [Extremist groups] had plans to disrupt communications and transport and tamper with municipal services. . . . I doubt if any government would have tolerated such movements to grow to the extent which we have. Campaign of hate and calumny had become hysterical and the objective of the Opposition was to bring the Central Government to standstill and to create anarchy. As you know, the newspapers were deliberately provocative, encouraging such elements. It became necessary to prevent disruptive activities. Therefore Emergency has been declared under the provision of our Constitution.
- The number of persons arrested is about nine hundred. About two-thirds of them are anti-social elements and one-third are political, most of them are left or right extremists whose ideology is violence and who, although not believing in democracy, are taking advantage of democratic freedom for their own purposes. Political leaders are not in jail but kept under detention, comfortably in houses.
- General public reaction is good; most people saying that such measures should have been taken earlier. There is tranquillity all over the country. . . .
- You know what has been happening in Parliament and outside. Freedom was being misinterpreted as license by a majority and democracy was being derailed. Our measures are intended to enable a return to normal democratic functioning.
- Delay in giving news is due to suddenness of events and to necessity of legal and administrative arrangements. Although this has caused some confusion it has also contributed to the peaceful atmosphere.

Pupul Jayakar, *Indira Gandhi: An Intimate Biography*. New York: Pantheon Books, 1992, pp. 202–203.

by cutting her off from lower levels in the system, and it allowed the various states to be more, not less heterogeneous—the opposite of her intentions. However limited Nehru's influence at the state level may have been, his accommodative routine leadership gained him far more leverage than Mrs. Gandhi had.

Our second example concerns her approach to state governments controlled by opposition parties. In 1983, Congress was defeated for the first time in the major southern state of Andhra Pradesh by a new party led by an aging film star, N.T. Rama Rao (he was known as NTR). He proved an inaccessible, eccentric, and incompetent chief minister. His legislators and civil servants rarely saw him since he was available to visitors only between four and six o'clock in the *morning.* He made next to no political resources available to his legislators, so that they had no way to respond to constituents' needs. As one of them told this writer, "Ours is a party of heroes and zeroes, and the number of heroes is one." By mid-1984, most legislators were close to open revolt against NTR, and given time, they would have rebelled. Mrs. Gandhi, however, felt unable to wait. Her aggressively centralist approach had already led her into unconstitutional acts and systematic campaigns of bribery in attempts to topple two other opposition-run state governments. In August 1984, she used both means to engineer the premature defection of a large number of NTR's legislators and the imposition of a new chief minister amenable to Congress. She moved too soon, however, to ensure enough defections and NTR kept his majority, mounted a huge protest campaign, and was swept back into office a month later on a massive wave of sympathy. Instead of destroying him, Mrs. Gandhi had thrown him a lifeline.

Central Irony

Thus . . . Mrs. Gandhi's career was marked by irony. Her drive to centralize power and to homogenize India left her weakened and the nation less well integrated, as the natural heterogeneity of the states asserted itself. More devastatingly ironic was the outcome of her use, after mid-1982, of Hindu chauvinism and fears of religious minorities. This was intended to sustain her in power at the election due in early 1985, but instead she lost her life to Sikh extremists whom she had actively encouraged at an earlier stage in an attempt to give the Hindu majority something to be anxious about.

Mrs. Gandhi's overriding aims in foreign policy, which brought numerous innovations in their train, were to maximize Indian power and to make forceful use of it. During her first premiership (1967–1977), détente between the U.S. and the USSR made the world a less dangerously polarized place, so that there was less need for nonaligned nations to serve as intermediaries between the major power blocs. But her deemphasis of nonalignment in Indian foreign policy, in favor of a 1971 treaty of friendship and cooperation with the Soviets and a pro-Moscow posture thereafter, had less to do with détente than with her eagerness to acquire greater international muscle. She viewed her father's delight in the more idealistic elements of nonalignment as dangerously naive, since it blinded him to the need to prepare India militarily for the inevitable perfidy of the likes of China. The Chinese intrusion in 1962 had severely undermined the political power and personal equanimity of Nehru. His daughter was as fiercely determined to avoid a recurrence of such an embarrassment as she was to cut down regional barons in domestic politics. This did not of course prevent her from making use of Nehruvian moralism or of India's prominent place in the Nonaligned Movement to advance the nation's interests (although amid the drive for realpolitik, such rhetoric seemed hypocritical to many). But her basic aims were to make India both a major force in the second rank of world powers alongside Britain, France, and China, and the dominant power within its own region, South Asia.

To that end, military spending was increased, the new relationship with the Soviets was cultivated, an aircraft carrier was purchased, and a "peaceful nuclear device" was detonated in 1974. Her greatest moment in what some have seen as a Gaullist phase in Indian foreign policy arose in late 1971 when Bengali resistance to a brutish and predominantly Punjabi military regime in East Pakistan gave India the opportunity to dismember its principal adversary. Mrs. Gandhi sent Indian-army regulars in mufti into East Pakistan to bolster the armed insurgency and, when it became clear that the regime was tottering, Indian forces undertook a full-scale, open intervention to bring into being the new state of Bangladesh. Since then, India has been a vigorous force in the affairs of South Asia, but its neighbors' complaints that they have occasionally been bullied owe as much to their own extravagant anxieties—particularly those of Sri Lanka—as to heavy-handed doings from New Delhi.

Mrs. Gandhi had a virtually free hand to make these foreign

policy innovations. This was particularly true after she achieved clear ascendancy in her party in 1969, but even before that her rivals had regarded foreign affairs as a helpful distraction that might keep her from meddling in domestic politics. Her innovations also won wide acceptance, partly because they were advertised as an embellishment of rather than a departure from Nehru's approach, and partly because they made considerable sense, given India's situation.

During her last premiership (1980–1984), when she largely abandoned new domestic programs for the betterment of society, and when galloping corruption in her party deprived most existing programs of funds, foreign policy and foreign ties provided a number of "spectaculars" that she offered as a substitute. Among these were the Commonwealth Heads of Government Meeting, separate visits by the Queen and Prince Charles, the Asian Games, the flight of an Indian cosmonaut in a Soviet capsule, and the conference of the Nonaligned Movement in New Delhi. In mid-1984, amid doubts about reelection chances at the forthcoming election, Rajiv Gandhi spoke openly about the possibility of a modest war with Pakistan. Many regarded this as a preparation for the ultimate election stunt, again using foreign affairs to compensate for domestic inertia. All such talk ceased, however, once the murder of Indira Gandhi on October 31 provided her son and her party with the certainty of an election landslide eight weeks later.

Indira Gandhi was much less effective than she thought she was at undermining the old political routines and the substance of political institutions. Some of them, especially her party, are so severely decayed as to be beyond reviving. . . . But she did not leave behind an entirely barren landscape. Indeed—to mention a further irony—one result of her loss of contact with and influence over state-level politics was the emergence within Indian states of governments that revived the old routines of the Nehru years and turned them to reformist, redistributive purposes. Some of these governments were headed by opposition leaders and some by Congressmen who were what she failed to become after her progressive posturing in 1971. . . .

A Comparative Viewpoint

Mrs. Gandhi inherited [an array of democratic institutions]. And yet she felt herself confined and threatened by them. She also took power at a time when the increasing sophistication and impatience of the mass electorate was becoming apparent. She therefore set about undermining the strength of institutions—cautiously and selectively at first, but aggressively and more generally later. She also adopted postures and slogans that would yield broad popular mobilization—at first stressing radical promises to uplift the poor, but then emphasizing competence and law and order in 1980, and the parochialism of the Hindu right after mid-1982.

All three leaders [M.K. Gandhi, Nehru, and Mrs. Gandhi] sought to acquire and then to retain power for themselves, but Gandhi and Nehru were intensely conscious of the importance of self-restraint in selecting the means of achieving this. Mrs. Gandhi's drive for personal dominance was far more unrestrained. This explains her ability to move from radical leftish postures in the early 1970s to the far right a few years later. Virtually any means were admissible.

The arresting irony in all of this was that her lack of restraint in the pursuit of power—seen most crucially in her willingness to destroy institutions—left her far less powerful than her two more cautious predecessors had been, or than she herself might otherwise have been.

Ironies, of course, attend the career of every political leader—including . . . those of Gandhi and Nehru. But in this, they differed from Mrs. Gandhi in one important respect. Both of them were aware that their efforts would produce certain incongruous results. The antistatist Gandhi built up a Congress organization that later took over and strengthened existing state structures. Nehru, a would-be reformer, created a routine mode of politics that enhanced the strength of prosperous groups. But both Gandhi and Nehru recognized such ironies and accepted them as inevitable. Mrs. Gandhi was unaware of the ironies that attended her actions. She was not only less restrained than her predecessors but less perceptive. So where their innovations were measured and thus largely creative, hers tended to be undertaken blindly, and this made them overwhelmingly destructive.

India Under Rao: 1991 to 1996

By Ranbir Vohra

According to Indian historian Ranbir Vohra, when Narasimha Rao became India's prime minister in 1991 he inherited complex political, social, communal, and particularly economic problems. In a bold new economic strategy, Rao departed from Gandhi's model of economic self-reliance and Nehru's socialism to launch India into an open-market capitalist economy. On the political front Rao was less successful, and resorted to some of the authoritarian tactics of Indira Gandhi. His failure to avert massive Hindu-Muslim violence, which broke out in late 1992 in connection with a dispute over a site for the construction of a mosque and Hindu temple, escalated into outbreaks of communal violence all over the country. Rao lost further credibility with accusations of crime and corruption in his administration. Amidst public disgust with political wranglings, Rao was defeated in the 1996 elections and the Congress Party lost the monopoly hold on power that it had exercised almost exclusively since 1947.

In July 1991 Narasimha Rao was sworn in as the ninth prime minister of India. No Congress prime ministers before him had ever faced as complex and difficult a set of problems. Most of these problems—associated with secessionist movements, terrorism, the Mandal Report [a controversial political initiative to help members of the historically disadvantaged castes], hardening of caste and regional identities, and the BJP [a political party that stands for the greatness of Hindu culture]—had produced a situation of ungovernability and political instability. But the issue that took precedence over all others was that of the economy, which had hit the lowest point since independence and was in a state of collapse.

However harshly historians may condemn Rao for the handling of the other crises, they must laud him for the boldness

Ranbir Vohra, *The Making of India: A Historical Survey*. New York: M.E. Sharpe, Inc., 1997.

with which he introduced reforms that altered the direction of the Indian economy and gave it fresh impetus for growth. Rao's government, by reducing controls on the private sector, liberalizing the foreign trade regime, and opening the country to foreign direct investment and joint enterprises, practically jettisoned the Nehruvian model that had guided India's economy for forty-three years.

The New Economic Face of India

When Rao assumed power, the country was in the throes of a terrible economic crisis. The growth rate of the GDP had halved in the previous year, the wholesale price index had more than doubled, inflation was soaring, and industrial production was stagnating. In 1991 India's foreign exchange reserves had been depleted to such a degree that the Reserve Bank of India was forced to sell some of its gold stock to keep the country from defaulting on its international debt. India's fragile economy appeared to be on the verge of total collapse.

It goes to Prime Minister Rao's credit that despite his weak position in the Parliament as head of a minority government, he appointed a farsighted economist, Manmohan Singh, to introduce economic policies that many industrialists and political parties were certain to find unpopular: the industrialists, who had a monopoly on a growing, closed market, felt uneasy at the prospect of competing with better-manufactured foreign goods in an open market; and political parties, such as the socialists, the Janata, and the BJP, on principle were against foreign intervention in the national market.

Within days of being sworn in as finance minister, Manmohan Singh declared that he planned to cut government spending, devaluate the rupee (to make exports cheaper and imports dearer), deregulate the licensing system (easing controls on the private sector), expose the economy to foreign competition by opening the market to foreign investment and joint enterprises, and stop subsidizing sick public-sector industries. Singh's short-term aim was to gain a loan from the International Monetary Fund, which had insisted that India take such actions to gain the loan; his long-term goal was to stabilize the Indian economy by reducing internal and foreign debt, and to integrate India with the global economy. By adopting these policies, India had made a deliberate decision to move away from the Gandhian belief in self-reliance, which had resulted in isolationism, and Nehruvian socialism, which had resulted in economic stagnation and low productivity.

Positive Results

Singh's bold initiatives surprised the world, but many doubted the possibility of a minority government's carrying out programs that did not find favor with vested interests in the public and the private sectors in India. However, even though the path chosen was not easy, and the execution of the reform policies had to be periodically tempered to suit changing political needs, the critics by and large were silenced by the very positive results that followed in the wake of the reforms. Within a year India's foreign exchange reserves, which had touched a low of $1 billion (a two week's import cover) in 1991, rose to $2 billion, and then to $6 billion in 1993, $9.5 billion in 1994, and $14.67 billion in 1995. The budget deficit dropped from 8.4 percent of the GNP in 1991 to 4.8 percent in 1995, while in real terms the GDP grew from 2.5 percent in 1991 to 5.5 percent in 1994–95.

The new market-friendly approach began to draw a response from foreign investors as approvals for projects involving up to 51 percent foreign equity were made automatic, and important sectors such as petroleum production, refining, and distribution, energy projects, telecommunications, and automobile manufacturing were opened to foreign companies. The response of the foreign investors was cautious in the beginning but speeded up as they realized that the reforms were there to stay. Direct foreign investment was less than $200 million a year in 1990–91. It rose to $585 million in 1992–93 and then to $4.7 billion in 1993–94. In 1995, when the United States had identified India as a "big emerging market" with a middle class of nearly 150 million, Commerce Secretary Ronald Brown visited India and within days concluded transactions worth $7 billion. The figures above, of course, indicate commitments and not the actual utilization of the moneys.

Today foreign investors from America, Japan, Germany, France, Italy, and other advanced economies, though still wary of the Indian political climate, have begun to establish their industries and businesses in India; American corporations such as IBM, McDonnell Douglas, Motorola, Texas Instruments, Ford Motor Company, Kellogg, and Pepsi-Cola, are "the second biggest foreign investors, after expatriate Indians." In 1994 even the Communist government of West Bengal revamped its industrial policy to welcome private corporations to invest in that state. As a result, West Bengal attracted $2.6 billion in domestic and foreign investments between January and August 1995, 380 percent more than in the corresponding period in 1994.

Dynamic Economic Environment

India is still a poor country and has a long way to go before it joins the ranks of industrialized nations. It has yet to eradicate poverty and illiteracy and provide clean water, proper sanitation and health facilities to millions of its citizens. Its infrastructure (power supply, roads, railway system, telephone and electronic networks) is backward and cannot handle rapid industrial growth. More important, the government has yet to dismantle the huge, money-losing public enterprises. However, what the new economic policies have done is to initiate the process of liberating India from the thralldom of suffocating bureaucratic controls. This has already created a dynamic, new social-economic environment that is perhaps best described in an article published in the *Business World* by Gurcharan Singh, a well-known playwright, novelist, columnist, and former chief executive officer of Procter & Gamble. To write this piece, Singh spent several months in 1995 traveling through India's remote villages and its bustling cities. Although several of the prominent personalities he met in his travels differed sharply in their comments, either praising Rao ("He doesn't realize it, but Narasimha Rao came out of the *Jurassic Park* in 1991 to become the biggest revolutionary in India since Gautam Buddha") or condemning him with equal vigor ("Do we really need Kellogg's corn flakes?"; "We are unleashing a culture of greed and permissiveness"), Gurcharan Singh himself was very impressed with what he witnessed in his travels:

> The defining image of my journey is 14-year old Raju in khaki half pants in Maraimalainagar village, between Madras and Pondicherry, who hustles around tables serving . . . south Indian coffee and spends the Rs 400 a month [$13] that he earns in the cafe on computer lessons. He says that he wants to grow up and run a computer company one day, just like his [U.S.] role model Bilgay [Bill Gates of Microsoft fame], the rich-

est man in the world. Raju defines a profound new mindset as social scientists call it, a new way of looking at the world, that I found again and again during my travels around India from June to September 1995. I encountered it every day, in the hopes of the young, in the way people talked, in the way they stood at street corners, in the way mothers thought about their daughters. . . .

The spirit of the age—of an India approaching the end of the 20th century—is reflected in the vast number of rags-to-riches stories. . . . [Because of reforms and prosperity in the 1980s] the middle class started to grow rapidly, but rural demand also exploded for everything from washing powders to black and white TVs. However, by far the single biggest factor in opening the floodgates of entrepreneurship is the liberalization of 1991. It has unleashed pent-up energies and created a new confidence among young people and a feeling that "they can do it." . . .

It is slowly beginning to dawn on Indian business that superior companies are built by superior people. . . . Almost every industrialist I talked to said that his biggest challenge is to find men and women of ability to manage crucial positions in his company. This is the most profound change I witnessed in the business world after the reforms. . . .

If there is one word that captures the mood of the country after the reforms, it is "confidence." Everybody I talked to, without exception, believed that their children and grand children would be better off than they had been. This was true in the slums of Bangalore, among the residents of Bartoli village in Uttar Pradesh, in middle class homes in Calcutta, among teachers, taxi drivers, shopkeepers, lawyers, politicians, painters, trade unionists, and bureaucrats across the country.

Several critics of the government feared that the reforms would make the rich richer (which they have) but not help in alleviating poverty. This, too, has been proved false. The poverty level, according to official data, fell from 25.5 percent of the population in 1987–88 to 18.9 percent in 1993–94. "In the subsequent two years GDP has exceeded 6 percent annually, and this must have reduced poverty [further]."

The Decline of the Congress Party

Prime Minister Rao was far less successful in handling the country's political problems than he was in dealing with its economic ones. Most of the political problems had emerged before he came to power, however the rise of the BJP as a contender for national power was a wholly new issue.

In dealing with these problems, Rao was handicapped not only because he headed a minority government that was constantly under attack by the opposition parties but also because Rao's uncharismatic personality and style of work encouraged Congress leaders, who had strong power bases in their own states, to put themselves forward as challengers for leadership. Rao managed to ride out the troubles and complete the entire first term of office despite predictions that he would fail. Nevertheless, his predilection for postponing decisions on crucial issues in the hope that somehow time would resolve them, his manipulation of the party to preserve his position, and his tacit acceptance of corruption reduced his effectiveness and damaged his image and that of the Congress Party.

Despite the political uncertainty that surrounded him at the time he assumed office, at the beginning of his ascendancy Rao managed to gain popular favor by appearing to establish a style of government that emphasized a conciliatory, consultative, and moderate approach. This gave Rao time to consolidate power; however, within a year he was to reveal a different face.

One of Rao's early actions concerned the Ramjanambhoomi-Babri Masjid issue (hereafter, the Temple-Mosque issue) that had begun to overshadow national politics. In September 1991, Rao managed to get a bill through Parliament that sought to return both places of worship to the status quo of August 15, 1947. The BJP government in Uttar Pradesh tried to bypass this legal hurdle by acquiring a parcel of land next to the mosque where Vishwa Hindu Parishad could build the temple, but the Supreme Court, then in the process of hearing the claims of Hindu and Muslim bodies, issued a stay for the construction of any structures on that land.

With the Ayodhya issue temporarily out of the way, Rao

turned his attention to Punjab, where by 1992 anti-insurgency operations had weakened the militant separatist movement to such a degree that Rao, against the advice of more cautious advisers, decided to risk holding elections in the state. Though all Akali parties boycotted the elections, and though the turnout was a mere 20 percent of the electorate, the elections of February 1992 brought back civil government to the state. The return of normalcy was welcomed by the majority of the people, as became evident when municipal elections later in the year saw a turnout of more than 70 percent, despite calls for boycott by several Akali factions. The days of terrorism were not quite over, but militancy had finally been crushed. Punjab had returned to the national fold. Normalcy was also brought back to Assam, where the militants, led by the United Liberation Front, had also become a spent force and were subdued by the end of 1992. Rao could do nothing, however, to reduce the state of turbulence in Kashmir, which remained the last major dark spot on the Indian political scene through the five years of Rao's tenure.

In another potentially very positive action, soon after assuming power Rao decided to bring back democracy to the Congress Party by holding intraparty elections, last held twenty years earlier. This was a massive exercise and held great promise, but the promise was never fulfilled. After the elections, it appears that Rao had second thoughts about their impact on his position within the party. Fearing that some of the members of the elected Central Working Committee, the policy-making body of the Congress, might prove too powerful to handle, Rao, in his capacity as the elected president of the party, managed to get half the committee to resign. Although the reason he gave for this rather undemocratic action was that the committee lacked representation from women, Scheduled Castes, and Scheduled Tribes, in actuality Rao was safeguarding his dominance of the party by keeping new leaders from emerging. Among those who had been pressured to resign were Sharad Pawar from Maharashtra and Arjun Singh from Madhya Pradesh, both very able and highly respected leaders of the party.

Rao's desire to dominate the party was also revealed in his refusal to establish the Congress Parliamentary Board, which took decisions on crucial legislative matters, and the Congress Central Election Committee, which made final decisions regarding candidates for elections. As a result, the party's democratic process was perverted, and Rao used the pliant Central Working Committee and the powerless Provincial Congress Committees to maintain himself in absolute power in the style of Indira Gandhi. If Rao had had any intention of ending nepotism and corruption within the party and rehabilitating the image of the moribund Congress, he would never have followed this path. Rao's maneuvers gained him the reputation of an amoral politician willing to sacrifice the party to keep himself in power. The fund of popular goodwill that he had so far earned began to dwindle.

The Ayodhya Incident

However, in immediate terms it was Ayodhya that proved to be Rao's nemesis. In July 1992, after months of relative inaction, the VHP heated up the Ayodhya issue by declaring that it had decided to go ahead and lay the foundation of the temple. Rao should have responded to this threat with resolute action, such as the dismissal of the BJP government in Uttar Pradesh and the imposition of central control over the state, or the dispatching of central forces to occupy the disputed site, as many in the Congress had advised him. But he did not do so because either action would have cost Hindu votes. Hoping that the courts would somehow relieve him from confronting the problem, Rao thought it more prudent to negotiate with the VHP for a postponement of action for three months.

The result of Rao's vacillation was that, on December 6, 1992, a mob of 300,000 fanatical volunteers (*kar seva*) of the VHP, who had tired of waiting, took matters in their own hands; in defiance of the center and the courts, but with the tacit backing of the BJP government, they stormed the mosque and demolished it within a few hours. Rao reacted to the Ayodhya incident by dismissing the BJP government in Uttar Pradesh (later, the governments in the three other states under BJP control were also dismissed), arresting some of the BJP leaders and banning five "ultracommunal" organizations, including the VHP and the RSS. Rao also made a hasty promise to build a mosque and a temple on the Ayodhya site.

None of this, however, kept the Muslims and secular-minded Hindus from blaming Rao for not having taken firm action during the preceding months when it had become obvious that a flare-up was in the making.

Nor could Rao's belated actions stop the outbreak of communal violence, the worst that India had witnessed since 1947. As many Hindus gloated over their victory and angry Muslims took to the streets to protest, religious hatred engulfed the country, spreading death and destruction through most of its major cities. Both Hindus and Muslims were killed in the riots, though it was the Muslims who suffered the most. By the end of December, over 1,000 persons had died in communal violence. Communalism was already a fact of everyday life in India, but this was a wholly new kind of communalism. It was espoused by organized parties that were openly using religion for political purposes to poison Hindu-Muslim relations at the national level.

The Ayodhya incident appalled the nation. Many believed that the country was on the verge of breaking up. Every thinking person deplored the bigotry that had led to the senseless destruction of the mosque. Liberal-minded intellectuals, particularly Westernized ones, wrung their hands in anguish because they saw secular India being taken over by militant Hindu fundamentalists. One scholar, referring to the "rottenness afflicting the Indian state," wailed that "in today's India religion is the first refuge of scoundrel politicians, patriotism the last retreat of the baffled and defeated."

The situation was actually far more complex than reflected in these responses. Though the savagery released by religion-based passions cannot be condoned, one has to look at the larger picture of post-1947 developments to comprehend the Ayodhya explosion. After Nehru, whose unrealistic notion of secularity died with him, not much effort had been made to understand the issue of nation building in a socioreligious society. Because Hinduism is *not* a religion in the sense the term is used for Judaism, Christianity and Islam—with a common scripture, creed, or rituals—the emergence of Hindu fundamentalism, per se, is impossible. However, there is a national ethos associated with Hinduism that pervades the everyday life of the majority of the people in the country. The BJP had managed to exploit this ethos temporarily to produce a broad sense of Hindu nationalism, but it was impossible for the BJP, as it soon learned, to use this ethos to create a monolithic Hindu society in a population deeply divided by caste, language, and region. The Ayodhya incident may yet provide the impetus for Indian thinkers to abandon Western models that are inapplicable to India and to produce an Indian paradigm that integrates secularism with the national ethos.

Bombay was worst hit by the riots. Hindu policemen had deliberately allowed Hindu mobs, directed by the militant Shiv Sena (Army of Shivaji, named after the Maratha hero who had defeated the Mughals and established a Hindu kingdom) to seek out and kill Muslims and loot their property. The Muslim response came on March 12, 1993, when Muslim underworld criminals in Bombay carried out seven sophisticated car-bomb explosions that damaged the stock exchange and other Bombay landmarks, killed 270 persons, and injured 1,200 in a conspiracy that led from Bombay to Pakistan and Dubai. Altogether, nearly 1,300 died in the Bombay riots and over 1,000 were wounded. The Bombay bombings revealed for the first time the extent to which organized criminal elements were being protected by crooked politicians, and it was this nexus of crime, corruption, and politics that would soon become the main target of public outcry.

To the credit of the cosmopolitan citizenry of Bombay, however, because of their universal outpouring of sympathy for the victims and their condemnation of the police, the riots did not produce long-lasting scars; in Bombay, the Muslims and Hindus more or less returned to their traditional relations based on mutual tolerance. Peace was also restored to other parts of India, though the Muslim-Hindu divide had widened in most areas. Just as the prospect of rebuilding the temple had temporarily galvanized Hindu sentiment, the destruction of the once-decrepit mosque had "become a symbol of identity for millions of Muslims." However, it is significant that in a nationwide poll carried out immediately after the Ayodhya incident, 52.6 percent of the respondents disapproved of the demolition of the mosque, and 52.9 percent felt that the BJP had broken the law. At the same time, ironically, popular opinion in all the states (except Gujarat and the four southern states) had swung in favor of the BJP at the expense of the Congress.

Rao came under much public criticism for his handling of the Ayodhya issue. His image within the party declined further when he silenced his critics in the cabinet by packing off one to become the chief minister of Maharashtra and downgrading the post of another.

Rao and Corruption

In 1993, Rao's reputation, and that of the Congress Party, suffered another setback when a broker involved in a $1.7 billion security-trading scam revealed that he had personally handed Rao a suitcase filled with 10 million rupees (over $300,000) in cash as a secret campaign donation. Rao was later exonerated by the Central Bureau of Investigation (CBI), but no one believed the CBI, a bureau under Rao's control; during his remaining years in office Rao never could overcome the general impression that he was a corrupt politician. Rao's loss of credibility gave an impetus to the Congress factions opposed to Rao to reposition themselves for a possible change in the leadership. All of this infighting and the loss of cohesiveness in the Congress encouraged the BJP to launch a *Rao-hatao* (Remove Rao) campaign.

To make matters worse, the Bofors scandal, believed to involve a $200 million payoff to Rajiv Gandhi's coterie, resurfaced in late 1993 when the Geneva Cantonal Court decided to release certain code-named bank accounts to Indian authorities. This in itself did not provide concrete proof of any wrongdoing, but the opposition made capital of the two scandals and introduced a no-confidence motion in Parliament. Rao, with 251 seats in a House of 533, barely managed to scrape through with a 265-251 vote. Rumors later suggested that he had given massive bribes to several MPs for their support.

Social Reform

Politics became further complicated when Rao undertook the sensitive task of implementing the Mandal recommendations in the form approved by the Supreme Court. In 1992, the Supreme Court had stipulated that the advanced sections of the Backward Castes, "the creamy layer," were not entitled to reservation quotas, nor were the poor among the "forward" castes, as had been recommended by Rao; that the Backward Castes were to be divided into Backward Castes (already well represented in government services) and More Backward Castes, and that only the latter should receive Mandal benefits; the quotas should apply at the time of appointment (certain categories of skilled jobs, such as medicine and engineering, were excluded from the list) and that promotions should be based on merit only. The Mandal reforms, along with reservations already in place for Scheduled Castes and Scheduled Tribes, raised the total percentage of reservations to 49.5 percent. This large-scale affirmative action plan had the potential of fracturing society even further because it politicized the lower castes and prompted them to strengthen their separate caste identities. Of course, upper-caste Hindus, about to lose their privileged status because of Mandal, found these developments distasteful.

But the Mandal reforms were the logical product of the directive principles of the Constitution and the evolving democratic system that had already witnessed a growing self-assertion of the Backward and Untouchable Castes (the Scheduled Castes) that had given themselves a new name, Dalit (Oppressed). Rao handled the complicated issue with tact and established a National Commission for the Backward Classes to oversee the reforms and handle complaints. However, since V.P. Singh and his Janata Dal had taken the lead in representing the cause of the lower castes in the Hindi heartland (which contains a third of India's population), the Congress had to scramble to regain support in this crucial area. The anti-Congress Backward Caste of Yadav's had already captured power in Bihar and Uttar Pradesh, and the new reservation system meant that they could advance their position through patronage. The Congress's attempt to exploit the frustration of the "creamy layer" of the Backward Castes in these states proved of little tactical value.

The November 1993 State Elections and Their Impact

When Rao called the elections in the three northern states where the BJP governments had been dismissed (Uttar Pradesh, Madhya Pradesh, Himachal Pradesh, and Rajasthan) and in the Metropolitan Council of Delhi in November 1993, he hoped to see his policies, particularly his attack on the BJP for having created the Ayodhya crisis, succeed in regaining ground for the Congress.

The elections brought mixed results. The Congress won in Madhya Pradesh and Himachal Pradesh; since the latter is a very small state, success there provided some psychological satisfaction but no real national gain. In the larger state of Madhya Pradesh, the Congress victory was truly impressive: the Congress tripled its pre-election assembly strength and the BJP lost over 50 percent of its seats. The Congress came to power in Madhya Pradesh with a clear majority. However, in two other states, Delhi and Rajasthan, the BJP succeeded in forming governments. The Janata Dal did poorly in all these states.

Uttar Pradesh, the home of the Temple-Mosque conflict, provided a real shock to the BJP, the Congress, and the Janata Dal.

The BJP lost 34 seats, which reduced its strength from 211 seats to 177 (total assembly seats: 425); the Congress was humiliated, and its strength reduced from 46 seats to 28; but it was V.P. Singh's Janata Dal that was totally disgraced, and its representation was decreased from 91 to 27. The shock was that Mulayam Singh Yadav's Samajwadi Party (SP) (representing the Backward Castes), in alliance with the Bahujan Samaj Party (BSP) (representing the Dalits) and with the backing of the Muslim voters, gained a combined total of 176 seats, up from 42 in the previous assembly. Though the BJP had still emerged as the biggest party, it could not form a government because none of the smaller parties was ready to support it. Yadav, heading the SP-BSP alliance supported by the minor parties and the Congress, became the chief minister. Caste politics had reached an unanticipated height.

New Political Directions

The BJP defeats gave heart to the Congress Party, but as India entered 1994 it became abundantly clear that Indian politics had advanced to a new stage. First, though the BJP and the Janata Dal (heading the National Front—Left Front coalition of centrist and left-oriented parties) had suffered setbacks, they remained viable parties and serious contenders for national power; this was particularly true of the BJP. Second, the era of the Congress single-party domination of Indian politics was over. Third, the BJP's well-defined platform of *Hindutva,* and the National Front—Left Front (NF-LF) program for "social justice for the backward and down-trodden in the country," meant that the Congress could no longer afford to be an umbrella organization that promised all things to all peoples and that it must have an issue-based program of its own. Fourth, and most important, neither the Congress nor the BJP could ignore the emergence of Backward-Caste and Lower-Caste politics. In 1994, Kanshi Ram, the dynamic leader of the Bahujan Samaj Party, traveled from state to state to create a national consciousness among the Dalits and spread the BSP network; his efforts met with considerable success.

THE HISTORY OF NATIONS

Chapter 5

Current Challenges

The Hindu Fundamentalist Movement

By the Bharatiya Janata Party

In May 1996, India's 48-year legacy of secular government ended with the victory of the Hindu fundamentalist Bharatiya Janata Party (BJP), which defeated the Indian National Congress party again in 1998 and 1999. The following description of the BJP's nationalist philosophy, known as "Hindutva," excerpted from the party's website, talks of the great Hindu awakening that is changing the face of Indian politics and society. The BJP's view of Indian history is one of an overly tolerant Hindu majority pandering to the interests of Muslim minorities. In the name of secularism, the party maintains, Muslim groups have been given preferential treatment. The BJP also asserts that India was not free at independence, but instead was subject to intellectual slavery by Western values and economic strategies. Only now under BJP authority has India been able to express with pride Hindu culture, history, and heroes, the party concludes.

The Hindu awakening of the late twentieth century will go down as one of the most monumental events in the history of the world. Never before has such demand for change come from so many people. Never before has Bharat, the ancient word for the motherland of Hindus—India, been confronted with such an impulse for change. This movement, Hindutva, is changing the very foundations of Bharat and Hindu society the world over.

Hindu society has an unquestionable and proud history of tolerance for other faiths and respect for diversity of spiritual experiences. This is reflected in the many different philosophies, religious sects, and religious leaders. The very foundation of this lies in the great Hindu heritage that is not based on any one book, teacher, or doctrine. In fact the pedestal of Hindu society stems from the great Vedic teachings Ekam Sat Viprah Bahudha Vadanti—Truth is One, Sages Call it by Many Names, and Vasudhaiva Kutumbakam—The Whole Universe is one Family. It is this philosophy which allowed the people of Hindusthan (land of the Hindus) to shelter the Jews who faced Roman persecution, the Zoroastrians who fled the Islamic sword and who are the proud Parsi community today, and the Tibetan Buddhists who today face the communist secularism: persecution of religion.

During the era of Islamic invasions, what [U.S. historian] Will Durant called the bloodiest period in the history of mankind, many Hindus gallantly resisted, knowing full well that defeat would mean a choice of economic discrimination via the jaziya tax[1] on non-Muslims, forced conversion, or death. It is no wonder that the residents of Chittor,[2] and countless other people over the length and breadth of Bharat, from present-day Afghanistan to present-day Bangladesh, thought it better to die gloriously rather than face cold-blooded slaughter. Hindus never forgot the repeated destruction of the Somnath Temple, the massacre of Buddhists at Nalanda, or the pogroms of the Mughals.

Thus, the seeds of today's Hindu Jagriti, awakening, were created the very instant that an invader threatened the fabric of Hindu society which was religious tolerance. The vibrancy of Hindu society was noticeable at all times in that despite such barbarism from the Islamic hordes of central Asia and Turkey, Hindus never played with the same rules that Muslims did. The communist and Muslim intelligentsia, led by Nehruvian ideologists who are never short of distorted history, have been unable to show that any Hindu ruler ever matched the cruelty of even a moderate Muslim ruler.

Abuse of Hindu Tolerance

It is these characteristics of Hindu society and the Muslim psyche that remain today. Hindus never lost their tolerance and willingness to change. However Muslims, led by the Islamic clergy and Islamic society's innate unwillingness to change, did not no-

1. A tax levied on the Hindu community by the Mughal emperors. 2. During the siege of Chittor in 1567, Muslim emperor Akbar slaughtered 30,000 Hindus.

tice the scars that Hindus felt from the Indian past. It is admirable that Hindus never took advantage of the debt Muslims owed Hindus for their tolerance and non-vengefulness.

In modern times, Hindu Jagriti [awakening] gained momentum when Muslims played the greatest abuse of Hindu tolerance: the demand for a separate state and the partition of India, a nation that had had a common history and culture for countless millenia. Thus, the Muslim minority voted for a separate state and the Hindus were forced to sub-divide their own land.

After partition in Pakistan, Muslim superiority was quickly asserted and the non-Muslim minorities were forced to flee due to the immense discrimination in the political and religious spheres. Again, Hindus did not respond to such an onslaught. Hindu majority India continued the Hindu ideals by remaining secular.

India even gave the Muslim minority gifts such as separate personal laws, special status to the only Muslim majority state—Kashmir, and other rights that are even unheard of in the bastion of democracy and freedom, the United States of America. Islamic law was given precedence over the national law in instances that came under Muslim personal law. The Constitution was changed when the courts . . . ruled that a secular nation must have one law, not separate religious laws. Islamic religious and educational institutions were given a policy of non-interference. The list goes on.

More painful for the Hindus was forced negation of Hindu history and factors that gave pride to Hindus. Hindu customs and traditions were mocked as remnants of a non-modern society, things that would have to go if India was to modernize like the west. The self-proclaimed guardians of India, the politicians of the Congress Party who called themselves secularists, forgot that it was the Hindu psyche that believed in secularism, it was the Hindu thought that had inspired the greatest intellectuals of the world such as Thoreau, Emerson, Tolstoy, Einstein, and others, and that it was Hindus, because there was no other land where Hindus were in a significant number to stand up in defence of Hindu society if and when the need arose, who were the most nationalistic people in India.

When Hindus realized that pseudo-secularism had reduced them to the role of an innocent bystander in the game of politics, they demanded a true secularism where every religious group would be treated the same and a government that would not take Hindu sentiments for granted. Hindutva awakened the Hindus to the new world order where nations represented the aspirations of people united in history, culture, philosophy, and heroes. Hindutva successfully took the Indian idol of Israel and made Hindus realize that their India could be just as great and could do the same for them also.

Hindu Revivalism

In a new era of global consciousness, Hindus realized that they had something to offer the world. There was something more than tolerance and universal unity. The ancient wisdom of sages through eternity also offered systems of thought, politics, music, language, dance, and education that could benefit the world.

There have been many changes in the thinking of Hindus, spearheaded over the course of a century by innumerable groups and leaders who made their own distinct contribution to Hindu society: Swami Vivekananda, Rabindranath Tagore, Gandhiji, Rashatriya Swayamsevak Sangh, Swami Chinmayananda, Maharishi Mahesh Yogi, International Society for Krishna Consciousness, Muni Susheel Kumarji, Vishwa Hindu Parishad, Bharatiya Janata Party, and others. Each in their own way increased pride in being a Hindu and simultaneously showed Hindus their greatest strengths and their worst weaknesses. This slowly shook the roots of Hindu society and prompted a rear-guard action by the ingrained interests: the old politicians, the Nehruvian intellectual community, and the appeased Muslim leadership.

The old foundation crumbled in the 1980s and 1990s when Hindus respectfully asked for the return of their most holy religious site, Ayodhya. This demand promptly put the 40-year old apparatus to work, and press releases were chunked out that spew the libelous venom which called those who represented the Hindu aspirations "militant" and fundamentalist, stigmas which had heretofore found their proper place in the movements to establish Islamic law. Hindus were humble enough to ask for the restoration of an ancient temple built on the birthplace of Rama, and destroyed by Babar, a foreign invader. The vested interests were presented with the most secular of propositions: the creation of a monument to a national hero, a legend whose fame and respect stretched out of the borders of India into southeast Asia, and even into Muslim Indonesia. A hero who existed before there was anyone in India who considered himself separate from Hindu society. The 400-year old structure at one of the holiest sites of India had been worshipped as a temple by Hindus even though the Muslim general Mir Baqi had partially built a non-functioning mosque on it. It was very important that no Muslims, except those who were appeased in Indian politics, had heard of anything called Babri Masjid before the pseudo-secularist apparatus started the next to last campaign against the rising Hindu society. It was also important that no Muslim had offered prayers at the site for over 40 years.

Hindus hid their true anger, that their most important religious site still bore the marks of a cruel slavery that occurred so very recently in the time span of Hindu history. It was naturally expected in 1947 that freedom from the political and economic

Pragmatism Dominates BJP Performance

Despite BJP rhetoric for Hindutva, according to Barbara D. Metcalf and Thomas R. Metcalf in the following excerpt from A Concise History of India, *published in 2002, since coming to office many of the goals of Hindu fundamentalism have been put aside by the BJP coalition government in the interests of pragmatism.*

Once in power the BJP party pragmatically sought to distance itself from many aspects of its earlier policies and promises. To maintain support from its coalition partners it could do no other. In the economic sphere, the BJP, for all its tradition of swadeshi [using home-grown products] found the move to liberalization irreversible. As for Hindutva, there were no steps towards building the Ayodhya temple, still under judicial scrutiny; there was no effort to move towards a Uniform Civil Code (that would replace the personal law of the minority communities); there was no action on abrogating Article 370 of the Constitution that prohibited outsiders from owning land in Kashmir. The BJP claimed to be offering 'genuine secularism', in contrast to what the

chains of Great Britain would mean that the systems and symbols that had enslaved India and caused its deterioration and poverty would be obliterated. Forty years after independence, Hindus realized that their freedom was yet to come.

So long as freedom to Jews meant that symbols of the Holocaust in Europe were condemned, so long as freedom to African-Americans meant that the symbols of racial discrimination were wiped out, and so long as freedom from imperialism to all people meant that they would have control of their own destinies, that they would have their own heros, their own stories, and their own culture, then freedom to Hindus meant that they would have to condemn the Holocaust that Muslims reaped on them, the racial discrimination that the white man brought, and the

Parivar liked to call Nehruvian 'pseudo-secularism', which meant, they insisted, that minorities were coddled and favoured.

Arguably, anti-Muslim sentiment was deflected on to the international scene where a range of issues identified Muslims as a threat surrounding India, whether in Kashmir, Bangladesh (with 'infiltrators' across the border), or the Middle East, where India dramatically reversed its tradition of Palestinian sympathy to recognize and support Israel. The decision to test nuclear weapons in May 1998 was justified as a response to China, but was understood by Pakistan, who immediately responded with their own tests, as a challenge to them. Nuclear capability was clearly intended as further assertion of India's hegemony in its region. Pakistan's inept intrusions in Kargil across the Line of Control in the spring of 1999 were widely condemned not only in India but beyond, and provoked a major crisis and loss of lives on both sides. In all these actions, [Indian prime minister Atal Bihari] Vajpayee had support far beyond his own party. Tough in relation to Muslims outside India, the party distanced itself from much in the Hindutva ideology.

Barbara D. Metcalf and Thomas R. Metcalf, *A Concise History of India.* Cambridge: Cambridge University Press, 2002, pp. 287–89.

economic imperialism that enriched Britain. Freedom for Hindus and Indians would have to mean that their heroes such as Ram, Krishna, Sivaji, the Cholas, Sankaracharya, and Tulsidas would be respected, that their own stories such as the Ramayana and the Mahabharata would be offered to humanity as examples of the brilliance of Hindu and Indian thinking, and that their own culture which included the Bhagavad Gita, the Vedas, the temples, the gods and goddesses, the art, the music, and the contributions in various fields, would be respected. Freedom meant that as the shackles of imperial dominance were lifted, the newly freed people would not simply absorb foreign ideas, they would share their own as well.

Indians as Intellectual Slaves

In India, something went wrong. The freedom from Britain was supposed to result in a two-way thinking that meant that non-Indian ideas would be accepted and that Indian ideas would be presented to the world. So long as the part of India giving to the world was suppressed, the freedom was only illusory and the aspirations of the freedom hungry would continue to rise in temperature.

The freedom could have been achieved if a temple to Rama was built and the symbol of foreign rule was moved to another site or demolished. The battle was never really for another temple. Another temple could have been built anywhere in India.

The humble and fair demand for RamaJanmabhoomi[3] could have resulted in a freedom for India, freedom from the intellectual slavery that so dominated India. This freedom would have meant that all Indians regardless of religion, language, caste, sex, or color would openly show respect for the person that from ancient times was considered the greatest hero to people of Hindusthan. For the first time, Hindus had demanded something, and it was justifiable that a reasonable demand from an undemanding people would be realized. Imagine if the Muslim leadership had agreed to shift the site and build a temple in Ayodhya. How much Hindu-Muslim unity there would have been in India? India could then have used that goodwill to solve the major religious, caste, and economic issues facing the country.

3. For the building of a Hindu temple to mark the birthplace and ancient capital of the Hindu god, Lord Rama.

But some of the vested interests in politics and in the Muslim community saw that such a change would mean that their work since 1947 would be overturned and that this new revolution would displace them. Rather than join forces and accept the rising tide, the oligarchy added fuel to the greatest movement in Indian history. One that on December 6, 1992 completely shattered the old and weak roots of Indian society and with it, the old political and intellectual structure. The destruction . . . of the dilapidated symbol of foreign dominance was the last straw in a heightening of tensions by the government, and the concomitant anger of more and more Hindus to rebuffs of their reasonable demands.

The ruthless last-ditch effort of the powers-that-be was the banning and suppression of the leaders of the Hindu Jagriti. The effort of the rulers reminds one of the strategy of all ill-fated rulers. Throughout history, when monumental upheavals have taken place, the threatened interests have resorted to drastic measures, which in turn have hastened their own death.

Freedom at Last

Hindus are at last free. They control their destiny now and there is no power that can control them except their own tolerant ethos. India in turn is finally free. Having ignored its history, it has now come face to face with a repressed conscience. The destruction of the structure at Ayodhya was the release of the history that Indians had not fully come to terms with. Thousands of years of anger and shame, so diligently bottled up by these same interests, was released when the first piece of the so-called Babri Masjid was torn down.

It is a fundamental concept of Hindu Dharma that has won: righteousness. Truth won when Hindus, realizing that Truth could not be won through political or legal means, took the law into their own hands. Hindus have been divided politically and the laws have not acknowledged the quiet Hindu yearning for Hindu unity which has until recently taken a back seat to economic development and Muslim appeasement. Similarly, the freedom movement represented the supercedence of Indian unity over loyalty to the British Crown. In comparison to the freedom movement though, Hindutva involves many more people and represents the mental freedom that 1947 did not bring.

The future of Bharat is set. Hindutva is here to stay. It is up to the Muslims whether they will be included in the new nationalistic spirit of Bharat. It is up to the government and the Muslim leadership whether they wish to increase Hindu furor or work with the Hindu leadership to show that Muslims and the government will consider Hindu sentiments. The era of one-way compromise of Hindus is over, for from now on, secularism must mean that all parties must compromise.

Hindutva will not mean any Hindu theocracy or theology. However, it will mean that the guiding principles of Bharat will come from two of the great teachings of the Vedas, the ancient Hindu and Indian scriptures, which so boldly proclaimed—*Truth is one, sages call it by many names*—and—*The whole universe is one family.*

India as a Nuclear Power

By Arundhati Roy

On May 11, 1998, twenty-two days after his government's inauguration, BJP prime minister Vajpayee read a statement informing the world that India had exploded three nuclear bombs underground at Pokhran, sixty miles from Pakistan's border. The BJP's 1998 election manifesto had advocated India joining the exclusive "nuclear club" and the new government wasted no time in fulfilling the election promise.

While the measure met with strong public approval in India, there were those who were horrified by the new government's actions. Arundhati Roy, the Indian author of The God of Small Things, *wrote a provocative essay called "The End of Imagination" in response to the BJP government's nuclear program. Roy adapted the following extract from her essay, which was influential in the debate in India on nuclear proliferation. Roy refutes the official arguments for building the bomb and argues that India has sold out its democratic ideals in an effort to gain international status.*

"The desert shook," the Government of India informed us (its people).

"The whole mountain turned white," the Government of Pakistan replied.

> By afternoon the wind had fallen silent over Pokhran. At 3:45 PM, the timer detonated the three devices. Around 200 to 300 m deep in the earth, the heat generated was equivalent to a million degrees centigrade—as hot as temperatures on the sun. Instantly, rocks weighing around a thousand tons, a mini mountain underground, vapourized. . . . Shockwaves from the blast began to lift a mound of earth the size of a football

> field by several metres. One scientist on seeing it said, "I can now believe stories of Lord Krishna lifting a hill."

"These are not just nuclear tests, they are nationalism tests," we were repeatedly told.

This has been hammered home, over and over again. The bomb is India. India is the bomb. Not just India, Hindu India. Therefore, be warned, any criticism of it is not just antinational, but anti-Hindu. (Of course, in Pakistan the bomb is Islamic. Other than that, politically, the same physics applies.) This is one of the unexpected perks of having a nuclear bomb. Not only can the Government use it to threaten the Enemy, they can use it to declare war on their own people. Us.

In 1975, one year after India first dipped her toe into the nuclear sea, Mrs. Gandhi declared the Emergency. What will 1999 bring? There's talk of cells being set up to monitor antinational activity. Talk of amending cable laws to ban networks "harming national culture." Of churches being struck off the list of religious places because "wine is served." Artists, writers, actors, and singers are being harassed, threatened (and succumbing to the threats). Not just by goon squads but by instruments of the government. And in courts of law. There are letters and articles circulating on the Net—creative interpretations of Nostradamus's predictions claiming that a mighty, all-conquering Hindu nation is about to emerge, a resurgent India that will "burst forth upon its former oppressors and destroy them completely." That "the beginning of the terrible revenge [that will wipe out all Muslims] will be in the seventh month of 1999." This may well be the work of some lone nut, or a bunch of arcane god-squadders. The trouble is that having a nuclear bomb makes thoughts like these seem feasible. It creates thoughts like these. It bestows on people these utterly misplaced, utterly deadly notions of their own power. It's happening. It's all happening. I wish I could say "slowly but surely"—but I can't. Things are moving at a pretty fair clip. . . .

My world has died. And I write to mourn its passing.

Admittedly it was a flawed world. An unviable world. A scarred and wounded world. It was a world that I myself have criticized unsparingly, but only because I loved it. . . .

I loved it simply because it offered humanity a choice. It was a rock out at sea. It was a stubborn chink of light that insisted that there was a different way of living. It was a functioning possibility. A real option. All that's gone now. India's nuclear tests, the manner in which they were conducted, the euphoria with which they have been greeted (by us) is indefensible. To me, it signifies dreadful things. The end of imagination. The end of freedom actually, because, after all, that's what freedom is. Choice.

On the fifteenth of August last year we celebrated the fiftieth anniversary of India's independence. Next May we can mark our first anniversary in nuclear bondage.

Why did they do it?

Political expediency is the obvious, cynical answer except that it only raises another, more basic question: Why should it have been politically expedient?

Official Justification for the Bomb

The three Official Reasons given are: China, Pakistan, and Exposing Western Hypocrisy.

Taken at face value, and examined individually, they're somewhat baffling. I'm not for a moment suggesting that these are not real issues. Merely that they aren't new. The only new thing on the old horizon is the Indian Government. In his appallingly cavalier letter to the US President (why bother to write at all if you're going to write like this?) our Prime Minister says India's decision to go ahead with the nuclear tests was due to a "deteriorating security environment." He goes on to mention the war with China in 1962 and the "three aggressions we have suffered in the last fifty years [from Pakistan]. And for the last ten years we have been the victim of unremitting terrorism and militancy sponsored by it . . . especially in Jammu and Kashmir."

The war with China is thirty-five years old. Unless there's some vital state secret that we don't know about, it certainly seemed as though matters had improved slightly between us. Just a few days before the nuclear tests General Fu Quanyou, Chief of General Staff of the Chinese People's Liberation Army, was the guest of our Chief of Army Staff. We heard no words of war.

The most recent war with Pakistan was fought twenty-seven years ago. Admittedly Kashmir continues to be a deeply troubled region and no doubt Pakistan is gleefully fanning the flames. But surely there must be flames to fan in the first place? Surely the kindling is crackling and ready to burn? Can the Indian State with even a modicum of honesty absolve itself completely of having a hand in Kashmir's troubles? Kashmir, and for that matter, Assam, Tripura, Nagaland—virtually the whole of the Northeast—Jharkhand, Uttarakhand, and all the trouble that's still to come, these are symptoms of a deeper malaise. It cannot and will not be solved by pointing nuclear missiles at Pakistan.

National Security and Respect

In the following extract from BJP prime minister Vajpayee's speech to the Indian people on August 15, 2000, he summarized his party's achievements and goals for the nation, placing India's nuclear program at the center of its accomplishment.

In the middle of the last century, Mother India won her freedom after a long and exemplary struggle against colonial rule. We have many proud achievements to our credit in nation building in the first five decades of Freedom. However, we also have many dreams that are yet unrealized. Learning proper lessons from the past, we must re-dedicate ourselves to the task of building a strong, prosperous, and egalitarian India; an India that is free of every trace of underdevelopment; a caring and compassionate India; and an India that regains her rightful role in shaping the destiny of the world in the new century and the new millennium . . . The most important achievements [since the BJP came to power in 1998]—and this is an achievement not so much of the Government, but of the entire country—has been that India is a stronger, more secure, and much more self-confident nation today than in the past. When we approached the people of India for a mandate . . . we had promised that national security would be one of our first and foremost priorities. We fulfilled this promise with our historical action of exercising the nuclear option at Pokharan in May 1998 . . . the very countries that imposed sanctions against us . . . [now] view India with greater respect than in the past.

Vajpayee, quoted in Barbara D. Metcalf and Thomas R. Metcalf, *A Concise History of India*. Cambridge: Cambridge University Press, 2002, pp. 286–87.

Even Pakistan can't be solved by pointing nuclear missiles at Pakistan. Though we are separate countries, we share skies, we share winds, we share water. Where radioactive fallout will land on any given day depends on the direction of the wind and rain. Lahore and Amritsar are thirty miles apart. If we bomb Lahore, Punjab will burn. If we bomb Karachi, then Gujarat and Rajasthan—perhaps even Bombay—will burn. Any nuclear war with Pakistan will be a war against ourselves.

As for the third Official Reason: Exposing Western Hypocrisy—how much more exposed can it be? Which decent human being on earth harbors any illusions about it? These are people whose histories are spongy with the blood of others. Colonialism, apartheid, slavery, ethnic cleansing, germ warfare, chemical weapons—they virtually invented it all. They have plundered nations, snuffed out civilizations, exterminated entire populations. They stand on the world's stage stark naked but entirely unembarrassed, because they know that they have more money, more food, and bigger bombs than anybody else. They know they can wipe us out in the course of an ordinary working day. Personally, I'd say it is more arrogance than hypocrisy.

We Have Sold Out

We have less money, less food, and smaller bombs.

However, we have, or had, all kinds of other wealth. Delightful, unquantifiable. What we've done with it is the opposite of what we think we've done. We've pawned it all. We've traded it in. For what? In order to enter into a contract with the very people we claim to despise. In the larger scheme of things, we've agreed to play their game and play it their way. We've accepted their terms and conditions unquestioningly. The Comprehensive Test Ban Treaty ain't nothin' compared to this.

All in all, I think it is fair to say that we're the hypocrites. We're the ones who've abandoned what was arguably a moral position: i.e., we have the technology, we can make bombs if we want to, but we won't. We don't believe in them.

We're the ones who have now set up this craven demoning to be admitted into the club of Superpowers. . . . For India to demand the nexus of a Superpower is as ridiculous as demanding to play in the World Cup finals simply because we have a ball. Never mind that we haven't qualified, or that we don't play much soccer and haven't got a team.

Since we've chosen to enter the arena, it might be an aim to begin by learning the rules of the game. Rule number one is Acknowledge the Masters. Who are the players: The ones with more money, more food, more bombs.

Rule number two is Locate Yourself in Relation to Them: i.e., make an honest assessment of your position and abilities. The honest assessment of ourselves (in quantifiable terms) reads as follows:

We are a nation of nearly a billion people. In development terms we rank number 138 out of the 175 countries listed in the UNDP's Human Development Index. More than four hundred million of our people are illiterate and live in absolute poverty, over six hundred million lack even basic sanitation, and over two hundred million have no safe drinking water.

So the three Official Reasons, taken individually, don't hold much water. . . .

Questionable National Consensus

According to opinion polls, we're expected to believe that there's a national consensus on the issue. It's official now. Everybody loves the bomb. (Therefore, the bomb is good.)

Is it possible for a man who cannot write his own name to understand even the basic, elementary facts about the nature of nuclear weapons? Has anybody told him that nuclear war has nothing at all to do with his received notions of war? Nothing to do with honor, nothing to do with pride? Has anybody bothered to explain to him about thermal blasts, radioactive fallout, and the nuclear winter? Are there even words in his language to describe the concepts of enriched uranium, fissile material, and critical mass? Or has his language itself become obsolete? Is he trapped in a time capsule, watching the world pass him by, unable to understand or communicate with it because his language never took into account the horrors that the human race would dream up? Does he not matter at all, this man? . . .

I'm not talking about one man, of course; I'm talking about millions and millions of people who live in this country. This is their land too, you know. They have the right to make an informed decision about its fate and, as far as I can tell, nobody has informed them about anything. The tragedy is that nobody could, even if they wanted to. Truly, literally, there's no language to do it in. This is the real horror of India. The orbits of the powerful and the powerless spinning further and further apart from each other, never intersecting, sharing nothing. Not a language. Not even a country.

Who the hell conducted those opinion polls? Who the hell is the Prime Minister to decide whose finger will be on the nuclear button that could turn everything we love—our earth, our skies, our mountains, our plains, our rivers, our cities and villages—to ash in an instant? Who the hell is he to reassure us that there will be no accidents? How does he know? Why should we trust him? What has he ever done to make us trust him? What have any of them ever done to make us trust them?

The nuclear bomb is the most antidemocratic, anti-national, antihuman, outright evil thing that man has ever made. . . . India's nuclear bomb is the final act of betrayal by a ruling class that has failed its people.

If you are religious, then remember that this bomb is Man's challenge to God.

It's worded quite simply: We have the power to destroy everything that You have created.

If you're not religious, then look at it this way. This world of ours is 4,600 million years old.

It could end in an afternoon.

The Crisis in Kashmir

BY THE *ECONOMIST*

The Indian Muslim–dominated state of Kashmir has been the cause of two Indo-Pakistani wars and is the scene of mounting tension that could spark a third such conflict. Stakes are ever higher following the demonstration of the nuclear capacity of both countries in 1998.

According to the following article from the January 19, 2002, Economist, *the conflict over Kashmir is based on ideological differences between India's "one-nation" theory (that what unites India is a common culture and shared geography) and Pakistan's "two-nation" theory (that Kashmir should be part of Pakistan because it is predominately Muslim and not Hindu). The article describes the state's unusual history, the distrust of the Kashmiri people for India's central government, and the vulnerability of Kashmiri separatist politicians to reprisals from Pakistan and unpopularity in Kashmir. The* Economist *concludes that unless India can convince the people of Kashmir that they will be treated fairly and humanely, violence and terrorism are likely to continue.*

Srinagar hardly looks like the capital of a state belonging to the world's largest democracy. Soldiers—helmeted, flak-jacketed and in camouflage—can be seen everywhere, behind sandbags, in open-backed lorries covered by netting against hand grenades, arrayed along pavements like lethal bits of shrubbery. The armour and guns are supposed to protect them from armed insurgents opposed to India's rule in Jammu and Kashmir, its only Muslim-majority state. But the security forces provoke hostility among ordinary Kashmiris that feeds and justifies the insurgency. Nearly every merchant in Srinagar's Maisuma Bazaar claims to have been beaten by them. A man who sells utensils says the security forces arrested him and demanded 100,000 rupees (about $2,100) to let him go. Any provocation turns the bazaar into a battlefield.

Kashmir has been the cause of two wars between India and Pakistan, in 1947 and in 1965. It is now threatening to cause another, the first since India and Pakistan declared themselves nuclear powers in 1998. On December 13th [2001] terrorists attacked India's parliament in an apparent plot to wipe out its leadership. India blamed groups fighting its rule in Kashmir, and Pakistan for harbouring them. It has responded by moving its armed forces into a threatening posture not seen since the last war in 1971 (fought over the breakaway of East Pakistan, now Bangladesh). Pakistan has mobilised in response.

Tensions have now eased a bit. . . . Under the pressure of India's guns and western diplomacy, Pakistan's self-appointed president, General Pervez Musharraf, went on television on January 12th to denounce religious extremism at home and forswear the use of terrorism to achieve Pakistan's objectives abroad. He banned the two groups India blames for the attack on its parliament, Lashkar-e-Taiba and Jaish-e-Muhammad, and has arrested nearly 2,000 people belonging to those and other groups. India cautiously welcomed General Musharraf's promises and is awaiting further evidence that he intends to carry them out. Meanwhile, its armed forces will remain poised. So tense is the potential front-line that war could well begin by accident.

Cause of the Conflict

It is not obvious why India and Pakistan are prepared to take such risks over a mountainous, landlocked territory with a small population and few natural resources. Kashmir's main asset is the beauty of the Kashmir Valley, which drew tourists until violence in the 1990s drove them away. Investors are equally gun-shy. Agriculture and construction are the mainstays of its economy.

The state is not of vital strategic significance to India. Pakistan largely satisfied its strategic needs in the first war, when it conquered a third of Kashmir's territory, including the areas closest to Rawalpindi, the headquarters of its army. It is unlikely ever to give up that third, which is nominally independent. Nor do many people seriously dispute India's claim to most of low-lying Jammu, which is inhabited mainly by Hindus, and Buddhist Ladakh. The heart of the conflict is the high Kashmir Valley, inhabited mostly by Muslims, which India is determined to keep.

Ideology is the germ of the dispute. Pakistan was created in 1947, at a cost of 1m lives, as a homeland for the sub-continent's Muslims. So Kashmir should be ours, say Pakistanis. But if Kashmir's Muslim majority disqualifies it from belonging to India, what becomes of India's identity as a nation based upon shared culture and geography rather than a common religion? The battle between India's "one-nation" and Pakistan's "two-nation" theories is almost as fierce and as fundamental as that between communism and capitalism.

Enmeshed in it are struggles between principles more familiar to the rest of the world, which each side uses to press its case. Pakistan's main slogan is "self-determination": the people of Jammu and Kashmir have the right to choose which of the two countries to join, a position upheld by non-binding Security Council resolutions. On its side India has democracy (Pakistan is under one-man rule and has been for half its history) and multiculturalism (Pakistan is avowedly Islamic and has not integrated its own small minority groups).

Above all, after September 11th, India has the issue of terrorism. The cause of liberating Kashmir from India is kept alive by violence, some of which can only be described as terrorist. Pakistan sponsors such violence by providing refuge and, probably, training and money to the terrorists. India, understandably, is using that sin to bash Pakistan and the whole cause of Kashmiri separatism. Its prime minister, Atal Behari Vajpayee, casts himself as a George Bush on the South Asian front of the international war on terrorism. Unlike Mr Bush, however, Mr Vajpayee cannot go to war without risking the lives of millions of his countrymen.

Kashmir's History

Despite Pakistan's claims, Muslim Kashmir was not fated to rebel against mainly Hindu India. It opted for India in 1947 because, 100 years before, India's British rulers sold rulership of the Muslim state to a Hindu maharajah for 7.5m rupees ($50m at current prices). When India and Pakistan were split apart, the then-maharajah tried to dodge the obligation of the 562 princely states of the Raj to join one of the two countries. An invasion by Pakistani tribesmen forced his hand: the maharajah acceded to India in return for military help. Pakistan held on to what it had conquered.

Almost everything about the accession is disputed. Did the maharajah persecute his Muslim subjects? Did the tribesmen leap spontaneously to their defence, or were they agents of Pakistan's new government? Were the British in cahoots with Jawharlal Nehru, India's first prime minister, to obtain accession?

These questions might not have mattered so much if India had continued the policies it started with in Kashmir. In acceding, the maharajah surrendered to India powers in just three areas: defence, foreign affairs and communications. Until 1965 the leader of the state's government was allowed to call himself prime minister. Nehru was eager to get popular ratification for the accession. It was he who brought Pakistan's invasion of Kashmir to the notice of the United Nations, which subsequently called on Pakistan to withdraw its forces in preparation for a plebiscite, which would allow Kashmiris to choose between joining India or Pakistan.

Nehru had reason to believe that India would win such a plebiscite. Kashmir's pre-eminent leader at the time was Sheikh Muhammad Abdullah, a Muslim who opposed the maharajah's rule but preferred the secular socialism of Nehru's India to the Muslim ideology of Pakistan. He became Kashmir's prime minister in 1948, and could surely have swung a plebiscite India's way. It never happened, partly because the Pakistanis never withdrew and partly because Nehru, feeling that Kashmir was India's anyway, did not see why he should put accession to a vote.

In 1953, just six years after accession, Sheikh Abdullah was dismissed as prime minister and sent to jail for 11 years on ill-founded suspicions that he was consorting with Pakistan and the United States. Thus began a five-decade fall from grace, during which India progressively integrated Kashmir and alienated it at the same time. In 1957 Kashmir accepted most of the Indian constitution; in 1964 the Indian president's right to dismiss state governments was extended to Kashmir. Sheikh Abdullah made his peace with integration and came back as chief minister in the 1977 elections, the state's first genuinely free ones. But in 1984 his son and successor, Farooq Abdullah, was ousted from power by Indira Gandhi, India's prime minister and Nehru's daughter.

Kashmiris thus came to associate the central government in Delhi and India's brand of democracy with the thwarting of the popular will. Anti-government groups contested the 1987 state elections under the banner of the Muslim United Front. In some areas their victories were annulled with Delhi's help, returning to power a tamed Farooq Abdullah. The cheated victors became founders of the insurrection. Succour came from Pakistan, which now looked a friendlier partner than India. Although Pakistan does not share Kashmir's culture and has fewer adherents to its Sufist version of Islam, it does profess support for self-determination.

Sumit Ganguly, who teaches at the University of Texas at Austin, has argued that the insurgency stems from democracy's success in raising popular expectations and its simultaneous failure to build institutions to meet those expectations. This points to the nub of the problem. Most Indians think their democratic constitution, applied faithfully, could provide the liberation Kashmiris seek; to most Kashmiris, that constitution is a prison.

The Kashmiri Viewpoint

A dozen years of insurgency have left Kashmir with a cast of dazed characters. The Kashmiri people themselves prefer independence to merger with Pakistan but may be (as the Indian government insists) more tired of war than they are eager for either. The militants, who still want a fight, started as a movement of local young men who had "exfiltrated" into Pakistan's side of Kashmir for arming and training, became a more lethal force of Pakistanis and other non-Kashmiris acting at Pakistan's bidding, and may now, after Pakistan's crackdown, mutate again. The Kashmiri government, headed by Farooq Abdullah, is deeply unpopular, and must face the voters again in 2002.

Separatist politicians, most of them part of the 23-member All-Party Hurriyat Conference, claim to speak for Kashmir's Muslims and probably come closer than anyone else to doing so. But they have yet to test their popularity in elections. Often they are the ventriloquist's dummy for Pakistan, though several would rather have independence than join Pakistan and resent its overbearing role in their struggle. The United States and its allies, which now have troops in the region, are looked upon by many Kashmiris, unrealistically, as potential saviours: when India has finished threatening war, perhaps the big powers can push it to a settlement in Kashmir. Last in this list of actors are the governments of India and Pakistan, the real arbiters of Kashmir's fate.

Until now, India has vacillated between inaction and ill-fated attempts to talk, either with Pakistan or with the separatists. Two events could now change that pattern. One is the crackdown on terrorism. Most Indians put little trust in General Musharraf's promises, a cynicism fuelled by reports that groups such as Lashkar-e-Taiba are still in business under different names. Indian officials, though, seem hopeful that the crackdown will moderate the militancy. "A lot of pressure on Pakistan immediately translates itself to Kashmir," says a senior Indian official.

Some speculate that Pakistan will dodge charges of backing cross-border terrorism by shifting support back to mainly Kashmiri outfits, such as Hizbul Mujahideen. That could mean a less lethal militancy, involving fewer suicide attacks and, perhaps, a willingness to talk. Hizbul Mujahideen, or at any rate a faction of it, had announced a short-lived ceasefire in July 2000. India has not spelt out how much and what sort of violence it is prepared to tolerate before demobilising its army and resuming talks with Pakistan. It has demanded an end to "all infiltration", but is willing to give General Musharraf "all due time" to accomplish this. An end to militant violence could start a hopeful cycle, prompting India to scale back its oppressive 400,000-strong security force in Kashmir, which in turn would lessen the rage that feeds the militants.

A Vital Election

The second event that might bring change is [a] state election. . . . Persuading separatist politicians to participate would be a coup. Candidates proclaim themselves Indians by taking part under the constitution. Demands for secession would thus be converted into less threatening demands for reform within India. The way might then be open to the settlement that many Indian policymakers are thought to favour: the partition of Kashmir into Indian and Pakistani states along the de facto border, called the Line of Control (LoC), plus some degree of autonomy for both sides. Without some separatists, however, the election will be a fiasco: Kashmiri Muslims will mock it again as phoney, and the government it produces will have no mandate to negotiate peace on their behalf.

The Indian government has made overtures of a sort to the separatists. In 2000 Mr Vajpayee called a unilateral ceasefire during Ramadan, the Muslim holy month, and extended it three times in the hope that the insurgents would respond in kind. They did not, and the ceasefire ended. Mr Vajpayee has promised that Kashmir's next election will be free and fair, and has appointed an intermediary to talk to Kashmiri groups.

Such efforts are undermined, however, by India's failure to understand how deeply the separatists mistrust it and how vulnerable they are to reprisals by Pakistan and—should they settle too cheaply—the scorn of Kashmiris themselves. None trusts India's election commission to guarantee the fairness of the forthcoming vote; most want foreign monitors to do that job, a condition they know the Indian government will reject. Separatist leaders suspect every Indian offer may be another betrayal. Yasin Malik, a member of the Hurriyat's executive council, describes the intermediary as "a clerk who wants to dialogue with 32 parties", 28 of which are already pro-Indian. Abdul Ghani Lone, another Hurriyat leader, points to the toll of a dozen years of violence: 70,000 Kashmiris dead, he claims (several times the official estimate), 5,000 women "dishonoured", 3,000 disappearances. "How can we participate in elections?" he asks.

Many Indian analysts believe that Mr Malik and Mr Lone, who, like most Kashmiris, favour azadi (independence) over merger with Pakistan, would in the end accept some version of "LoC plus", Indian shorthand for partition plus autonomy. "Azadi can be accommodated within India," says Amitabh Mattoo of Jawaharlal Nehru University, in Delhi. The harder task may be to persuade Pakistan.

General Musharraf has conceded much since terrorists attacked America in September. He withdrew support for the Taliban in Afghanistan, and has started to shut down a proxy war against India that is Pakistan's only way of promoting its claim to Kashmir. Yet he has declared that "Kashmir runs in our blood" and has called on outside powers to push India into a resolution of the dispute. India rejects outside mediation, as it does a "triangular" discussion with Pakistanis and Kashmiris at the same table, because that would suggest that its sovereignty over Kashmir, or at least the part it now controls, is negotiable. India's best offer is, in effect, a more democratic and humane version of the status quo that Pakistan has been fighting for 50 years to overturn.

Could General Musharraf ever accept this? Indians point to the burden that fighting India has placed on Pakistan's frail economy and to the disfiguring effect on its society of employing Islamic fanatics in that fight. General Musharraf, they hope, would rather modernise Pakistan than continue a futile struggle over Kashmir. Perhaps they are right. But if India is to continue to fly its flag in Srinagar with the consent of Pakistan and the Kashmiri people, democracy and humanity will have to come in torrents. If the drought continues, so will the strife.

Economic Performance and Prospects

By Alok Sheel

In the following selection, Indian economist Alok Sheel explains that India's economic performance since the restructuring of the early 1990s has been impressive, showing growth rates of around 6.5 percent and a reduction in the level of poverty from 36 to 26 percent of the population. Strengths of the Indian economy include the large population and potential market, a growing consumer-oriented middle class, and a stable political and legal system conducive to encouraging foreign investment. Underlying weaknesses that must be addressed if India is to realize her full potential relate to the country's poor state of physical infrastructure, particularly in the transport and energy sectors. In addition, the agricultural sector, which supports the majority of the poorer groups, has thus far not benefited from economic liberalization measures. Alok Sheel is the Economics Counselor at the Indian Embassy in Washington, D.C.

The Indian economy was relatively closed till 1991, following which sweeping reforms opened up trade, industry and financial sectors to domestic and foreign competition. The economic restructuring process has its protagonists and detractors. The latter consider the reform process too slow and partial, especially when compared to East Asia and China in particular, which have achieved much faster growth rates. Protagonists, on the other hand, point out that India has had one of the fastest growing economies during the nineties, averaging around 6.5 percent GDP growth per annum. Poverty levels have fallen from 36 percent to 26 percent over this period. Its international balance of payment is very comfortably placed. Growth rates recovered comparatively fast after the initial adjustment, and

Alok Sheel, "Political Economy of India, 1800–2001," *International Journal of Commerce and Management*, vol. 11, Summer 2001.

it escaped the more deleterious effects of the Latin American and East Asian debt and currency crises. Reform and growth, moreover, is being achieved in a much more challenging political environment, which reduces future political risk.

Following the collapse of the Soviet model of development, there is now a global consensus on the mix of policies for growth and development. The real debates now revolve around pace and sequencing. As India moves into the twenty-first century and integrates into a global economy where all barriers are fast breaking down, it is worthwhile to do a quick . . . analysis of India's political economy. Its greatest strengths derive from its numbers: its vast size, population and economy, and, in particular, its huge, ever expanding, middle class. This provides a powerful demand stimulus for boosting and sustaining growth rates, foreign investment and international trade. A stable political environment supplements this. Despite razor thin coalition-based majorities in parliament, the transition from one government to another has been smooth and through the ballot box. Close and heated parliamentary debates might slow down the policy reform process, but they also make the outcomes durable with little risk of reversal, thereby reducing political risk. India also has a robust legal system based on Anglo-Saxon jurisprudence, and English is widely spoken, thereby greatly facilitating its integration into the global economic mainstream.

The flip side of the state's disproportionate expenditure on higher education has been the creation of a big pool of skilled, white collar labor, whose global impact has been felt most tellingly in the Information Technology sector which is, not surprisingly, fast becoming the engine of growth of the Indian economy, as indeed it has been of the United States for some time now. The Indian Software industry growth rate exceeds 50 percent per annum, and India appears to be on track to becoming a global IT superpower with US$50 billion exports by 2008, according to a recent influential survey done by McKinsey and NASSCOM [India's National Association of Software and Service Companies].

A Bright Outlook

India enters the twenty-first century on a relatively buoyant note. Despite global recessionary trends, especially in the leading IT sector, GDP growth in the financial year 2000–01 was around 6 percent, and export growth around 20 percent. Foreign currency reserves have been sustained at a historic peak of USS 40 billion, despite the recent 75 percent rise in oil prices. Cumulative foreign investment stocks are touching US$ 30 billion. IT technology export projections have been scaled down, largely on account of the IT downturn in the U.S., but these are, nevertheless, in excess of 40 percent. There is also good news on the fiscal front, with the fiscal deficit having been contained at the estimated level of 5.1 percent of the GDP for the first time in several years, as the expected tax buoyancy arising out of tax reform is beginning to be felt. The decline in interest rates is likely to improve the fiscal position still further, as interest payments on government debt is a major component of the government's budget deficit. The dip in inflation rates also makes it more likely that the drop in interest rates will be sustained in the market, making a virtuous cycle of lower deficits, with higher investment and growth a distinct possibility. The privatization efforts of the government have also picked up momentum with the first privatization of a profit making state owned enterprise, namely, the Bharat Aluminum Company. A number of major reform bills, such as the Fiscal Responsibility Bill, Information Technology, Communication and Entertainment Bill (or ICE which seeks to set up a unified regulatory framework to harness the synergy between these sectors in a bold attempt to convert India into an IT powerhouse), the Electricity Bill (which seeks to remove regulatory bottlenecks standing in the way of the financial closure of new power projects), and Competition Bill are being placed before parliament to be enacted into law.

India has the potential to become one of the fastest growing economies in the coming decade, and to emerge as a major economic power in the new millennium. However, certain fundamental weaknesses in the Indian economy will have to be addressed before this great potential is translated into concrete results. Huge investments in, and rapid development of, the infrastructural sectors, social and physical, are a necessary precondition for sustaining high rates of growth. Poverty indices have declined gradually over the years, but India still has a major share of the world's poor, which acts as a drag on the economy. Poverty reduction has a huge demand side upside, for it is well-known that the multiplier effect of putting more income into the hands of the poor is much higher than what it is in the hands of the more affluent.

The critical importance of a quantum jump in infrastructural investments cannot be over-emphasized. The IT sector, for instance, rides piggyback on the telecommunications network. But India's telephone density is below 2 percent, compared to over 7

A Bleaker Forecast

In contrast to the optimistic economic projections made by government economist Alok Sheel, in the following extract from India Changes Course: Golden Jubilee to Millennium in Historical Perspective, *American author Paul R. Dettman paints a far bleaker picture of India's economic future given population trends and the continued divergence by the government of scarce resources from poverty-alleviation programs to its nuclear arsenal.*

An indication of what lies in store over the next half century for the India that has joined the nuclear club was provided by a report issued by the Washington-based World Watch Institute following the May 1998 nuclear bomb tests. The report painted a picture of the state of India's natural resources, as it entered the third millennium, that raised serious questions regarding its ability to sustain a 1 billion plus population:

> As the '90s unfold, the rise in grain productivity is slowing, as it is in many other countries. Against this backdrop, the continuing shrinkage of crop land per person now threatens India's food security. In 1960, each Indian had an average of 0.21 hectares of grain land. By 1999, the average had dropped to 0.10 hectares per person, or less than half as much. And by 2050, it is projected to shrink to a meager 0.07 hectares per person. . . .
>
> Falling water tables are also threatening India's food production. . . . In a country where irrigated land accounts for 55 percent of the grain harvest and where the lion's share of irrigation water

percent in China and over 11 percent in Thailand. Rail, road, port and air links, and the energy sector, in particular are in need of huge investments for expansion, without which Indian industry cannot become internationally competitive in an increasingly

comes from underground, falling water tables are generating concern. The Water Management Institute estimates that aquifer depletion could reduce India's grain harvest one-fourth. Falling water tables will likely lead to rising grain prices on a scale that could destabilize not only grain markets, but possibly the government itself. With 53 percent of all children undernourished and underweight, any drop in food supply can quickly become life-threatening. India's population is projected to reach 1.5 billion by 2050, but there are doubts as to whether the natural resource base will support such growth. . . .

In some ways, India today is paying the price for its earlier indiscretions, when, despite its impoverished state, it invested in a costly effort to design and produce nuclear weapons and succeeded in becoming a member of the nuclear club. As a result, it has a nuclear arsenal capable of protecting the largest concentration of impoverished citizens on earth. Even today, India spends 2.5 percent of its GNP for military purposes but only 0.7 percent on health, which includes family planning. Unless India can quickly reorder priorities, it risks falling into a demographic dark hole, one where population will begin to slow because death rates are rising. It may be time for India to redefine security. The principal threat now may not be military aggression from without, but population growth from within.

Paul R. Dettman, *India Changes Course: Golden Jubilee to Millennium in Historical Perspective.* Westport, CT: Praeger, 2001, pp. 202–204.

globalized economy. Fiscal consolidation in the center and states, including deepening of tax reforms, privatization and rollback of the state, would be necessary to release resources for infrastructural development. Indian customs tariffs are excessive, and these translate into distorted resource flows and inhibit the growth of international trade. Inflexibilities in the labor market and bankruptcy laws also act as barriers to investment and growth. Finally, the agricultural sector has been barely affected by economic reform, so far.

Democracy in India: Creative Chaos

By the *Economist*

The following article, which originally appeared in the May 22, 1999, Economist, *underlines the paradox of India as a vigorous democracy in which the majority have asserted their right to vote, but also a society in which the poor have had little success improving their economic plight. According to the* Economist, *democracy in India is in chaos. No one central party can win a clear majority at the federal level; with the rise of regional parties, power has shifted from the center to the states and in some cases state authorities have further devolved power to people at the village level. Political fragmentation is a serious concern, but as experiments at the local level empower people to make decisions about their own lives, there is cause for optimism that in time India's democracy may cure its own flaws.*

"The world's largest democracy": India's boast has many subtexts. You are meant to understand that India is not just big (which makes it important) and democratic (which makes it better than, say, China), but also that there is a tension between the two characteristics. India's diversity and size sometimes make it difficult to enact reforms or to be totally fastidious about human rights. The appellation is partly a plea for understanding.

As an accolade, it is largely deserved. India is indeed vibrantly democratic, and democracy is one of the few things that command the universal reverence of a diverse people. Voters eagerly exercise their rights: a study by the Election Commission found that in the past 11 parliaments an MP had on average only a 25%

Economist, "Creative Chaos: India's Democracy Is a Work in Progress," *Economist*, vol. 351, May 22, 1999.

chance of being re-elected to the lower house. According to Yogendra Yadav, a political scientist at the Centre for the Study of Developing Societies in Delhi, India experienced a "second democratic upsurge" in the 1990s, with a sharp increase in voting and other forms of political participation by dalits (formerly untouchables) and members of tribes and other economically and socially deprived groups. India may be the only country in the world, says Mr Yadav, where the lower down the social scale people are, the more likely they are to vote.

This makes India the world's largest paradox: a land of appalling poverty and stunning social inequality, despite the assertiveness of the downtrodden. Some 300m people still live below a meanly defined poverty line. According to a recent report by Human Rights Watch, based in New York, violence against India's 160m former untouchables (a status formally abolished by the constitution in 1950) is rising. Indians sometimes wonder whether democracy has denied them the relative well-being and equality that China enjoys. All the same, there are reasons to hope that Indian democracy is beginning to find ways of curing its own defects.

Democracy in Chaos

Few would deny that Indians have a talent for political revolution. They showed it when Nehru and Gandhi demolished the British Raj, and again after independence, when lower-caste leaders demanded access for their constituents to government jobs and education. But they have shown no equivalent flair for social or economic revolution. This is not to deny that for most of them living conditions have improved dramatically since independence, thanks to higher agricultural productivity and better health care. The disappointment is that India has done so much less well than it might have done.

Once elected, politicians join what amounts to a political caste, consumed with intrigues and minutiae of no interest to the voters. Detachment is encouraged by ideologies that at best address only one dimension of a citizen's well-being. Thus the Communists of Kerala are good at promoting literacy but bad at encouraging growth. The Bharatiya Janata Party, ousted from government in April, is good at instilling pride in India's Hindus, but bad at making Muslims and other members of minority groups feel like fully fledged Indians. Caste-based parties do wonders for the self-esteem of lower castes, but little for their living conditions. Laloo Prasad Yadav, the popular former chief minister of Bihar, was once accosted by a constituent who complained about the quality of roads in the state. His retort was, roughly: "You elected me to build roads? I thought it was to give you dignity." As India has become more democratic, it has become more chaotic. The erosion of the Congress party's monopoly of power, which began in 1967, opened the door to a host of regional parties. Most ideological and caste-based parties are also, in effect, regional parties. Indeed, there are only two truly national parties: Congress, which has not won a majority in parliament in 15 years, and the Hindu-nationalist BJP, which has never had one. The chances are that whichever of these comes out on top in [future elections] will still have to scrabble around for coalition partners among the minnows.

The government that collapsed on April 17th, 1999, an 18-party fricassee, had been the fifth since 1996. During its 13 months in office barely a day went by when one of its constituent parties did not hold it to ransom. Some people hope for a two-party system, or at least a two-block system, and see signs of it in the decline of a "third force" that had opposed both national parties but has constituents that are now gravitating towards Congress. The clash between Congress's secularism and the BJP's emphasis on the Hindu way of life (Hindutva) is titanic enough, they believe, to become the principle around which politics is organised. But there are complications. Several states have their own two-party systems in which at least one of the main players is not one of the two national parties.

The Advantages of Having Many Parties

It is easy to overlook what India has gained from democratic profusion. For one thing, small parties have had a tempering effect. The BJP's coalition partners curbed the party's nationalist agenda, insisting that it drop ideas such as the withdrawal of Kashmir's constitutional right to autonomy and the introduction of a uniform civil code, which would have denied Muslims their personal law.

Caste-conscious politics began in southern India, which in the 1950s expanded reservations in government jobs from the lowest ("scheduled") castes to intermediate ("other backward") castes. States such as Karnataka and Kerala now reserve more than half their government jobs for members of lower castes. Reservations have created the core of the lower-caste middle class, opening avenues that would have been closed by religious and

Caste as the Unit of Social Action

In the following extract, political scientist Myron Weiner says that while caste social divisions are condemned in contemporary Indian society on an ideological level, they are the common practice. Furthermore, as the lower castes have banded together to form political action groups, castes have become the unit of social action.

Perhaps no other major society in recent history has known inequalities so gross, so long preserved, or so ideologically well entrenched. In the traditional civilizations of Islam and China, the ideal if not always the practice of equality had an honorable and often commanding place in the culture. But in India the notion that men should remain in the same occupation and station of life as their forefathers was enshrined in religious precepts and social custom. . . . It was not simply that India has had gross inequalities in material standards, but more profoundly, social relations were marked by indignities: the kissing of one's feet by a beggar and supplicant for a job, the outstretched hands of the groveling poor, the stooped backs of low-caste sweepers.

The principle of equality [introduced when India became independent], implied a revolutionary transformation. The nationalist elite that took power in 1947 wrote a constitution that contained the full panoply of democratic institutions—parliament and legislatures, elections, universal suffrage, freedom of assembly, freedom of the press, legal rights—all based on the principle of equal political rights. Equality was to be achieved in part through democratic institutions and procedures, particularly universal suffrage without a literacy requirement, equality before the law, legislation banning discrimination, and through the establishment of a system of reservations that would guarantee represen-

social stigma. "Other backward castes" got reservations for central-government jobs only in 1990. If the south's relative prosperity and better governance are linked to the early assertiveness

tation to members of scheduled castes and tribes. . . . Equality of opportunity, they said, would come through universal and compulsory elementary education and an expanded system of higher education. The nationalist elite did not promise a classless society, but they did offer the promise of a casteless society in which social status would not be based upon hereditary social rankings and individuals would not be denied opportunities because of their birth.

The revolutionary transformation did not of course take place. Caste as an ideology may be (almost, but not quite) moribund, but as a lived-in social reality it is very much alive. The demise of orthodoxy, right beliefs, has not meant the demise of orthopraxy, right practice. Castes remain endogamous. Lower castes, especially members of scheduled castes, remain badly treated by those of higher castes. But the gap between beliefs and practices is the source of tension and change. The lower castes no longer accept their position in the social hierarchy, no longer assume that their lower economic status and the lack of respect from members of the higher castes are a "given" in their social existence. But the movement for change is not a struggle to end caste; it is to use caste as an instrument for social change. Caste is not disappearing, nor is "casteism"—the political use of caste—for what is emerging in India is a social and political system which institutionalizes and transforms but does not abolish caste. Thirty-five years ago India's distinguished anthropologist, M.N. Srinivas, presciently wrote that "caste is so tacitly and so completely accepted by all, including those who are most vocal in condemning it, that it is everywhere the unit of social action".

Myron Weiner, "The Struggle for Equality: Caste in Indian Politics," *The Success of India's Democracy*, edited by Atul Kohli. Cambridge, MA: Cambridge University Press, 2001.

of its lower castes, there may yet be hope for Mr Yadav's constituents in Bihar.

With the rise of regional parties able to dictate terms to the centre, power has shifted from Delhi to the states. Thanks also to liberalisation, they now compete for investment and negotiate directly with lenders such as the World Bank. India is not a federation, but unlike Pakistan it has used federalism in the past to contain regional yearnings. Yet federalism can go too far. A battle is looming in 2001 when the allocation of seats by state in the lower house of parliament, which has been frozen for more than 20 years, is due to be revised to reflect shifts in population. States that have done a good job controlling their population, such as Tamil Nadu and Punjab, are already arguing that they should not be penalised for their good performance. If their argument succeeds, it could lead to one of India's worst constitutional crises since language riots forced the redrawing of state boundaries 43 years ago. India might gradually begin to resemble a confederation, something very different from the dreams of its founding fathers.

Power to the People

After a half century of democracy, the gears of politics may at last be meshing with the concerns of ordinary people. There is something of a fad among states for panchayati raj, rule by elected village bodies. Amendments to the constitution in 1992 required states to hold their first panchayat elections, but gave states considerable discretion over how much power to devolve to panchayats and the other two tiers of local government. Plenty of states, jealous of their powers, have starved the panchayats of money and power. But a few have been willing to give them a try.

West Bengal, for example, is using panchayati raj to reform an education system that had been compromised by the ruling Communist Party's penchant for appointing party hacks as teachers and leaving them in the jobs for life. The state is establishing new types of primary schools supervised by management committees on which parents hold three-quarters of the seats. Teachers are now appointed on renewable one-year contracts. The West Bengal government also turned the management of tube wells for irrigation over to their users.

Panchayati raj speeds up social change as well, since under the constitution elected bodies must reserve a third of their seats for women and a portion for scheduled castes. Even where states are reluctant to cede much power to the panchayats, the reservations bring new blood into politics. Kripa Ananthpur, an academic who has produced a series of radio programmes to popularise panchayati raj in Karnataka, tells of several devadasis—women bound to a form of religious prostitution—who became members of their village assemblies and "felt recognised as human for the first time".

Chandrababu Naidu, the visionary chief minister of Andhra Pradesh, is trying to make government more transparent and responsive by making it electronic. He has automated the recording and issue of property titles, cutting down waiting times from days to minutes and eliminating middlemen who funnelled bribes from citizens to bureaucrats. With the help of McKinsey, a consultancy, Mr Naidu has produced a report called Vision 2020 that offers an inspiring picture of what Andhra Pradesh might be like in two decades: a state free from poverty and illiteracy, a government made responsive and efficient by high technology, a business environment that beguiles investors.

Digvijay Singh, his counterpart in Madhya Pradesh, is more interested in grass roots than fibre optics. He is devolving power to villages and has set up an innovative education guarantee scheme, which promises a school within three months to every community with 40 potential students that demands one. During the first 18 months of the scheme, nearly 20,000 new schools were created. Mr Singh's re-election last November shows other politicians that devolving power may be a good way to retain it.

These experiments are still too new to judge. Mr Naidu in particular has his critics. His high-tech passions, they say, leave the countryside cold, and he may not win re-election later this year. Yet Mr Naidu is making a point which India desperately needs to take note of: that there is no conflict between efficiency and social justice, and that enterprise need not be the enemy of equality. The sort of revolution Mr Naidu is aiming for in Andhra Pradesh—a managerial, not an ideological one—is exactly what India needs.

Chronology

Ancient Empires

ca. 6000 B.C.

Neolithic settlements are established in Baluchistan.

3000s B.C.

Settlements emerge in the Indus Valley.

2800–2600 B.C.

The Indus civilization begins.

2300–1700 B.C.

The great cities in the Indus Valley (Mohenjo Daro, Harappa), in the Punjab (Kilibangan), and in Gujarat (Lothal) are established.

ca. 1500–1200 B.C.

The Vedic Aryans immigrate to India.

ca. 1200–900 B.C.

The Early Vedic period (Rig Veda).

900–600 B.C.

The Late Vedic period (Brahmanas); the Aryans settle in the central and eastern Gangetic Plain.

ca. 563 B.C.

Buddhism is founded.

ca. 320 B.C.

Chandragupta Maurya establishes the Mauryan dynasty.

ca. 272–232 B.C.

Ashoka reigns as emperor.

261 B.C.

Ashoka conquers Kalinga and converts to Buddhism.

A.D. 320
Chandra Gupta I establishes the Gupta dynasty.

376–415
During Chandra Gupta II's reign, the Gupta Empire is at the peak of its power.

455–467
The first attack of the Huns occurs.

ca. 500–527
The Huns rule over northern India; the classical urban culture of the north declines.

711
Arab invaders establish an Islamic presence in India.

Growth of Islam and the Mughal Period

997–1027
Mahmud of Ghazni raids the Indian subcontinent from Afghanistan.

1206
The Delhi Sultanate, the principal Muslim state in India before the Mughal Empire, is founded.

1293
Marco Polo visits south India.

1398
Timur invades Delhi.

1414–1450
The Sayyid dynasty; the Delhi Sultanate is renewed.

1498
Portuguese explorer Vasco da Gama reaches Calicut.

1510
The Portuguese conquer Goa.

1526
Babur lays the foundation of the Mughal Empire; wins first battle of Panipat.

1556–1605
Akbar expands and reforms the empire; wins second battle of Panipat.

1600
The British East India Company is founded in London.

1602
The Dutch East India Company is founded.

1605–1627
Jahangir reigns as emperor; Persian court culture flourishes in India.

1612
The East India Company opens its first trading post.

1628–1658
Shah Jahan rules India.

1658–1707
Aurangzeb, the last great Mughal ruler, reigns.

1664
The French East India Company is founded.

1707–1858
During the period of weaker Mughal emperors, the Mughal Empire declines.

British Period

1751
British colonialist Robert Clive captures and defends Arcot.

1757
Clive defeats the nawab of Bengal in the battle of Plassey.

1760
British troops defeat the French in the battle of Wandiwash.

1764
The joint forces of the Mughal emperor Shah Alam and the nawabs of Bengal and Oudh are defeated in the battle of Baxar.

1765
Clive returns to India as governor of Bengal.

1773
Warren Hastings becomes governor-general.

1835
English education and other reforms are instituted.

1857–1858
Indian rebels capture large swaths of territory before the revolt is put down by the British.

1858
The British abolish the East India Company and put India under the authority of the British Crown, marking the formal end of the Mughal Empire.

1877
Queen Victoria becomes empress of India.

1885
The Indian National Congress is formed.

1906
The Muslim League is founded.

1907
The Indian National Congress splits into moderates and extremists.

1919
The British implement the repressive Rowlatt Acts, leading Mohandas Gandhi to begin his satyagraha campaign; British troops kill sixteen hundred protesters in the Amritsar Massacre.

1920–1922
Gandhi begins his noncooperation campaign and the Khilafat agitation of the Muslims.

1928
The Simon Commission visits India.

1930

As part of his civil disobedience campaign, Gandhi leads a "salt march" to protest the repressive British government's laws; the Round Table Conference in London is boycotted by Congress.

1930–1931

The Great Depression hits India.

1935

The British Government of India Act provides for the establishment of an autonomous Indian nation.

1939

World War II begins; Congress ministers resign.

1940

The Muslim League adopts the Lahore Resolution, the "two nations" theory articulated by Mohammed Ali Jinnah.

1942

The Cripps Mission visits India and the "Quit India" resolution is passed.

1946

On August 16, "Direct Action Day" is declared by the Muslim League.

Independent India

1947

The Islamic Republic of Pakistan is established in the Indian subcontinent on August 14; India gains its independence from Britain on August 15; the Kashmir conflict, and undeclared war with Pakistan, begins.

1948

Mohandas Gandhi is assassinated on January 30.

1950

The Constitution of the Republic of India is inaugurated.

1952

The first general election is held; the Congress Party wins.

1957
The second general election is held; Congress wins.

1961
The Non-Aligned Conference takes place in Belgrade.

1962
Congress wins the third general election; a border war with China begins.

1964
Prime Minister Jawaharlal Nehru dies; he is succeeded by Lal Bahadur Shastri.

1965
A second war with Pakistan occurs.

1966
Indira Gandhi becomes prime minister.

1971
A third war with Pakistan occurs; Bangladesh becomes independent after an Indian invasion of East Pakistan.

1975
A state of emergency is proclaimed by Indira Gandhi.

1977
Morarji Desai serves as head of the Janata Party coalition, India's first non-Congress government.

1979
Chaudhary Charan Singh serves as prime minister for the Janata Party–led coalition.

1980
Indira Gandhi is reelected as the head of Congress.

1984
Indira Gandhi is assassinated in New Delhi; Rajiv Gandhi succeeds her as prime minister of Congress.

1989
Vishwanath Pratap Singh becomes prime minister of the National Front–led coalition.

1990

Chandra Shekhar becomes prime minister of the Samajwati Janata Party government.

1991

Rajiv Gandhi is assassinated near Madras; Narasimha Rao becomes prime minister of the Congress Party government.

1992–1993

The Babri Masjid mosque in Ayodhya is destroyed by Hindu activists; widespread communal violence follows the mosque's destruction.

1996

General elections for Lok Sabha oust the Congress Party government; in May, the minority Bharatiya Janata Party (BJP) government, led by prime minister Atul Behari Vajpayee, is elected, then resigns after thirteen days; Haradanahalli Deve Gowda, head of the thirteen-party United Front, is sworn in as India's eleventh prime minister.

1998

The BJP coalition is reelected; underground nuclear tests occur at Pokharan.

1999

The BJP government returns to power; the conflict in Kashmir sparks the Kargil War; India's population reaches 1 billion.

2001

A terrorist attack on the Indian Parliament occurs in December.

2002

In February, Muslims firebomb a train of Hindus coming from Ayodhya, killing fifty-seven people; a terrorist attack in Jammu, Kashmir, in May brings India and Pakistan to the brink of war.

For Further Research

General

James Heitzman and Robert L. Worden, *India: A Country Study.* Washington, DC: U.S. Government Printing Office, 1996.

Barbara D. Metcalf and Thomas R. Metcalf, *A Concise History of India.* New York: Cambridge University Press, 2001.

D.P. Singhal, *A History of the Indian People.* London: Methuen London, 1983.

Stanley Wolpert, *A New History of India.* New York: Oxford University Press, 2000.

Ancient India

A.L. Basham, *The Wonder That Was India: A Survey of the History and Culture of the Indian Subcontinent Before the Coming of the Muslims.* New York: Taplinger, 1967.

A.L. Basham, ed., *A Cultural History of India.* Oxford, England: Clarendon Press, 1975.

William T. De Bary, ed., *Sources of Indian Tradition.* New York: Columbia University Press, 1960.

Ainslie T. Embree, ed., *The Hindu Tradition: Readings in Oriental Thought.* New York: Vintage Books, 1972.

Klaus K. Klostermaier, *Hindu Writings: A Short Introduction to the Major Sources.* Oxford, England: Oxford University Press, 2000.

Gregory Possehl, ed., *The Harappan Civilization.* London: Aria and Phillips, 1982.

Romila Thapar, *Interpreting Early India.* New Delhi, India: Oxford University Press, 1992.

Mughal India

Bamber Gascoigne, *The Great Moghuls.* New York: Harper and Row, 1971.

Irfan Habib, ed., *Medieval India. Vol. 1: Researchers in the History of India, 1200–1750.* New Delhi, India: Oxford University Press, 1992.

S.M. Ikram, *Muslim Civilization in India.* New York: Columbia University Press, 1964.

R.C. Majumdar, ed., *The Cambridge History of India.* Vol. 8: *The Mughal Empire.* Bombay, India: B.V. Bhavan, 1969.

M.N. Pearson, *The New Cambridge History of India.* Vol. 1: *The Portuguese in India.* Cambridge, England: Cambridge University Press, 1987.

I.H. Qureshi, *The Muslim Community of the Indo-Pakistan Subcontinent, 610–1947: A Brief Historical Analysis.* 's-Gravenhage, The Netherlands: Mouton, 1962.

S.A.A. Rizvi, *The Wonder That Was India.* Vol. 2: *A Survey of the History and Culture of the Indian Subcontinent from the Coming of the Muslims to the British Conquest, 1200–1700.* London: Sidgwick and Jackson, 1987.

British India

Michael Adas, "Twentieth Century Approaches to the Indian Mutiny of 1857–58," *Journal of Asian History*, vol. 5, 1971.

John Beecroft, *Kipling: A Selection of His Stories and Poems.* New York: Doubleday, 1956.

Larry Collins and Dominique Lapierre, *Freedom at Midnight.* New York: Simon and Schuster, 1975.

E.M. Forster, *A Passage to India.* New York: Harcourt Brace Jovanovich, 1924.

Philip Mason, *The Men Who Ruled India.* London: Cape, 1985.

Louis Mountbatten, *Time Only to Look Forward: Speeches of the Viceroy of India and Governor-General of the Dominion of India, Including Related Addresses.* London: N. Kaye, 1949.

Paul Scott, *The Raj Quartet.* New York: Morrow, 1976.

The Independence Movement

Mohandas K. Gandhi, *An Autobiography: The Story of My Experiments with Truth.* Boston: Beacon Press, 1972.

Peter Hardy, *The Muslims of British India.* Cambridge, England: Cambridge University Press, 1972.

Ved Mehta, *Mahatma Gandhi and His Apostles.* New York: Viking Press, 1977.

V.P. Menon, *The Transfer of Power in India.* Princeton, NJ: Princeton University Press, 1957.

Jawaharlal Nehru, *Toward Freedom: An Autobiography.* New York: Day, 1941.

C.H. Philips, *The Evolution of India and Pakistan: Select Documents on Indian History.* London: Oxford University Press, 1962.

Anil Seal, *The Emergence of Indian Nationalism.* Cambridge, England: Cambridge University Press, 1968.

Hugh Tinker, *Experiment with Freedom, India and Pakistan.* London: Oxford University Press, 1967.

T. Walter Wallbank, *The Partition of India: Causes and Responsibilities.* Boston: D.C. Heath, 1966.

Stanley Wolpert, *Gandhi's Passion.* New York: Oxford University Press, 2001.

———, *Jinnah of Pakistan.* New York: Oxford University Press, 1984.

Independent India

Granville Austin, *The Indian Constitution: Cornerstone of a Nation.* Oxford, England: Clarendon Press, 1966.

Paul R. Brass, *The New Cambridge History of India.* Vol. 4: *The Politics of India Since Independence.* Cambridge, England: Cambridge University Press, 1994.

Milton Israel, *Nehru and the Twentieth Century.* Toronto, Canada: University of Toronto, 1991.

Jawaharlal Nehru's Speeches, 1946–64. 5 vols. Delhi, India: Indian Press, 1949–1968.

Pupul Jayakar, *Indira Gandhi: An Intimate Biography.* New York: Pantheon Books, 1992.

Ravindar Kumar, *The Emergence of Modern India.* New Delhi, India: Oxford University Press, 1990.

Ved Mehta, *Rajiv Gandhi and Rama's Kingdom.* New Haven, CT: Yale University Press, 1994.

Stanley Wolpert, *Nehru: A Tryst with Destiny.* New York: Oxford University Press, 1996.

Contemporary India

Ainslie T. Embree, *Utopias in Conflict: Religion and Nationalism in Modern India.* Berkeley and Los Angeles: University of California Press, 1990.

Francine Frankel, "India's Democracy in Transition: The Search for a New Consensus," *World Policy Journal,* Summer 1990.

Robin Jeffrey, *What's Happening to India?* London: Macmillan, 1986.

Atul Kohli, *Democracy and Discontent: India's Growing Crisis of Governability.* Cambridge, England: Cambridge University Press, 1990.

Atul Kohli, ed., *The Success of India's Democracy.* Cambridge, England: Cambridge University Press, 2001.

Yogendra K. Malik and V.B. Singh, *Hindu Nationalists in India: The Rise of the Bharatiya Janata Party.* San Francisco: Westview Press, 1994.

V.S. Naipaul, *India: A Million Mutinies Now.* New York: Viking Penguin, 1990.

Salman Rushdie, *Mirrorwork: 50 Years of Indian Writing, 1947–1997.* New York: H. Holt, 1997.

Peter Ronald de Souza, ed., *Contemporary India: Transitions.* New Delhi, India: Sage Publications, 2000.

INDEX